STRATFORD-UPON-AVON STUDIES 7

General Editors
JOHN RUSSELL BROWN
& BERNARD HARRIS

Already published in this series:

*Under the general editorship of John Russell Brown and Bernard Harris

STRATFORD-UPON-AVON STUDIES 7

AMERICAN POETRY

Associate Editor
IRVIN EHRENPREIS

EDWARD ARNOLD

© EDWARD ARNOLD (PUBLISHERS) LTD 1965

First published 1965 by
Edward Arnold (Publishers) Ltd
25 Hill Street, London W1X 8LL

Paperback edition first published 1973

Reprinted 1975

ISBN: 0 7131 5526 4

Printed in Great Britain by
Whitstable Litho Ltd., Whitstable, Kent

Contents

Preface

Stratford-upon-Avon Studies began to be published some four years ago. Their editors have sought to provide a series of books on important literary and theatrical themes that would avoid the narrowness of a single scholar's work and be comprehensive, up-to-date and varied: so each volume depends on the collaboration of writers with differing skills and interests, and offers not one guide to understanding and appreciation, but several. Their chapters are especially commissioned to be complementary to each other. Such a co-operative book is needed to present *American Poetry* to readers on both sides of the Atlantic.

The General Editors of the *Studies* have been joined by Irvin Ehrenpreis as associate editor for this volume, and together we have commissioned chapters from poets and critics in the United States and England. At the head of the book is a study of the poets of the South, from Louis D. Rubin who writes of their work, ideas and background from an intimate and practised acquaintance. A wider but similar view follows, relating three poets to American history and the idea of America; in this chapter, J. Albert Robbins looks back to Whitman, the earliest mark in the range of this volume. Generally the focus of the book is upon the last few decades, and Irvin Ehrenpreis establishes this in a detailed study of Robert Lowell, the poet we have chosen for the most extensive individual study. Several chapters are concerned with poetic ideals and techniques: Walter Sutton writes of the interactions of criticism and poetry; David Ferry and Elizabeth Jennings, both poets, write respectively of diction and metrical experiment. Two English writers have contributed wide perspectives, A. R. Jones tracing the European origins of 'Imagism' and its effects in America, and Dennis Welland following the theme of the sea in poets from Emerson, Longfellow and Whitman to some writing today. Malcolm Bradbury interprets three short poems by Wallace Stevens to illustrate the unique style of this poet and exemplify the detailed attention his work invites. A final chapter by George Garrett, a poet and the poetry editor of *The Transatlantic Review*, surveys the work of other young poets writing today.

No chapter deals directly with Robert Frost, but contributors have been encouraged to use this poet, readily available and familiar on both sides of the Atlantic, as a kind of touchstone for 'placing' and comparison.

In choosing poems for discussion writers have considered their availability to readers without extensive libraries of modern American writing. Often the poems are available in cheap anthologies; among these are: *American Poetry Now*, ed. Sylvia Plath, *Critical Quarterly Poetry Supplement*, No. 2 (1961); *Contemporary American Poetry*, ed. Donald Hall (Penguin, 1963); *Fifteen Modern American Poets*, ed. George P. Elliott (Rinehart, 1956); *New Poets of England and America: Second Selection*, eds. Donald Hall and Robert Pack (Meridian, 1962); *The Oxford Book of American Verse*, ed. F. O. Matthiessen (1950); *The Penguin Book of Modern American Verse*, ed. Geoffrey Moore (1954); *The New American Poetry 1945–1960*, ed. Donald M. Allen (Grove, 1960); *The New Poets of England and America*, eds. Donald Hall, Robert Pack and Louis Simpson (Meridian, 1957).

Prefatory notes to each chapter give bibliographical and, sometimes, biographical information, and suggestions for further reading.

The next volumes of *Stratford-upon-Avon Studies* to be issued are *Late Shakespeare*, *Victorian Poetry*, *Elizabethan Theatre* and *American Theatre*.

JOHN RUSSELL BROWN
IRVIN EHRENPREIS
BERNARD HARRIS

Acknowledgements

THE editors and publisher wish to express their thanks to the following for permission to reprint extracts from copyright works:

Laurence Pollinger Ltd. and Alfred A. Knopf, Inc., for extracts from *Selected Poems* by John Crowe Ransom; the author and University Press, Minnesota, for extracts from three poems by Donald Davidson; the author, Eyre & Spottiswoode Ltd. and Charles Scribner's Sons, for extracts from *Collected Poems* by Allen Tate; Eyre & Spottiswoode Ltd., the William Morris Agency and Random House, Inc., for extracts from *Promises* and *Selected Poems, 1923–1943* by Robert Penn Warren; Liveright Publishing Corp., for extracts from *The Collected Poems* by Hart Crane; Laurence Pollinger Ltd., and Holt, Rinehart and Winston, Inc., for extracts from *Complete Poems* and *In the Clearing* by Robert Frost; Farrar Straus & Co., Faber & Faber, Ltd. and Harcourt, Brace & World, Inc., for extracts from *Lord Weary's Castle*, *Life Studies* and *Imitations* by Robert Lowell; Faber & Faber, Ltd. and Macmillan & Co., New York, for extracts from *Collected Poems* by Marianne Moore; Mr. A. V. Moore and New Directions, Inc., for extracts from *Cantos* and *Personae* by Ezra Pound; Routledge & Kegan Paul, Ltd., for extracts from *Speculations* by T. E. Hulme; McGibbon & Kee Ltd. and New Directions, Inc., for extracts from *Collected Earlier Poems* and *Collected Later Poems* by William Carlos Williams; the author and Houghton Mifflin Co., for *Night Clouds* by Amy Lowell; Faber & Faber, Ltd. and Harcourt, Brace & World, Inc., for extracts from the poems of T. S. Eliot; Faber & Faber, Ltd. and Alfred A. Knopf, Inc., for extracts from *The Collected Poems* by Wallace Stevens; Martin Secker & Warburg, Ltd., for extracts from *Basement Apartment* and *Elegy for a Dead Soldier* by Karl Shapiro; Wesleyan University Press for extracts from *Apples From Shinar* by Hyam Plutzik; Grove Press, Inc., for extracts from *The Distances* by Charles Olson; New Directions, Inc., for extracts from *The Jacob's Ladder* by Denise Levertov; the authors and Mr. George Garrett for extracts from *New Writing from Virginia* by Harriet Hodges and R. H. W. Dillard; the author and *Atlantic Monthly* for extracts from *Euripides* by DeWitt Bell; Macmillan & Co., New York, for extracts from *The Self-Made Man* by Reed Whittemore; Alan Swallow, Publisher, for extracts from *Seascape with Snow* by Elizabeth Harrod; the author, *The Listener* and *BBC Television Review* for an extract from the talk 'Huck and Oliver' (*The Listener*, 1st October, 1953) by W. H. Auden; the author and Wesleyan University Press for extracts from *The Man Whom the Sea Kept Awake* by Robert Bly; the author and Alfred A. Knopf, Inc., for extracts from *Collected Poems* by Stephen Crane; Totem Press and Corinth Books, Inc., for extracts from *Preface to a 20 Volume Suicide Note* by LeRoi

Jones; Mrs. Theodore Roethke and Doubleday & Co., Inc., for an extract from *Words for the Wind* by Theodore Roethke; the author and Houghton Mifflin Co., for an extract from *The Fish* by Elizabeth Bishop; the author, The Bodley Head, Ltd. and Houghton Mifflin Co., for an extract from *Ars Poetica* by Archibald Macleish; the author, Chatto & Windus, Ltd. and Oxford University Press, New York, for extracts from *Collected Poems* by Richard Eberhardt; Grove Press, Inc., for an extract from *Thank You and Other Poems* by Kenneth Koch; the author and Grove Press, Inc., for an extract from *Praise to You, My Country* by Ray Bremser; the author and Auerhahn Press for an extract from *The Hotel Wentley Poems* by John Weiners; The New Yorker Magazine, Inc., for an extract from *Seed Leaves* by Richard Wilbur; Harcourt, Brace & World, Inc., for extracts from *Poems 1923–1954* by E. E. Cummings, and Harcourt, Brace & World, Inc. and Faber & Faber, Ltd., for an extract from *Next to of course god america i* by E. E. Cummings; Laurence Pollinger, Ltd. and the Estate of the Late Mrs. Frieda Lawrence for *Aware* by D. H. Lawrence; the author and Farrar Straus and Co., for an extract from *Nine Dream Songs (III)* by J. Barryman; the author and Alfred A. Knopf, Inc., for extracts from *The Open Sea and Other Poems* by William Meredith; the author and Oxford University Press for an extract from *Leviathan* by W. S. Merwin; Oxford University Press for extracts from the poems of D. G. Hoffman; Random House, Inc., for extracts from *The Selected Poetry of Robinson Jeffers* and *The Double Axe* by Robinson Jeffers.

Note

Biography. John Crowe Ransom, born in Pulaski, Tennessee, 1888, was educated at Vanderbilt University and, as a Rhodes Scholar, at Oxford. He served in France during the first world war, returning afterwards to Vanderbilt to teach. In 1937 he moved to Kenyon College in Ohio, where the next year he established the *Kenyon Review*. Retired now from academic work and editing, Mr. Ransom lives in Gambier, Ohio.

Donald Davidson, born in Campbellsville, Tennessee, 1893, received bachelor and master of arts degrees from Vanderbilt, before serving overseas as a lieutenant during the first world war. Since 1920 he has been a member of the English Department of Vanderbilt.

Allen Tate, born in Clark County, Kentucky, 1899, graduated from Vanderbilt in 1922, and has taught at numerous colleges, for the past twelve years at the University of Minnesota. In 1944-6 he edited *The Sewanee Review*.

Robert Penn Warren, born in Guthrie, Kentucky, 1905, graduated from Vanderbilt in 1925, and subsequently studied at the University of California, Yale University, and, as a Rhodes Scholar, at Oxford. He has taught at several colleges, most recently at Yale. At the Louisiana State University he edited *The Southern Review* with Cleanth Brooks. Warren and Brooks have written highly influential textbooks, including *Understanding Poetry* (1938). He now lives in Fairfield, Connecticut.

Works. Ransom's first book of poems was *Poems About God* (1919). His second, *Chills and Fever* (1924), won a wide reputation, and was followed by *Two Gentlemen in Bonds* (1927). In 1945 Ransom published *Selected Poems*; a new edition (1963) contains a somewhat larger selection, as well as several earlier poems revised extensively. Ransom's collections of essays include *God Without Thunder* (1930), *The World's Body* (1938) and *The New Criticism* (1941). There is a paperback *Poems and Essays* (1955).

Davidson's books of poems are *An Outland Piper* (1924), *The Tall Men* (1927), *Lee in the Mountains and Other Poems* (1938) and *The Long Street* (1961). His essays in *The Attack on Leviathan* (1938) constitute an articulate defence of the Southern tradition.

Tate published his first book of poems, *Mr. Pope and Other Poems*, in 1928. Later collections are *Poems 1928-1931* (1932), *The Mediterranean and Other Poems* (1936), *Selected Poems* (1937), *The Winter Sea* (1944) and *Poems 1922-1947* (1948, reissued, with additions, 1960). Many of Tate's widely influential essays are available in *Collected Essays* (1959); *The Man of Letters in the Modern World* (1957) is a paperback collection.

Robert Penn Warren's first collection of poems was *Thirty-Six Poems* (1935). *Eleven Poems on the Same Theme* appeared in 1942, followed by *Selected Poems, 1923-1943* (1944). *Brother to Dragons*, a verse tale, was published in 1953. His most recent volumes of verse are *Promises: Poems 1954-1956* (1957) and *You, Emperors, and Others: 1957-1960* (1960). Warren has written *John Brown: The*

I

Four Southerners

LOUIS D. RUBIN, JR.

★

THERE had always been poetry, of a sort, in the South. For young men of sensibility it had been a kind of accomplishment, exquisitely romantic, properly suspected by the solid, political-minded lawyers, planters and merchants of the Old South. One thinks of its poets as pallid, thin-faced young men, writing slender lyrics after the style of Shelley. 'My life is like the summer rose/That opens to the morning sky,/But, ere the shades of evening close,/Is scattered on the ground—to die!' began Richard Henry Wilde's 'The Lament of the Captive' (though in point of fact, Wilde was six feet tall and huskily proportioned). Most of the poems written by his ante-bellum contemporaries are of comparable vigour; the Southern singers were Romantics after their time, writing tender nature poetry long after Shelley and Byron were dead and Wordsworth had gone over to the Establishment. There were only two

---

Making of a Martyr (1929), eight novels and a collection of short stories. His non-fiction work includes *Segregation* (1956), *Selected Essays* (1958) and *The Legacy of the Civil War* (1961).

Criticism. An extensive historical and critical study is Louise Cowan's *The Fugitive Group* (1959). John Bradbury's *The Fugitives: A Critical Account* (1958) discusses both the group and individual Fugitives in subsequent years. Essays on the Fugitives appear in two collections, edited by Louis D. Rubin, Jr., and Robert D. Jacobs: *Southern Renascence: The Literature of the Modern South* (1953) and *South: Modern Southern Literature in its Cultural Setting* (1961). The summer 1948 issue of *The Sewanee Review* contains essays on Ransom, and the autumn 1959 number on Allen Tate. Two important essays on Ransom and Tate are by Howard Nemerov in *Poetry and Fiction: Essays* (1963). The autumn 1963 issue of the *South Atlantic Quarterly* contains essays on Warren. A book-length study of Warren is Leonard Casper's *Robert Penn Warren: The Dark and Bloody Ground* (1960). The Agrarian symposium, *I'll Take My Stand*, by Twelve Southerners, (1930; paperback ed., 1962) contains essays by all four poets.

notable exceptions: Edgar Allan Poe, and a South Carolina poet named Henry Timrod who but for the Civil War might have produced lyric poetry worthy of his Metaphysical taste for sensuous imagery. Poe of course is *sui generis*, a Southerner who took literature seriously and thus was forced to live in want for most of his short life. His poems are perhaps the best known and most often recited of any American's; yet it is difficult to find any great merit in them. As a poet he lacked taste, and his verse exploits all manner of exaggerated sound effects that work so crudely against the meaning of his poems as to make them largely ridiculous. His importance, so far as the development of American verse is concerned, lies in his insistence on the poem's integrity as a work of art, in contrast to the Platonising tendencies of his New England contemporaries. The French, to be sure, responded to him. What he had to show them was the way whereby the controlled use of tone could be made to create psychological moods. It was his created morbidity that entranced them; beneath the surface of his poems—all too excessively on the surface, for English readers—was the accent of irrationality, despair, disenchantment. He helped Baudelaire and Mallarmé to perceive the language of spleen.

After Poe, except perhaps for Timrod, there was very little. The post-Civil War period produced Sidney Lanier, a heavy, lush technician who like Poe cared principally for sound, and so was willing, in his best poem, to rhyme 'emerald twilights' with 'virginal shy lights'. One may say of him that he did what Swinburne did, only not nearly so well. Like Poe he was a brave man: he tried to live by his artistry in the South, and so died at the age of 39.

Poetry as an important art, therefore, occurred in the South for the first time in the 1920's. It was then only that persons born and residing in the Southern states produced a body of poems that intelligent, informed readers might take seriously. For these poets—John Crowe Ransom, Allen Tate, Robert Penn Warren and Donald Davidson—there was little in the verse written by Southerners before their own time that was of any important use to them. Their models were those of other places—Frost, Edwin Arlington Robinson, Thomas Hardy, more importantly Eliot and Pound. Whatever the value of the regional tradition that nurtured them, it was not one that importantly involved literature. And this, indeed, is part of the story. For what they are as poets has much to do with the contrast, and the conflict, between what they were taught as Southerners growing up in a still largely agricultural community, and what they discovered as intellectuals who had grown apart from that community. The contrast produced a highly distinctive body of literature.

*   *   *

The Southern Renascence, as it is called, in poetry took place not only in a single geographical region of the United States of America during a single decade of the twentieth century, but indeed in a particular city, at a single university. The chief Southern poets did not simply exist in the same place together; they actually belonged to a kind of literary club, at which they read each other's poems and criticised them. They even published their early work in a joint magazine established for that purpose. The Nashville Fugitives, as they styled themselves, were all natives of the Upper South, of Tennessee and Kentucky. They attended Vanderbilt University in Tennessee, consciously and enthusiastically joined forces, contributed to each other's development, sought to (and to a large extent did) arrive at a common aesthetic and a common poetics, and a few years subsequent, extended their literary operations to take in a cultural and social programme for the South. In the process they acquired another name, the Agrarians. This was in the early 1930's, after publication of their book about the South entitled *I'll Take My Stand*. There were other Fugitives besides Ransom, Tate, Warren and Davidson, and also other Agrarians, including the novelists Andrew Nelson Lytle and Stark Young. Also associated with them at Vanderbilt during much of the period was the literary critic Cleanth Brooks. All have long since gone their separate ways; only Donald Davidson remains at Vanderbilt University.

Save perhaps for Ransom, who had published a volume of verse in 1919, one first began to hear of the Fugitive poets in the early 1920's, when their magazine, *The Fugitive*, began to attract attention both in the United States and England.[1] *The Fugitive* was not unlike numerous other 'little magazines' which sprung up during the years after the first world war. Its slender issues have the same sense of self-importance, of conscious rebellion against the Victorian muse. There were, however, important differences, apparent even at the time and in retrospect seemingly quite clear. Among the chief Fugitives there was a commitment to form, an insistence upon the poem as existing within its language and on the page, with the responsibility for creating its own

[1] Cf. Chapter VIII, pp. 182-3, below.

meaning, that contrasted sharply with the loose, undisciplined, form-less experimentalism of so much little magazine verse of the period. What interested the Fugitives most was language, its properties, its concreteness; their poetry tended towards the tightly-seeded, packed line, with the energy of the poem focused on the way in which images worked with and against other images to produce a kind of poetry which, however complex and even dense it might appear on quick reading, developed from beginning to end a controlled, cohesive mean-ing in which each image, each line, was part of the total movement of the poem. It is not surprising that Ransom, Tate, Warren and their somewhat younger friend Cleanth Brooks were to prove the leading proponents of the critical development which Ransom was to christen the New Criticism. Though it lies outside the scope of this chapter, one might well contend that important though the poetry that these men wrote proved to be, they are at least equally influential in the development of American poetry because of what they were as critics. They taught a generation of students how to read poems.

*   *   *

Few of the poems published in *The Fugitive*, with the notable excep-tion of some by John Crowe Ransom, have survived that magazine's demise. When the magazine ceased publication in 1925, only Ransom had really begun to develop his characteristic style. Older by eleven years than Tate, and by seventeen than Warren, by the second number of the magazine in 1922 he had begun publishing the poems which, with slight revisions, were subsequently brought out in the two volumes of verse, *Chills and Fever* (1924) and *Two Gentlemen in Bonds* (1927), on which his poetic reputation was primarily built, and, with still further revisions, still chiefly rests. It was Ransom who dominated the early meetings of the Fugitive group. A former Rhodes Scholar, he had taught Davidson in his literature classes at Vanderbilt before the war, and after returning from service in France he had Allen Tate, Robert Penn Warren, and, later, Cleanth Brooks for his pupils. Dry, a touch formal, he was logical, factual as he brought to bear his incisive analytical powers on the carbon drafts of the new poems that each Fugitive brought to the twice-monthly evening sessions.

Yet though Ransom was teacher, he was student as well. Indeed, it was he who perhaps most of all benefited from membership in the group. The naïveté, the looseness, the tendency towards excessive posturing that was apparent in his pre-Fugitive work was largely purged away by the Fugitive insistence upon concretion, precision of language and metaphor. In particular he had much to learn from his younger colleague Allen Tate, who, very much the ardent modernist in those days, brought to the Fugitive group the poems, the poetics, the attitudes of the post-war literary generation which under the leadership of Eliot, Pound and others was so thoroughly demolishing the old poetry of easy idealism and Poetic Diction, and replacing it with the disciplined, intellectually-demanding poetry of modernism.

For Ransom this did not come naturally. When *The Waste Land* appeared, for example, Ransom prepared an attack on it, in which he criticised the poem for its obscurity, its irrationality, its ellipses of thought. Tate responded at once with a defence so strongly worded that it momentarily jeopardised friendly relations between the two. Yet in retrospect it can be seen that much of Ransom's best poetry arises from the tension created by the clash, within his own sensibility, of the rival appeals of these two divergent, apparently irreconcilable, attitudes. He is both traditionalist and modernist, mannered gentleman and ruthless satirist. The hallmark of his verse is the savage irony with which he confronts everyday experience.

Ransom, it has often been said, is a very 'Southern' sort of poet. His verse, on the surface at least, is gentle, polite, decorous. He is a gentleman, and he is aware of his station. There is never any straining for effect. His language, though erudite and even a trifle archaic ('Sweet ladies, long may ye bloom, and toughly I hope ye may thole'), is full of colloquialisms, down to earth in its choice of metaphor. His subject-matter is domestic, folksy. He writes of spinsters, housewives, children, gardens, trees, the seasons, farms, barnyard animals, old mansions; as befits the son of a Methodist minister, some of his best poems are on Biblical subjects. What could seem more 'Southern', than, for instance, the conclusion to 'Conrad in Twilight':

> Autumn days in our section
> Are the most used-up thing on earth
> (Or in the waters under the earth)
> Having no more color or predilection
> Than cornstalks too wet for the fire,
> A ribbon rotting on the byre,
> A man's face as weathered as straw
> By the summer's flare and winter's flaw.

It is a Tennessee pastoral, making full use of the Southern setting, colloquial diction, the rural referents of an American region whose life was still, during the years when he was growing up, predominantly agricultural.

Yet to picture Ransom as gentle squire of the Old South is to catch only the surface of what in fact is a very complex poetic attitude. His poetry is filled with the awareness of a world in which irrationality, brutality and despair are everyday occurrences. His view of human experience is not of something serene; the apparent serenity and order are contrasted with the most appalling kind of inner disorder and rage, so that the surface calmness becomes a desperate insistence on decorum at all costs, as the only strategy, however forlorn, whereby a civilised man may confront that which is mindless, barbarous, terrible.

Consider a typical Ransom poem, 'Blue Girls'. It begins with some none-too-scholarly young ladies attending classes:

> Twirling your blue skirts, travelling the sward
> Under the towers of your seminary,
> Go listen to your teachers old and contrary
> Without believing a word.
>
> Tie the white fillets then about your lustrous hair
> And think no more of what will come to pass
> Than bluebirds that go walking on the grass
> And chattering on the air.

The tone is whimsical, humorous, not one whit indecorous; the poet contemplates the youthful collegians and likens them to birds. It is enough that they are beautiful; he will tell the world about it:

> Practise your beauty, blue girls, before it fail;
> And I will cry with my loud lips and publish
> Beauty which all our power shall never establish,
> It is so frail.

Up to now the poem has seemingly done no more than comment on the briefness of mortal beauty. But then Ransom adds one more stanza, which changes the import of the description until it is something quite different:

> For I could tell you a story which is true:
> I know a lady with a terrible tongue,

Blear eyes fallen from blue,
All her perfections tarnished—and yet it is not long
Since she was lovelier than any of you.

He has pointed out the inevitable fate of human loveliness in time, but in such a way that one is made not wryly melancholic, but quite appalled at the loss of innocence, the physical decay. The bluebirds have turned into shrikes; lovely ladies are harridans. One word enforces it: 'blear'. The 'terrible' tongue is beautifully equivocal, for the expression is colloquial, and in everyday usage it means something less than 'that which is full of terror'. So too the 'tarnished' perfections, which but for the line before might not seem so bitter. But when Ransom says 'blear eyes fallen from blue', the image is so unmistakably physical that when Ransom ends his poem with the admonition that 'it is not long/Since she was lovelier than any of you', the remark is sharply, unmistakably ironic. Yet even so he will not permit us to contemplate, without reservation, the logic of his conclusion. The tone of the poem is too mocking, too fanciful for that. The benevolent sweetness of the opening stanzas, the leisurely pace of the lines, the quaint diction work against the shattering moral of the conclusion, so that we are held off at arm's length, as it were, by the poem's good manners, denied the right to participate fully in the rage against time.

The truth is that Ransom's poetry is filled with violence, gore, decay on a scale that at first reading is only slightly apparent. In another poem, 'Necrological', for example, a friar observes bodies on a battlefield:

Not all were white; some gory and fabulous
Whom the sword had pierced and then the grey wolf eaten;
But the brother reasoned that heroes' flesh was thus,
Flesh fails, and the postured bones lie. weather-beaten.

A Biblical poem tells of how Judith of Bethulia waylays the invader in his tent, whereupon the Lord's host went forth to dispose of his followers, and

smote them hiding in our vineyards, barns, annexes,
And now their white bones clutter the holes of foxes,
And the chieftain's head, with grinning sockets, and varnished—
Is it hung on the sky with a hideous epitaphy?
No, the woman keeps the trophy.

The violence is always disguised with the proper archaism, a sense of literary diction, which serves only to dramatise the horror of the action. The protagonist of Ransom's best-known poem, the mock ballad 'Captain Carpenter', is a gentleman of the old school, chivalric and true, who rides out to confront the modern world, with lamentable results. First he meets 'a pretty lady and all her train' who 'played with him so sweetly' but then seized a sword 'and twined him of his nose for evermore'. Next he encounters a stranger rogue, and at once the Captain

> drew upon him out of his great heart
> The other swung against him with a club
> And cracked his two legs at the shinny part
> And let him roll and stick like any tub.

The Captain loses one encounter after another. His difficulty is that he goes about his questing in the approved style of knightly chivalry, while his opponents will not observe the rules. The wife of Satan, who should have 'made off like a hind', instead 'bit off his arms at the elbows'. He 'parted with his ears' to a black devil, and he yielded up 'his sweet blue eyes' to another foe. Finally 'the neatest knave that ever was seen' stepped out and fell upon the Captain:

> I would not knock old fellows in the dust
> But there lay Captain Carpenter on his back
> His weapons were the old heart in his bust
> And a blade shook between rotten teeth alack.

'With gentle apology and touch refined', the knave thereupon 'pierced him and produced the Captain's heart'. So much for Captain Carpenter. Yet there is something admirable about the Captain, for all his ineffectiveness:

> God's mercy rest on Captain Carpenter now
> I thought him Sirs an honest gentleman
> Citizen husband soldier and scholar enow
> Let jangling kites eat of him if they can.

As for the Captain's murderer, why,

> The curse of hell upon the sleek upstart
> That got the Captain finally on his back
> And took the red red vitals of his heart
> And made the kites to whet their beaks clack clack.

Is not Captain Carpenter, in all his forlorn bravery, very much a Southern gentleman of the old school, who tries to go about his life in a traditional way, only to be hewn to pieces by vicious rogues with no compunctions about honour and dignity? Indeed, does not this renowned 'citizen husband soldier and scholar' fall before the onslaught of modernity? If so, it is a familiar theme in the literature of the modern South; the Captain's inability to handle the ways of the present is reminiscent of the troubles that the Sartorises and the Compsons have in handling the Snopeses in William Faulkner's Yoknapatawpha County tales. There is no doubt about where Ransom's sympathies lie; ironic he may be in describing the Captain's limitations for the kind of combat he faces, but Ransom is not on the side of the barbarians. There is the intimation, too, that though life has dealt unkindly with the Captain, he has done what he should even so, and his defeat is not entirely without compensations. Throughout the poem the ballad form, the quaint diction, the formality of the language, all contrast with the violence of the deeds described, so as to give the poem an ironic, mordant tone.

Throughout Ransom's poetry there is the same kind of irony, brought about by the conjunction of a stylised, formal attitude of discourse and some of the most violent, sanguinary subject matter in all of modern American poetry. Little children die; old maids see their lawns symbolically deflowered; spinsters are buried; country mountebanks boast of the bloodthirstiness of their pets; ladies of high degree die 'after six little spaces of chill, and six of burning'; Christ smites Antichrist; Judith waylays the heathen; chickens are stung to death; lovers 'with individual tigers in their blood' marry, then 'rend and murder trying to get undone'; old soldiers bleed to death; and so on.

Earlier I remarked that his poetry seems 'Southern' in its air of mannered politeness, its restraint, its colloquial diction, and its choice of subject-matter. But it is also 'Southern', it seems to me, in another and no less important sense. For its basic attitude seems strikingly to symbolise the historical circumstance out of which it came.

It should be remembered that of the four leading Fugitive poets, Ransom is the oldest. He was born in 1888, and was already twelve years old when the new century arrived. During the last decades of the nineteenth century and well into the new century, the American South was still predominantly agricultural, impoverished, untouched for the most part by the industrial revolution that had already transformed the

Northeast and the Midwest into their modern commercially-oriented, business-dominated society. In the South, the desolation of the Civil War and the Reconstruction, which had stripped the region of its chief capital investment, slavery, so retarded the coming of industrialism that, for all the propaganda for a 'New South' during the 1880's and 1890's, the region at the turn of the century was still but little changed from its rural ways. Southern society was static, closed; it was not urban-directed. Its folkways, its interests, its political and economic orientation were agricultural. It was a deeply traditional kind of society, highly conscious of the past, intensely and often narrowly religious in its preoccupations. It was a threadbare kind of existence, in which there was little capital, little wealth, and therefore little social flux and change. The Southern community, typically a small town or a small city, was largely self-sufficient, with a low-keyed but complex social ordering, and suspicious of change.

It was in the twentieth century that industrial society began to make a serious impact on Southern life, climaxing in the first world war, which touched off an industrial boom by bringing, for the first time since the Civil War, an abundant supply of capital to the region. Towns became cities, cities became metropolises; the rural South, so long isolated, was drawn into much closer relationship with the cities and the outside world. Good roads, mass communications, more and better schools, a vastly increased flow of newcomers into the region, all helped to disrupt and break up the long-settled patterns of Southern community life. Tenaciously-held attitudes, traditional ways of ordering and regulating one's existence, underwent swift and violent change as the tumult and flux of modern industrial society began having its impact. The South entered the modern world, which meant that it experienced vast and continuing upheaval as it sought to reconcile its unhurried, fixed ways with the demands of an urban, cosmopolitan, fluid society.

Now it is a tenuous business to attempt an immediate correlation between the work of a poet and the condition of the society from which the work grows—even when, as in Ransom's instance, the poet at one stage of his career did so very much writing about the condition of that society. Yet the poetry of John Crowe Ransom seems so very appropriate to his time and place that one is willing to draw the inference. Terror is played against decorum, violence against gentility. A traditional sensibility, a highly formal, erudite diction is made to confront the most appalling kind of subject-matter, and in the play of the one against the other, there results a most grim, sternly expressed balance.

The poet Randall Jarrell declares of Ransom that 'he has written poems that are perfectly realised and occasionally almost perfect— poems that the hypothetical generations of the future will be reading page by page with Wyatt, Campion, Marvell and Mother Goose'. And indeed, one might well compare such poems as 'Captain Carpenter', 'Janet Waking' and 'Blue Girls' to the Mother Goose poems; in both there is that curious mixture of childlike nonsense fantasy and incredible horror. What seems at first to be a kind of daydream turns out, on closer examination, to resemble a nightmare. A gentleman confronts, with chivalrous decorum of language, the ferocity, the turmoil of his crass times.

★   ★   ★

Though deeply Southern in tradition and attitude, Ransom's poetry is not strongly historical in theme. But for two of his Fugitive colleagues, Allen Tate and Donald Davidson, the South and its history provided theme and imagery for much of their best work. Davidson, the older of the two and closer to Ransom in age, had during the early and middle 1920's written poems that were romantic, musical, only occasionally satirical. One may search in vain through his first book, *An Outland Piper* (1924), for a single lyric that is overtly concerned with the South and its history. But as the decade drew to a close, Davidson began writing poems that were directly based on the South and its past. Graceful romanticism gave way to strident social commentary and fiercely elegiac invocations of the Southern tradition. When the city of Nashville, Tennessee, decided to construct a replica of the Parthenon as a public monument, Davidson's response was a bitter denunciation:

> Why do they come? What do they seek
> Who build but never read their Greek?
> The classic stillness of a pool
> Beleaguered in its certitude
> By aimless motors that can make
> Only incertainty more sure.

He depicts the replica of the Greek temple in the Southern city as a helpless, futile gesture towards tradition by modern men who have otherwise ignored and forgotten their past, and who have now 'raised up this bribe against their fate' while continuing to follow the goals of modern urban living.

Davidson's best-known poem, 'Lee in the Mountains', is as literally a Southern Agrarian poem as has ever been composed. The concerns and attitudes are directly those which provided the impulse for the symposium, *I'll Take My Stand*, which appeared in 1930 and behind which Davidson was the moving spirit. In the poem, the image of General Robert E. Lee, defeated but not dishonoured, living out his last years as president of a small college in the mountain town of Lexington, Virginia, and occupying himself with editing the memoirs of his father, General 'Light Horse Harry' Lee of the American Revolution, is of a man who still believes firmly in the rightness of the cause for which he fought so well:

> God too late
> Unseals to certain eyes the drift
> Of time and the hopes of men and a sacred cause.

He is resolved, unlike his father, never to write of the battles he has fought:

> The rest must pass to men who never knew
> (But on a written page) the strike of armies,
> And never heard the long Confederate cry
> Charge through the muzzling smoke or saw the bright
> Eyes of the beardless boys go up to death.

He asks himself whether the sordid present times justify the valour and sacrifice of the war:

> Was it for this
> That on an April day we stacked our arms
> Obedient to a soldier's trust? To lie
> Ground by heels of little men,
> Forever maimed, defeated, lost, impugned?
> And was I then betrayed? Did I betray?

He feels that the spirit of the cause is still alive, that if called upon to do so the Southern people would again rally to his standard and give battle to the invaders from the cities of the North:

> The sunken flag would kindle on wild hills,
> The brooding hearts would waken, and the dream

Stir like a crippled phantom under the pines,
And this torn earth would quicken into shouting
Beneath the feet of ragged bands—

But it is all over, just as he had foreseen long before, and it is not his
duty to summon the young men of the South to battle again. Rather,
it is his task to remind them of their duty to the land and to tell them
that despite military defeat the hope for them and their Southland rests
in submission to God's will:

                              a just
              And merciful God Who in this blood once shed
              On your green altars measures out all days,
              And measures out the grace
              Whereby alone we live;
              And in His might He waits,
              Brooding within the certitude of time,
              To bring this lost forsaken valor
              And the fierce faith undying
              And the love quenchless
              To flower among the hills to which we cleave,
              To fruit upon the mountains whither we flee,
              Never forsaking, never denying
              His children and His children's children forever
              Unto all generations of the faithful heart.

God's truth and solace are thus embodied in an agrarian image of the
flowering hills and fruited mountains, where earthly hope and cer-
tainty lie in a life close to nature. The passionate devotion of Lee to the
Southland, his faith in a just God, his belief that, though defeated in
war, the South remains strong in its resolve and devotion, all serve to
build up an image of a people bound by historical loyalties and blood
ties, imbued with a religious attachment to the land and to the past.

Davidson's use of the Southern historical tradition and the agrarian
heritage of the region is direct and uncomplicated. The historical birth-
right is available to him as a poet without irony or qualification, and
the image of the Old South can be thrown into immediate and telling
contrast with modern urban existence, as a rebuke to what he con-
siders is the aimlessness, the tawdry materialism of contemporary
society. His most ambitious poem, 'The Tall Men', is constructed
directly on the contrast between the uncomplicated, vigorous life of

the Tennessee frontiersman and the compromised plight of the modern city-dwelling Southerner. In what might be described as the quint-essential Nashville Agrarian attitude, he speaks of

> this gray city, blinded, soiled, and kicked
> By fat, blind fools. The city's burning up?
> Why, good! Then let her burn!

Davidson's more recent work, collected in a volume entitled *The Long Street* (1961), is less historical in choice of subject-matter, and more pastoral. But it too is frequently marked by sharp social satire. Perhaps because of their insistent historical literalness, Davidson's poems are less well known among most American poetry readers than those of his other Fugitive colleagues. They depend strongly on historical allusion; and most Americans who read contemporary verse, much though they may concern themselves with the function of tradition, are not greatly interested in American history, particularly when told from the standpoint of the losers.

*   *   *

No such difficulty characterises the poetry written by Allen Tate during the late 1920's and early 1930's, though much of it is equally concerned with Southern and American history. This I think is due in part to Tate's somewhat greater aesthetic distance from his subject. Tate's Civil War poems, which comprise some of his best-known work, are likewise history told from the loser's point of view, but as poet Tate is much more willing to acknowledge the fact that the defeat took place. He emphasises the distance between the historical occasion and the modern who would recall it, so that in his work the context and the attitude are clearly of the present day. This tactic provides Tate with a much broader frame of reference, so that the reader need not actually subscribe to the historical loyalties of the poet in order to grasp the import of the poem. Admirers of Tate's 'Ode to the Confederate Dead', for example, are not called upon to share the poet's personal interest in the Southern cause in order for the poem to have meaning for them. What is necessary is an awareness that there was a war, and perhaps the knowledge that the Confederates were on the losing side. The poem then becomes a meditation on dead soldiers, in which defeated valour is contrasted with modern uncertainty, and the dis-tance between a past historical moment and a present-day observer is used to comment on the nature of human existence in time. Thus, Southern history is made into a metaphor that transcends its literal and regional implications.

Tate's earlier work, little of which appears in his more recent collections, was *fin de siècle* in tone, and characterised by a world-weary romanticism that is almost entirely absent from his best poems. Its chief distinction was one which marks almost all his poetry: a kind of savagely intellectual imagery, shocking in its violence, alternating Latinate and colloquial diction to produce a characteristically apocalyptic tone. In an early poem, 'The Progress of Oenia', for example, he refers to

> the dry debility
> Of a spent wind in a winter tree.

The intrusion of the Latinate word produces a jolt that helps the lines achieve a sense of irrational despair. Tate's work of this period, the early 1920's, is not quite committed to any particular social attitude; he satirises the modern scene, but with a sense of romantic striving for an air of detachment that is not altogether convincing. The best of his early poems is probably 'The Death of Little Boys', which focuses on the individual's private desperation and the need to maintain decorum in public. In the unexpected death of a child there is chaos, the completely irrational happening, giving the lie to orderly processes of personal meaning and social convention. The emotional derangement of the speaker is paralleled by the derangement of senses, and the moment of absolute unreason produces a surrealistic madness:

> The bleak sunshine shrieks its chipped music then
> Out to the milkweed amid the fields of wheat.

Finally the mechanical order that comes from the funeral ceremony mocks the individual's own feeling of meaninglessness:

> There is a calm for you where men and women
> Unroll the chill precision of moving feet.

This poem, in which the tone and attitude are not forced, but grow out of the dramatic situation, sets forth one of Tate's characteristic themes, the sense of the inability of individuals to perceive order and meaning in modern experience. In the early poems this is personal and private, but always with the spokesman of the poem a created, third-person voice, never the poet himself. There is no thought, for example, that the individual who describes his reactions to the death of the little boy is necessarily or importantly the poet. During the middle 1920's this technique of anonymity is steadily developed, and the spokesman's private failure to recognise order in his own experience is deepened into a full-fledged critique of modern society.

A poem such as 'The Subway' is interesting in its display of Tate's social attitude just prior to his discovery of Southern history and experience as a theme for his work. The poem, a sonnet, describes the chaos and bedlam of modern urban life:

> Dark accurate plunger down the successive knell
> Of arch on arch, where ogives burst a red
> Reverberance of hail upon the dead
> Thunder like an exploding crucible!

The effect is of motion too furious and too violent to provide any sense of purpose or destination, producing a sensation of utter helplessness as the throbbing, plunging forward movement obliterates ideas of time, place and journey:

> I am become geometries, and glut
> Expansions like a blind astronomer
> Dazed, while the worldless heavens bulge and reel
> In the cold revery of an idiot.

Tate could not, any more than Eliot or Yeats, welcome the chaos and violence and try to make poetry out of it; indeed, the only poet of importance in America who tried to do this at the time was Hart Crane, and as Tate has pointed out in a brilliant essay, Crane was unable to bring it off. Much though he admired Crane, Tate was unwilling and unable to follow Crane's lead. Instead, from the middle 1920's on, his poetry constituted a search for order, an attempt to discover a traditional, moral and social perspective from which to master the explosive energy and trackless movement of contemporary experience. Like Eliot in England, he sought stability and order in tradition. But there was an important difference. Where Eliot's appeal was to an ideal order divorced from secular history, Tate had available to him—had, indeed, all but forced upon him—a concrete historical image, a ready-made loyalty, in the history and tradition of the region in which he was born.

For poets in search of a tradition there is much to be said for one which has not only strong, still binding loyalties, but a heritage of valour (and defeat) in war, and even a mythology of its own. All this the Confederate South must have seemed to a young poet who in the boom-and-bust confusion of the middle and late 1920's looked around for an image of something enduring. To be sure, there were drawbacks, and in due time they made themselves felt. Yet whatever reservations may be entered, in retrospect, concerning the appropriateness of the Old South as symbol and image for a rebuke to the chaos of modern industrial society, it furnished Allen Tate with the legendry for a body of distinguished poetry, the best work of his career.

The celebrated 'Ode to the Confederate Dead', which appeared in the first of its several versions in 1927, presents the problem squarely. A modern man peers through a cemetery gate at the gravestones of dead soldiers—a modern Southerner, at Confederate graves, to be exact, but any man and any war would do as well—and considers the inaccessibility of the historical situation. Separated from his history by an impenetrable gap in time, he not only lacks any access to it, but the ability to define reality through it. The dead soldiers are anonymous, removed beyond identification:

> Row after row with strict impunity
> The headstones yield their names to the element,
> The wind whirrs without recollection;
> In the riven troughs the splayed leaves
> Pile up, of nature the casual sacrament
> To the seasonal eternity of death;
> Then driven by the fierce scrutiny
> Of heaven to their election in the vast breath,
> They sough the rumour of mortality.

The watcher at the gate feels cut off, isolated, alien to whatever it was that the dead soldiers fought for. The sensation is that of drowning in time, submerged in opaque depths of space, without vision or direction:

> The brute curiosity of an angel's stare
> Turns you, like them, to stone,
> Transforms the heaving air
> Till plunged to a heavier world below
> You shift your sea-space blindly,
> Heaving, turning like the blind crab.

An attempt to bring the scene before him to a focus of meaning beyond that of mere physical spectacle collapses; the watcher at the gate is able to believe only in the inanimate scene before him, and repeats a refrain that will recur throughout the poem:

> Dazed by the wind, only the wind
> The leaves flying, plunge.

The dead soldiers, he thinks to himself, had at least known the reality of struggle, of the moment of battle that would not admit of equivocation, that demanded action, elemental response. They were able to fight and to die, to believe in a meaning for their experience that transcended mere survival:

> You know the unimportant shrift of death
> And praise the vision
> And praise the arrogant circumstance
> Of those who fall.

But such belief, such commitment are beyond his own experience, and he cannot credit it; he is still outside the cemetery, 'here by the sagging gate, stopped by the wall', and again there are only the leaves, the immediate scene. A prisoner in time, he feels locked within his own sensibilities:

> You hear the shout, the crazy hemlocks point
> With troubled fingers to the silence which
> Smothers you, a mummy, in time.

What insight may the modern watcher at the gate achieve for himself, and what knowledge can he find for his own situation, from the presence of the dead soldiers? Self-conscious scruples of conduct, hairsplitting nuances of right or wrong, seem weak, antiseptic, before the violent, whole-hearted engagement in life and death that the dead soldiers exemplify:

> What shall we say of the bones, unclean,
> Whose verdurous anonymity will grow?
> The ragged arms, the ragged heads and eyes
> Lost in these acres of the insane green?
> The grey lean spiders come; they come and go;
> In a tangle of willows without light
> The singular screech-owl's tight
> Invisible lyric seeds the mind
> With the furious murmur of their chivalry.

But the vision fails once more; he can see 'only the leaves/Flying, plunge and expire'; he is cut off from them in time, walled in by the thicket of the present. The one reality that is certain is that of time. The Confederate graves can at least mean that for the man at the gate; man is inextricably involved in time, is part of time, and the knowledge of that, while it is not solace, is at least the recognition of the mystery, the resolution of the poem:

> Leave now
> The shut gate and the decomposing wall;
> The gentle serpent, green in the mulberry bush,
> Riots with his tongue through all the hush—
> Sentinel of the grave who counts us all!

Tate's concern with Southern tradition was not limited to regional problems, even during his most intensely 'Agrarian' years. He saw the order and pattern of pre-industrial Southern life as a manifestation, however inadequate, of Western humanism, and the South of the early American Republic as having been modelled on the ideals of classical civilisation. His own training in the Greek and Latin classics, product as it was of an educational philosophy still based firmly on humane studies, lent itself naturally to such a comparison. Thus in 'Aeneas at Washington' he could liken the victory of the North in the Civil War, and the industrial democracy that emerged after the defeat of the plantation South, to the sack of Troy by the Hellenes:

> That was a time when civilization
> Run by the few fell to the many, and
> Crashed to the shout of men, the clang of arms.

In the plight of the tradition-minded Southerner contemplating the wreck of the agrarian republic his forefathers had helped build he saw repeated the plight of Aeneas as wanderer:

> Stuck in the wet mire
> Four thousand leagues from the ninth buried city
> I thought of Troy, what we had built her for.

In another poem, 'The Mediterranean', the legend of Aeneas is again used to delineate modern experience, in this instance the search of the poet for his tradition. Just as the Trojans recognise that they have arrived at their destination because in their famine they have eaten their very plates, thus fulfilling Anchises' prophecy, so the moderns come upon their own new land through discovery of their classical heritage, 'the famous age/Eternal here yet hidden from our eyes'. Only through his tradition may the poet find his theme, grasp the true meaning of the present, create his art:

> Now, from the Gates of Hercules we flood
>
> Westward, westward till the barbarous brine
> Whelms us to the tired land where tasseling corn,
> Fat beans, grapes sweeter than muscadine
> Rot on the vine: in that land were we born.

The real world—nature, the land of plenty—is the place of one's origins, the South, achievable through the classical heritage, the tradition. The Mediterranean becomes the South, becomes anywhere in which union is re-established with the past and its heritage of beauty: 'They, in a wineskin, bore earth's paradise.'

Drawing on the historical image of the Old South as metaphor for the kind of society best fitted for humane existence, Tate produced a dozen or more poems, many of them among his best work. And if, as critics have asserted, such a society never existed anywhere, and certainly not in the Old South, it is true even so that the legend of its existence, the complex fabric of loyalties, insights, beliefs involved in the Southern consciousness, provided Tate with a notable image for his critique of modern times.

During the late 1930's, however, Tate's interests began changing. There had always been a strongly religious aspect to his work; his contribution to the Agrarian symposium, *I'll Take My Stand*, had to do with the inadequacy of religious consciousness in the South. Now the cut-off-ness of the modern 'intellectual' man from the world became more and more a religious problem in his poetry. The transition is clearly evident in the two 'Sonnets at Christmas', published in 1934, which describe a man musing over his inability to feel the spiritual implications of the Christmas season. From that point onwards the imagery in his poetry became increasingly religious and Christian. In 1944 he brought out his major long poem, 'Seasons of the Soul'. Composed during wartime, it represents a personal stocktaking, in which the poet examines his own spiritual plight as it reflects that of Western man caught up in an era of savagery and barbarism. The four seasons correspond to the four elements of ancient science, chronicling man's four ages in relation to the four aspects of the universe. Summer is the present,

> a gentle sun
> When, at the June solstice
> Green France was overrun
> With caterpillar feet.

Autumn is a time of death, of growing isolation; the image is of a world peopled by ghosts, with the individual trapped in time, unable to achieve any meaningful unity with his past experience, alive only for the moment:

> I saw my downcast mother
> Clad in her street-clothes,
> Her blue eyes long and small,
> Who had no look or voice
> For him whose vision froze
> Him in the empty hall,

In Winter, the poet considers love. Religion, Christianity seem dead; all that remains is pagan delight in the body:

> You, Venus, come home
> To your salt maidenhead,
> The tossed, anonymous sea
> Under shuddering foam.

But the sea rages on, while 'Eternal winters blow/Shivering flakes', and from love without belief only lust is possible:

> The pacing animal
> Surveys the jungle cove
> And slicks his slithering wiles
> To turn the venereal awl
> In the livid wound of love.

Finally, in Spring, man faces his ultimate despair. There is, as in *The Waste Land*, no apparent hope of regeneration; man can place his trust only in an unknown hereafter. Like the inhabitants of the Platonic cave, who knew no reality save the shadows cast on the wall by the hidden light beyond, he can only wait, whether for animal extinction or spiritual rebirth he does not know. God, or no God? Belief, or unbelief? Only the 'mother of silences', whoever or whatever she is, can answer:

> Then, mother of silences,
>
> Speak, that we may hear;
> Listen, while we confess
> That we conceal our fear;
> Regard us, while the eye
> Discerns by sight or guess
> Whether, as sheep foregather
> Upon their crooked knees,
> We have begun to die;
> Whether your kindness, mother,
> Is mother of silences.

The poem ends without answering that question, for the poet does not know the answer. And while in his own life Tate professed to find the answer in Roman Catholicism, his only important published poetic work since the wartime 'Seasons of the Soul' has been three portions of a long poem, written in terza rima, in which the poet sets out to examine his past experience through the new perspective of religious faith. Again the scene is the South, the poet's childhood, but this time presented as allegory for religious meanings. Thus a lynching, as seen by a child, is related in terms of the Passion. Though almost a decade has passed since new portions of this poem have appeared in print, Tate is apparently still at work on it. At present we have only fragments of what may some day be his final, major accomplishment. If the poem is never completed, however, it would not be the first instance of a poet finding that his best and most enduring verse grows not out of belief, but of doubt. 'As I look back on my own verse, written over more than twenty-five years,' Tate wrote at one point, 'I see plainly that its main theme is man suffering from unbelief; and I cannot for a moment suppose that this man is some other than myself.' Seen in this light, Tate's 'Agrarian' poetry, written when his interest in Southern history and society was greatest, becomes an objective correlative, so to speak, for the larger, underlying problems of human faith and belief. So also, one might say, with Robert Frost's New England, Walt Whitman's Manhattan, and, indeed, Words-

worth's Lake Country; otherwise there would be no purpose in
reading poems at all.

★   ★   ★

Oddly enough, the fourth and youngest of the major Fugitive poets,
Robert Penn Warren, shows no such historical and regional preoccupa-
tion in his best lyric poetry, though as a novelist he has continually
drawn on the Southern theme. His earlier verse in particular is medita-
tive, pastoral, and almost never given to topical reference or historical
analogy. Where Tate's poetry so often assumes a shared regional ex-
perience—'we who count our days and bow/Our heads with a com-
memorial woe'—Warren's is solitary, introspective. John Crowe
Ransom's description of one as being 'instructed of much mortality'
might well describe Warren's characteristic poetic mode; his poems are
filled with images of the solitary individual contemplating his plight in
time.

As a novelist, one of the most distinguished of his century, Warren
has been primarily concerned with the individual's relationship to
power. As lyric poet, however, Warren has been largely without con-
cern for the public man in his society. His personae are characteristic-
ally locked in with their loneliness; for them it is not a mode of
thought, as it perhaps is with Tate's watcher at the cemetery gate, but
a literal fact, a condition of being. Typically his poems are filled with
nature imagery; like Wordsworth, Warren as nature poet wanders
lonely, and in forest and field discovers evidence of his mortality. But
unlike Wordsworth, and unlike Emerson or any of the other American
nature poets, even Frost, there is precious little comfort about it. Not
only is there no thought of transcendental harmony with the natural
world; there is a preoccupation with the bitter transience of man's
existence, the solitude of the human being in time. Growing fields,
harvest time, seasonal prodigality serve only to remind him of his
mortality. Of 'Croesus in Autumn' he writes:

> Should then gruff Croesus on the village bench
> Lament the absolute gold of summer gone?
>
> Though this grey guy be no Aurelius
> Surveying the ilex and the latin vine,
> He might consider a little piteous
> The green and fatal tribe's decline.

In another early lyric, 'The Last Metaphor', a man goes out to look at the wintertime landscape:

> After April and the troubled sod
> Fell summer on us with its deathly sheaf,
> Autumnal ashes then and the brittle leaf
> Whereunder fructified the crackling pod.
>
> Now flat and black the trees stand on the sky
> Unreminiscent of the year's frail verdure.
> Purged of the green that kept so fatal tenure
> They are made strong: no leaf clings mortally.

All things in nature are rumours of mortality to the man who views them. The poem entitled 'End of Season' depicts a man at the beach as the summer closes. He is reminded that it is all over with now, the friends of a summer season, the swimmers in the surf, the children playing on the shore, the whole ritualistic purifying by water. Now he must return to the world and confront time again,

> the essential face, which now wears
> The mask of travel, smudge of history. . . .

In the early poem entitled 'The Return: an Elegy', a man is riding a train back home to where his mother has died, and is trying to feel something meaningful in what has happened. Everything appears senseless, vain. He can manage only a self-conscious parody of the grief he knows he should feel:

> The wheels hum hum
> The wheels: I come I come
> Whirl out of space through time O wheels
> Pursue down backward time the ghostly parallels
> Pursue past culvert cut fill embankment semaphore
> Pursue down gleaming hours that are no more.
> The pines, black, snore.

He considers his childhood, his dead mother, his vain effort to discover some reason or logic to life:

> the old fox is dead
> what is said is said
> Heaven rest the hoary head
> what have I said?

> . . . I have said only what the wind said
> honor thy father and mother in the days of thy youth
> for time uncoils like the cottonmouth

One of the best of all Warren's poems, 'The Ballad of Billie Potts', depicts time in a similar fashion. The poem describes Billie's rise and fall in the world, with extended parenthetical commentary by the poet. Billie is the child of a frontier Kentucky innkeeper and his wife, who are in the habit of arranging for the waylaying and murder of their customers. When young Billie decides to have a try at the game himself, he is shot by an alert would-be victim for his pains. His parents thereupon give him money and tell him to head westward. Billie does so, and his fortunes prosper. Warren conceives the westward trek as constituting the essential engagement in time:

> Think of yourself riding away from the dawn,
> Think of yourself and the unnamed ones who had gone
> Before, riding, who rode away from *goodbye, goodbye,*
> And toward *hello,* toward Time's unwinking eye . . .

Man rides forth, into time, to act. Action is in time, and is innocent. Thus meaning, which is timeless and is spatial, cannot be discovered in action.

Eventually Billie decides to come back home to show his parents what he has accomplished. The trip homeward is Billie's manifestation of the need for identification, for self-realisation, which alone can provide meaning:

> You became gradually aware that something was missing
>   from the picture
> And upon closer inspection exclaimed: 'Why, I'm not in
>   it at all!'
> Which was perfectly true.

Whereupon the mortal man in time attempts to return to the place of his origins, to the 'land between the rivers', the Tigris-Euphrates Eden of man's first innocence and fall. The only hope of discovering earthly meaning lies outside of time, and each living creature struggles to escape the limitations of mortality by going back:

> The salmon heaves at the falls, and, wanderer, you
> Heave at the great fall of Time, and, gorgeous, gleam
> In the powerful arc, and anger and outrage like dew,

In your plunge, fling, and plunge to the thunderous stream:
Back to the silence, back to the pool, back
. To the high pool, motionless, and the unmurmuring dream.

But Billie's return home is not what he expected it to be. Instead, the
ostentatious wealth of the apparent stranger kindles the greed of his
parents. Before revealing his identity, Billie goes out to the spring for
a drink, and just as he sees a star reflected in the pool, unwinking, his
father murders him with a hatchet. Thus Billie's quest is thwarted by
the very conditions that made it possible.

Warren's continual use of nature in his earlier poetry as the index of
man's plight in time inevitably reminds one of that most distinguished
of twentieth-century nature poets, Robert Frost. In an excellent essay,
'The Themes of Robert Frost', Warren has shown how Frost's poems
commonly deal, not with the identity of man's concerns with those of
nature, but with the separateness. Frost, he says, never simplifies the
human position; however much man may learn from nature, his
capacity for thought, his human purposiveness set him apart from it.
Thus in Frost's 'Thrush Music' the man stands on the edge of the forest
and hears the bird singing:

> Far in the pillared dark
> Thrush music went—
> Almost like a call to come in
> To the dark and lament.
>
> But no, I was out for stars;
> I would not come in.
> I mean not even if asked,
> And I hadn't been.

The thrush's song, Warren declares, 'had seemed to be an invitation.
But it had not been an invitation after all. For the bird cannot speak to
the man. It has not the language of man.' Thus man is contrasted with
nature, though man has nature in him too, and Frost's poem concerns
itself with 'the contrast between the two kinds of beauty, and the idea
that the reward, the dream, the ideal, stems from action and not from
surrender of action'.

In general this distinction is likewise true of Warren's poems.
Though in the lines from 'The Ballad of Billie Potts' quoted above,
Warren identifies the homing instinct of man and animal alike as a

quest for meaning outside of time, there is no suggestion that man's proper condition is *in* nature. In the poem 'Pondy Woods', buzzards circling above a Negro fleeing from a lynch mob inform him that 'We swing against the sky and wait;/You seize the hour, more passionate/ Than strong, and strive with time to die—/With Time, the beaked tribe's astute ally.' The distinction is important; just as with Frost, the Southern poets do not confuse agrarianism with primitivism.

Indeed, the Southern poets, especially Warren, go even further than Frost does in this respect. For though, as Warren points out, Frost maintains a separateness between human identity and that of nature, the difference is discernible only because man so readily goes into nature, and can understand himself through what nature has to show him. For New England writers from Jonathan Edwards through Emerson, Thoreau, Dickinson and Frost, there has always been the sense of man's being able to discover his own essential self when in nature. One of Frost's finest poems begins with a fervent assertion of the need to maintain a close association with nature:

> Tree at my window, window tree,
> My sash is lowered when night comes on;
> But let there never be curtain drawn
> Between you and me.

Though the tree turns out to be 'so much concerned with outer' and the man 'with inner, weather', the two nevertheless complement each other, and the man would make sure that his habitat includes plenty of trees. One recalls Thoreau's famous dictum: 'I went to the woods because I wished to live deliberately, to front only the essential facts of life. . . .'

Like Frost, Warren too draws observations about the human condition from nature. But in his work, as in that of Tate, Ransom and Davidson as well, there is no sense of easy familiarity, no intimation that man's true fulfilment is in nature. What he learns from the contemplation of nature is the knowledge of his isolation, the conviction of his own mortality. Thus for an aged man looking at his orchard, 'the well-adapted and secular catbird/Whispers its enmity and invitation'. Nature is finally inscrutable, a mystery. Man may coexist with it; indeed, if he goes too far away from it, he is living an unnatural existence. Hence the Agrarian suspicion of modern urban life. But to coexist with nature is not to become as one with it.

One of the finest of Warren's earlier poems is 'Bearded Oaks', which is built on the realisation of man's mortal position when in nature. A man and woman are in woods so shaded that, though it is daytime, it is almost as if night were about to fall. Lying on the grass, surrounded by oaks laden with Spanish moss, they seem to be almost outside of time, in inanimate suspension from the world:

> Upon the floor of light, and time,
> Unmurmuring, of polyp made,
> We rest; we are, as light withdraws,
> Twin atolls on a shelf of shade.
>
> Ages to our construction went,
> Dim architecture, hour by hour;
> And violence, forgot now, lent
> The present stillness all its power.

The silence, the stillness of the scene seems to set at nothing all the passion, thought and frenzied activity of human life:

> All our debate is voiceless here,
> As all our rage, the rage of stone;
> If hope is hopeless, then fearless fear,
> And history is thus undone.

The sense of the unimportance of their existence when contrasted with the immense stillness of nature, the overwhelming conviction of the briefness of human life, the imminence of death, do not, the man tells the woman, cancel his human affection for her:

> I do not love you less that now
> The caged heart makes iron stroke,
> Or less that all that light once gave
> The graduate dark should now revoke.

It is rather that for this moment, life and death seem so much alike, phases of a single process, and the concerns of human experience in time so tentative and temporary, that ordinary preoccupations no longer seem important:

> We live in time so little time
> And we learn all so painfully,
> That we may spare this hour's term
> To practice for eternity.

Though the man and woman are fancifully 'of polyp made', they are nonetheless intruders on the scene. This, says the poet, is *like* death; and conversely, death will be *like* this. In life, all is different, for life is in time, and only for this hour, in this place, are time seemingly suspended and human concerns put out of mind. Their two lives, like the daylight and violence screened out by the heavy foliage, are customarily filled with the tumult of human life in time, and they come upon the stillness of the forest glade as strangers, for a little while. But there is no thought of not returning to life once the moment is past. Human beings live in time; there is no other way.

After Warren published his *Selected Poems 1923–1943*, from which all the poems thus far discussed are taken, he brought out no new collection of lyrical poetry for thirteen years. During this time he wrote four novels, a verse-play, a long poetic narrative, numerous critical essays and a volume of journalism. It was not until the early 1950's that new lyric poems by Warren began appearing in magazines. When *Promises: Poems 1954–1956* was published, readers familiar with his earlier work noted what seemed a significant difference. The new poems were, like the previous work, private, dealing with man in his solitude rather than in public situations, but they dealt directly and unashamedly with Warren's own personal experience and with the poet's reflections on that experience. Previously the sense of 'public' utterance was a characteristic of poems by Southerners; there was no assertion of uniqueness, of private personality, as for example in Yeats or Frost. In this respect Southern poetry has always been much more closely akin to the poetry of eighteenth-century England; it has been formal, mannered, holding the reader at arm's length, as it were, the product of a society so patterned and codified that inward emotion is expressed in formalised symbols, assuming common experience and shared attitudes. Even Tate's later work, in which the first person singular is habitually used, is not 'private'; it is public confession, which is another thing entirely.

In his recent work, however, Warren writes of his children, his boyhood, his parents, his present thoughts about them. Perhaps as a result of his extensive involvement with prose fiction, the language is much more colloquial than ever before, and the form of the poems considerably more free and relaxed, not nearly so concentrated. Though sometimes they seem little more than clever *vers de société*, the net result, it seems to me, is one of liberation from what for Warren at any rate had become an increasingly hampering restraint on his poetry. One cannot, for example, imagine Tate or Ransom writing a stanza such as this, from *Promises: Poems 1954–1956*:

> Sleep, my son, and smile in sleep.
> You will dream the world anew.
> Watching you now sleep,
> I feel the world's depleted force renew,
> Feel the nerve expand and knit,
> Feel a rustle in the blood,
> Feel wink or warmth or stir of spirit,
> As though season woke in the heart's cold underwood.
> The vernal work is now begun.
> Sleep, my son.
> Sleep, son.

A decently sound case could be made for the position that the reader need not know who Warren is to appreciate the poem, and that therefore it is an objectified emotion. This is quite true; but the whole tone of the poem, the choice of words, the easy flow of the irregularly metred lines, focuses our attention on the personality of the poet. We are inside his mind.

All but the very best of Warren's earlier work, that collected in the *Selected Poems 1923–1943* and written for the most part before he turned importantly to the writing of novels, seem, to the present writer at least, to involve a kind of victory of the intelligence over a too artificial notion of form. It is not that Warren does not write such poems well, but rather that the language and the sensibility seem somehow uncomfortable within the rigid form of a too impersonal, too conventional medium. In the later poetry it is as if he had decided to lay aside the mask of anonymity, to forget any pretension to an austere formal dignity. Devoid of pose, the later work recreates, through the poet's own honesty of perception, an experience of being human that is at times compellingly beautiful.

*   *   *

Of the four leading Fugitive poets, Warren has been the only one to produce any considerable body of verse in recent years. One might conjecture that, with the steady breakdown of the traditional agrarian, conservative society of the pre-industrial South before the forces of the twentieth century, the terms whereby a Southern poet might work his art demanded a much greater dependence on the individual's private, personal experience, the direct exploitation of his own personality, together with far less reliance upon communal myth, shared social attitude and public voice. If so, it would not be after all surprising that Warren, younger by far than the others, would turn out to be most able to adapt his muse to a different, more cosmopolitan, less communal cultural experience.

Significantly, I think, the poetry written by younger Southern poets, those who began publishing their work in the years during and after the second world war, is generally conceded to share very few of the qualities that one associates with Southern poetry. The foremost historian of the Fugitive group, Professor Louise Cowan, has demonstrated convincingly that the poetry of the leading Fugitives possesses certain characteristics—a classical form, a clear rational framework, dignity and elevation of style, loyalty and affection rather than the brooding loneliness and isolation of most modern poems, and the sense of a shared commitment between author and addressee, 'a bond between the two based on something outside themselves to which they acknowledged allegiance'. The poetry of Ransom, Tate, Davidson and the earlier Warren, Professor Cowan declares, is marked by these characteristics, in a way that the poetry of the later Warren, and that of such younger poets as Randall Jarrell, James Dickey and William Jay Smith, all of whom were born and reared in the South, is not so marked. The poetry of these latter writers, she says, is 'active, accomplished, and all but indistinguishable from poetry in the rest of the nation'.

By and large, it seems to me, this is true. Where in prose fiction there seems little or no abatement of the Southern Literary Renascence that began in the 1920's—Faulkner, Warren, Thomas Wolfe, Eudora Welty, Katherine Anne Porter, Andrew Nelson Lytle, Carson McCullers, Caroline Gordon have been followed by William Styron, Flannery O'Connor, James Agee, Peter Taylor, Reynolds Price, Elizabeth Spencer, Truman Capote, Madison Jones, George Garrett, Shirley Ann Grau, Shelby Foote, Walter Sullivan—there has been no comparable literary succession in Southern poetry. Jarrell, Dickey, Smith and others seem to have far less in common with Tate and Ransom, and far more in common with such other, non-Southern poets of their own generation as Robert Lowell, Karl Shapiro, Richard Wilbur, Howard Nemerov, John Berryman, William Meredith and Reed Whittemore, than is true for the novelists. Perhaps this is because of the far greater relative importance of technique in poetry, as compared with content. In any event, one would be hard put, I think, to single out, in the work of the younger poets of Southern origin, characteristics which seem importantly 'Southern'.

Robert Penn Warren's later work, as I have said, seems to mirror this transition. Yet if in this respect he seems to have travelled far from his fellow-Fugitives, in another sense he may be said to be writing, in his recent verse, as directly out of his region's experience as ever. For if the South has been undergoing great change as it enters the modern industrial world and loses its old social identity, its strong commitment to the community and the values of the community, then one result of this change must surely be that its writers are made conscious, to a heightened degree, of the impact of change, the passage of time, the distance they have travelled. And Warren's most recent poetry is, more so than even his earlier work, pervaded by the poet's awareness of time and change, his awe and wonder at how far in time and history he has come.

Thus in one of the best poems from *Promises*, the poet remembers a time when as a youth he had worked on the farm back in the rural South, and as he pictures to himself the scene, the thresher quiet after the harvest, the hired hands paid off, and the coming of night to the farm, he thinks of how far away he has travelled, until now he stands on a shore, across the ocean, and the years stretch out between what he is now and what he once knew and was. The ending of the poem, which is entitled 'Hands Are Paid', might well constitute an epitaph for all the writers of an American region, one which in our century has dislodged its young men to send them out in the world to create their art out of what they once knew and were, and which is now no more:

> And the years go by like a breath, or eye-blink,
> And all history lives in the head again,
> And I shut my eyes and I see that scene,
> And name each item, but I cannot think
> What, in their urgency, they must mean,

But know, even now, on this foreign shore,
In blaze of sun and the sea's stare,
A heart-stab blessed past joy or despair,
As I see, in the mind's dark, once more,
The field, pale, under starlit air.

Note

Biographies. Walt (Walter) Whitman (1819–92) was born in Long Island, New York; at 11 he was an office boy and later became printer, teacher, journalist and traveller. The first edition of *Leaves of Grass* appeared in 1855; and this was subsequently altered and enlarged in many further editions, the last in 1891–2. Whitman was a clerk in the offices of the Department of Interior and of the Attorney-General of the U.S., from 1865 to 1873 when he was afflicted with paralysis; he then lived in Camden, New Jersey, until his death.

Hart Crane (1899–1932) was born at Garretsville, Ohio, and moved to New York and his family's plantation in the West Indies. He was unsatisfied with jobs in advertising and the family business, and refused to go to college; later he spent much time in Europe. He was influenced by Christian Science, Rimbaud and Ouspensky. He ended his own life by throwing himself from the ship on which he was returning from Mexico.

Robert Frost (1874–1963) was born in San Francisco but brought up by his widowed mother in Lawrence, Massachusetts. After some time at Dartmouth College and Harvard University he worked in a textile mill, taught, edited a local paper, farmed and wrote verses. Travelling to England in 1912 he gained recognition, especially among the 'Georgian' poets; his first volumes *A Boy's Will* (1913) and *North of Boston* (1914) were published in England. Returning to the United States, Frost lived in the countryside of New England and was for a time a 'resident poet' for Amherst College and other campuses.

Modern Editions. No complete edition of Whitman is in print, but seven volumes of an anticipated fourteen of *The Collected Writings of Walt Whitman* have been recently published; the general editors are G. W. Allen and S. Bradley, the publisher New York University Press.

For the general reader a convenient source of the final version of *Leaves,* plus the rejected poems, is *Complete Poetry and Selected Prose,* edited by J. E. Miller, Jr. (1959). The significant first and third editions are available in paperback: *Walt Whitman's Leaves of Grass: The First (1855) Edition,* ed. M. Cowley (1959) and *Leaves of Grass, Facsimile Edition of the 1860 Text* with an introduction by R. H. Pearce (1961). Quotations in the following chapter are from the final edition, unless otherwise noted.

Frost's collected poetry is available in two volumes, *Complete Poems* (1949) and *In the Clearing* (1962).

The Complete Poems of Hart Crane, edited by W. Frank, are available in paperback (1958).

Criticism. Willard Thorp has written on Whitman in *Eight American Authors: A Review of Research and Criticism,* ed. F. Stovall (1956; paperback ed., 1963). Deficient in some respects but useful is *A Critical Guide to Leaves of Grass,* by James E. Miller, Jr., published 1957 but currently out of print. A centennial volume of essays was edited by M. Hindus in 1955 under the title, *Leaves of*

II

America and the Poet:
Whitman, Hart Crane and Frost

J. ALBERT ROBBINS

*

THERE was little in the early years of Whitman's life to predict that, in his thirty-sixth year, he would produce the astonishing 1855 edition of *Leaves of Grass* and revolutionise American poetry. Even now it is difficult to document how the ungifted writer of mediocre verse and tales could have conceived and executed the revolutionary volume. Whitman is no absolute pioneer, for it was Emerson who first had the full vision of the ideal America, but it was Whitman who first applied that vision fully to poetry. Surely, as Emerson surmised, Whitman's poem was long in preparation, as the boy came to know and feel the texture of life on his father's Long Island farm and the ocean shore near by, and as the young man absorbed the varied human scene in the village of Brooklyn and the metropolis of New York. 'Starting from fish-shape Paumanok[1] where I was born,' Whitman lived the continuum of American life from farm to village to metropolis. The wilderness he knew only by brief observation and by reading, but the awareness of it fills his poems. Among these levels of American life

[1] The Indian word for Long Island which Whitman was fond of using.

Grass One Hundred Years After. R. H. Pearce has edited *Whitman: A Collection of Critical Essays* (1962).

Three basic works on Whitman are G. W. Allen's *The Solitary Singer: A Critical Biography of Walt Whitman* (1955), *Walt Whitman Handbook* (1946) and Roger Asselineau, *The Evolution of Walt Whitman* (2 vols.; translated 1960-2).

A helpful critical study is L. S. Dembo *Hart Crane's Sanskrit Charge: A Study of 'The Bridge'* (1960).

The most adequate biography of Frost is Elizabeth S. Sergeant's *Robert Frost: The Trial by Existence* (1960), and a convenient sampling of criticism is *Robert Frost: A Collection of Critical Essays*, edited by James M. Cox (1962).

Whitman ranged freely in actuality and in imagination. Though he loved Brooklyn and Manhattan, he felt the pull back to woods and shores, and he never outgrew the love or need of solitudes. We see this in the way the themes are linked in adjoining passages of 'Song of Myself'; and we see also how fundamental to Whitman are fact and sensory experience:

> Alone far in the wilds and mountains I hunt,
> Wandering amazed at my own lightness and glee,
> In the late afternoon choosing a safe spot to pass the night,
> Kindling a fire and broiling the freshkilled game . . .
>
> . . . . . .
>
> The big doors of the country-barn stand open and ready . . .
> The clear light plays on the brown gray and green intermingled,
> The armfuls are packed to the sagging mow:
> I am there, I help, I come stretch'd atop of the load . . .
>
> . . . . . .
>
> The heavy omnibus, the driver with his interrogating thumb,
>   the clank of the shod horses on the granite floor . . .
> The hurrahs for popular favorites, the fury of roused mobs . . .
> The excited crowd—the policeman with his star quickly working
>   his passage to the centre of the crowd . . .

Whitman poised his life midway between country and city—first in the village of Brooklyn, with Manhattan beyond the East River; later in Camden, with Philadelphia across the Delaware. Though he spent his years in Brooklyn and Camden, and during the War in Washington, it is right that we do not associate him with any seat of residence, as we do Emerson and Longfellow. We think of him, as we should, not residing but moving—making forays, walking and absorbing the day's sensations and scenes. As in his poetry so in his life motion was vital for him—the motion of restlessness to be sure, but also a questing to fill a deep psychic need for humanity.

More went into the first *Leaves of Grass* than walking and observing, of course. Whitman's knowledge of Emerson had great force in shaping his idealisation of man, and the very vehemence with which Whitman later denied the influence betokens it. To a remarkable degree do the characteristics of Emerson's ideal new poet, announced in the 1844 essay, 'The Poet', describe the Whitman of the 1855 *Leaves*.[2] He fulfills

2 Cf. Chapter VIII, pp. 176-9, below.

what Emerson requires: the sayer and namer; committed not to metres but to metre-making argument; the seer of visions purer for a simple soul in a chaste body. In 1844 Emerson looked in vain for such a poet: 'We do not with sufficient plainness or sufficient profoundness address ourselves to life, nor dare we chaunt our own times and social circumstance. If we filled the day with bravery, we should not shrink from celebrating it.' Within eleven years the post delivered just such a poet into Emerson's hands and only Emerson was capable of instant recognition. 'I rubbed my eyes a little,' he wrote Whitman, 'to see if this sunbeam were no illusion.'

The circumstances of Whitman's appearance as poet attest to his high purpose. It was as though he had husbanded his powers in order to take the world by surprise. His paternal solicitude for the physical book shows his attitude. It was new in size, for Whitman needed an unusually wide page to accommodate his long lines; and the absence of the author's name on the title-page, with the unidentified portrait of the frontispiece looking one in the eye, the absence of titles for individual poems; the unconventional punctuation, the often 'unpoetic' vocabulary, the vigour and sweep of the words—all these announced a new era in poetry.

Such a break with tradition demanded explanation, and even here there is originality. The untitled preface is unconventional poetic prose, so close in manner and cadence to the poetry which follows that Whitman later easily converted portions of it into separate poems. (In this and in other ways, Whitman showed himself to be one of the first in prose or in poetry to assail the barriers of form.) Actually this important preface is a manifesto which announces, defines, and explains in most forceful terms. There is no arguing or convincing, no vituperation or sarcasm, but only calm and positive pronouncement. There is no formal order or logical progression of thought—something uncongenial to Whitman in both prose and poetry, but passionate rhetoric and moving cadence. 'The United States themselves are essentially the greatest poem', he tells us. The one complete lover who is the poet must be also 'arbiter of the diverse' and 'equalizer of his age and land'. He will have such resources of soul that he 'confronts all the shows he sees by equivalents out of the stronger wealth of himself'. He will not withdraw from worldly affairs, but be the voice of political liberty, to cheer slaves and horrify despots. He will 'flood himself with the immediate age' and be not merely the age but 'the age transfigured'. He will speak 'the dialect of common sense' in an American language brawny, limber and full. Such poems will not be 'distilled from other poems', but drawn directly from life, distilled through the soul and character of the poet, who speaks not definitively but procreatively, for, note, 'a great poem is no finish to a man or woman but rather a beginning'.

This last principle he rephrases early in 'Song of Myself', where he promises the reader not merely a poem but the *origin* of all poems. He is convinced that poetry has a power not just to describe but to shape life. 'By my life-bumps! becoming already a creator!' we find him exclaiming with wit and joy in 'Song of Myself'. The reader no longer is graciously admitted as a privileged observer into the poet's presence; he is seized ('My left hand hooks you round the waist') and forcefully shown the 'landscapes of continents' and universes. And this poet will not take no for an answer: 'I *will* you to be a bold swimmer',[3] he insists. Taking the brave specifications of Emerson's new poet, he has made them bolder and more inclusive in his preface, and then has proceeded, in 'Song of Myself' especially, to become and be that new poet.

This 'Song' has astonishing variety and immediacy. The shifts of cadence, tone, language, the breathless excitement of the poet's words, even with repeated reading, grip the responsive reader. The style hooks you round the waist, compelling you to see where Whitman sees, feel as he feels, and soar with him as he moves at will through time and space. The flood of images and emotions sweeps the reader along, not in straight but in circular or spiral courses. Whitman displays countless scenes and *personae*, many of them contradictory and baffling. He is the idler and drifter, but also the purposeful seer; he is the rebel, but also the uniter and transcender; the rough, but also the tender lover; despondent, but ecstatic. He forces eternal truths upon us one minute and the next confesses to fallibility.

The simplest experience becomes miraculous: 'To walk up my stoop is unaccountable, I pause to consider if it really be'; and meaning floods in upon him from both the unexpected and the familiar. 'A morning-glory at my window satisfies me more than the metaphysics of books', he tells us. All is a miracle, as he says explicitly in the poem 'Miracles', 'Whether I walk the streets of Manhattan . . ./Or stand under trees in the woods.' He constantly shifts stance and posture, one moment promising us 'the origin of all poems' if you 'stop this day and night

[3] Italics mine.

with me'; the next, warning us that 'You shall not look through my eyes either.' There is an air distinctly jocose in his keeping us constantly off balance, in talking one moment about universal truths and the next about the scent of arm-pits. He dares at one moment to assault with abrupt rhythms and commonplace monosyllables: 'Every kind for itself and its own, for me mine male and female'; and the next to delight with exquisite music: 'I am he that walks with the tender and growing night;/I call to the earth and sea half-held by the night.'

For Whitman to make his 'Song' appear random and inchoate was poetically right and intellectually astute. The questions we face seldom present themselves logically; our consciousness is less orderly than erratic. By sacrificing the rational forms of coherence Whitman was releasing the mind from arbitrary order and pointing to new possibilities in literature. As he develops his poem, he is fully free to elaborate, to juxtapose, to reiterate.

The true structure of 'Song of Myself' is not logical but dramatic. After the tentative thoughts of the opening, with conjecture upon purpose in life and with a masterful employment of the symbol of grass, Whitman at some length describes his search for identity and certitude. In the process, at first tentative and speculative, finally with conviction and certainty, the identity is achieved, the name announced: 'Walt Whitman, an American, one of the roughs, a kosmos'; thus he suggests a nationality, a personality and a purpose. With such new resources, the poet announces, 'I am afoot with my vision', and proceeds on an imaginative journey to cover all time and all modes of life. It is a journey of intense optimism in which the poet identifies himself with mankind: 'I am the man, I suffered, I was there.' The generalised experiences we have encountered earlier become here explicit recreations of actual historical events—the fall of the Alamo, the victory of the frigate *Bonhomme Richard*—which the poet imaginatively enters by identifying himself with men of the heroic and moving past.

The intense emotion and sense of power reach a sudden climax of surfeit and doubt as the poet exclaims: 'O Christ! My fit is mastering me!' Here is the dramatic pivot, the discovery and reversal, of the poem:

Enough! enough! enough!
Somehow I have been stunned. Stand back!
Give me a little time beyond my cuffed head and slumbers and
    dreams and gaping,
I discover myself on a verge of the usual mistake.

The succeeding allusions to crucifixion and resurrection are even more intensive and revealing:

> That I could look with a separate look on my own crucifixion and
>   bloody crowning! . . .
> The corpses rise, the gashes heal, the fastenings roll away.

Only in reflecting on this journey, impressive in its own way, do we realise that the earlier, generalised passing references to 'you' are completely absent. Whitman's trial flight of the spirit, for all its vigour and intensity, has been introverted and self-centred; by 'the usual mistake' he means a false involvement in the conventionally ideal and heroic. In actuality the meaning of life does not add up to noble last stands in a Texas mission-fort or to glorious sea victories over the British. Life has its mockers and insults, tears and blows. In the sudden reversal, therefore, Whitman dramatises the false poet he might have become and indeed for a moment did become. Only by a symbolic crucifixion and resurrection, only by a poetic reincarnation can he realise his true poetic purpose. A vital key, the word 'eleves', appears now, and this image permeates the remainder of the poem.

Up to this point the poet has merely addressed the vague, stereotyped 'you' at the very beginning of the 'Song', and that not often; now 'eleves' announces not only certitudes but profound purposes. Purely personal sensation and belief now become faith and purposeful action. The poet-celebrator of earlier lines becomes the poet-teacher, the saviour-poet, newly risen; and it is *after* the symbolic resurrection from falsity that this ministry begins. Whereas earlier Whitman merely identified himself with others ('I am the man, I suffered, I was there'), he now bestows himself ('When I give I give out of myself'— and in later revision he wisely deleted the words 'out of'). His sense of power, even over death, is not now merely for himself, but for others. What before had been vague symbol and intuition ('Or I guess it [the grass] is the handkerchief of the Lord . . ./Bearing the owner's name someway in the corners, that we may see and remark, and say "Whose?" ') is now certainty and confident metaphor ('I find letters from God dropped in the street, and every one is signed by God's name').

Near the mid-point of this last important segment of the poem, as though he were speaking cosmic truths from a pulpit, Whitman says, 'It is time to explain myself—let us stand up.' Man must approach full realisation in the posture of praise, which is as well the posture of inherent nobility. It is here that Whitman relates man to his God; for we are now prepared to hear the words: 'And nothing, not God, is greater to one than one's-self is . . ./And any man or woman shall stand cool and supercilious before a million universes.' After such loud affirmations, the poetry gives way to quiet and reflective assertions. The credo which began forthrightly with 'let us stand up', closes with a quiet plea, 'Do you see O my brothers and sisters?/It is not chaos or death—it is form, union, plan—it is eternal life—it is Happiness.' There remain only the closing lines, a verse coda, in which the words with memorable feeling direct our thoughts increasingly to nature, the source of both mystery and meaning, as the poet gently takes leave of mankind, his eleves, still affirming the promises that lie ahead for the seeker:

I depart as air. . . .
I bequeath myself to the dirt to grow from the grass I love,
If you want me again look for me under your bootsoles.

And the final words remind us of those at the poem's commencement ('A child said *What is the grass?* fetching it to me with full hands'):

Failing to fetch me at first keep encouraged,
Missing me one place search another,
I stop somewhere waiting for you.

We come again to the bountiful earth, where we saw the poet reclining as the poem opened, but with what a difference! The Whitman of the first line who said, 'I celebrate myself', is not the Whitman who at the close says, 'I bequeath myself'.

'Song of Myself' is meteoric poetry, flashing powerfully into view, then fading swiftly to leave burned on the retina of the mind and imagination the memory of a dazzling experience. Whitman's words seem to grow out of the experience itself, taking organic shape as we read and carrying an inherent authority. One has only to recall such a poem as Pope's 'Essay on Man' to realise the quite different world of feeling and intuitive truth which Whitman records. In speaking as the common man and for him, he shows us the beauty and power that lie there, common no longer but greatly uncommon.

★   ★   ★

'Song of Myself' was rich enough to include virtually all of the themes and convictions that were to occupy Whitman for the remaining

thirty-seven years of his life. Yet it is incomplete. For all his claim of
openness and honesty, Whitman held back from revealing the dark side
of his vision, associated with sexual experience: the conflict between the
poet in him and the lover. Only in reworking and enlarging his poems
for the third edition of *Leaves of Grass* did Whitman reflect a recent
personal crisis and allow himself to admit that sexual passion, for him,
was not the analogue of creation but the emblem of poetic sterility; and
even then he insisted on tying this revelation to an exactly opposed
assertion. The forms he gave these opposed expressions became two
series of poems, 'Children of Adam' and 'Calamus'.

The former celebrates procreation and the sexes and these themes can
be found throughout 'Song of Myself', along with early reference to
Adam and Eve in the final poem of the first edition. Even the sexual
preoccupations of the 'Calamus' poems are not wholly unexpected,
for the Whitman of 'Song of Myself' prefigures 'Calamus' by insistently
describing men and the male body. Much of the imagery of the 'Song',
too, prepares us for 'Calamus'. As we approach a central section of the
earlier work, we meet an astonishing concentration of these images:
'firm masculine coulter', 'milky stream pale strippings of my life',
'mixed tussled hay of head and beard and brawn', 'fibre of manly
wheat'; and it is even more notable that, in turning to nature, the
sexual imagery continues. The brooks to him are sweaty, the gentle
pressures of wind upon one's body are like the rub of soft-tickling
genitals and the fields are broad and muscular. But if the sexual
themes of the 'Calamus' poems are by no means new, their autobio-
graphical immediacy is. 'Calamus', however, is best approached
through the associated, counterbalancing 'Children of Adam'.

While Whitman's ordinary mode is to celebrate and expound, he
reserves for his major poems a special form of the dramatic or narrative.
This is true of the 'Song', as we have seen, and of other important
poems such as 'Out of the Cradle Endlessly Rocking' and 'When
Lilacs Last in the Dooryard Bloom'd'. If we apply the same principle
to these two sex clusters, it becomes apparent that 'Children of Adam'
is celebratory and non-dramatic, and thus is entertained rather than
vitally felt. It deals with heterosexual love and procreation in terms that
are mythic and visionary. But 'Calamus' follows another mode.
Dealing with sexual inversion, the love of man for man, these poems
are starkly biographic and real. 'Adam' is Whitman's ideal for mankind;
'Calamus' is for him the personal reality.

'Children of Adam' opens with joyous announcement:

> To the garden the world anew ascending,
> Potent mates, daughters, sons, preluding,
> The love, the life of their bodies, meaning and being,
> Curious here behold my resurrection after slumber . . .

and ends with a vision of a new, modern Adam walking in perfect joy and concord with Eve. Elsewhere Whitman calls himself 'chanter of Adamic songs,/Through the new garden the West, the great cities calling.' Through the imagery of these poems he dwells on themes of awakening, morning light and promise, the miracle of procreation ('the bath of birth') and the movement of life ('All is a procession . . . with measured and beautiful motion'). The word death appears just once— and then only as an inevitable part of the sequence from birth to immortality.

But 'Calamus' is largely a grim withdrawal from the main currents of life, a foreboding dirge, brooding, agonising, solitary and death-ridden. For the basic 'Calamus' images of forest, pond and sedges Whitman's imagination reaches back to a closing section of the 'Song', where he spoke of a turbid pool and an autumnal forest; and the transition from the garden image of 'Children of Adam' is found in 'These I Singing in Spring':

> I traverse the garden, the world—but soon I pass the gate,
> Now along the pond-side, where the old stones have accumulated,
> Wild-flowers and vines and weeds. Beyond these I pass,
> Far, far in the forest, before I think where I get,
> Solitary, smelling the earthy smell, stopping now and then in
>   silence . . .

With this quick transition, Whitman takes us from the sunny, fresh and hopeful garden of the world, past the abandoned relics of human society, and into the dark and solitary forest. We soon sense why these poems are unique: we are seeing Whitman the man, not Whitman the poet. Here the saviour-poet falters and loses sight of his previously announced mission. But these are significant poems because they show us with incredible frankness the real Whitman, not his masks, and because they reveal the dark underside of his psyche that is the necessary though little-seen counterpart of his more idealistic utterances.

Here 'in paths untrodden,/In the growth by margins of pond-waters', here 'away from the clank of the world', he can respond as he 'would not dare elsewhere' and 'tell the secret' of his 'nights and days'. What he has written heretofore he describes in the cancelled lines of the second poem: 'disclaiming all except what I had in myself'—'boasting how complete I was in myself'. But the self, even though it partake of all the wonder of life and creation, now does not suffice without 'a lover, a dear friend, [to] walk by my side'. He shows us the man in desperate conflict with the poet, whether gloomily convinced that 'my chant of lovers . . . must be for Death', or else hopefully trying to fuse it with his programme of universal love of men and women. Perhaps he can 'plant companionship, thick as trees along all the rivers of America', he says in a hopeful mood; but shortly thereafter we feel shocked to find in the eighth poem, never reprinted, an announcement of poetic abdication. All that he once thought vital and meaningful—knowledge, nation, heroes, 'the songs of the New World'—do not now suffice; and now he serves notice:

> I can be your singer of songs no longer—One who loves me is
>   jealous of me, and withdraws me from all but love,
> With the rest I dispense—I sever from what I thought would suffice
>   me, for it does not—it is now empty and tasteless to me . . .
> I am indifferent to my own songs—I will go with him I love,
> It is enough for us that we are together—We never separate again.

Few of these are hopeful poems. The limitless promise and sense of power have vanished, for Whitman realises that 'it is not for life I am chanting here my chant of lovers—I think it must be for Death'.

Unlike the thoughtful narrative plan of 'Song of Myself', the 'Calamus' narrative is fragmentary and disordered, necessarily and perhaps deliberately so. Whether this personal crisis merely burned itself out or whether Whitman regained the will and power to extinguish or suppress it, we are not told. What we do know, through the later poems, is that he did forsake the weedy margin of the pond and find his way out of the solitary forest of guilty love, returning to the streets and roads and shores where sun and stars glowed as before with promise. One thinks inevitably of Hart Crane, who later faced his own Calamus crisis, only to be submerged by it, though not before he had achieved in *The Bridge* his poetic vision of man's transcendence over self and time.

Whitman's best later poems show us the poet of old, who, if rather less ebullient, is more mature and eloquent, capable, for example, of combining deep elegiac feeling on Lincoln's death with a calm faith in man's ability to surmount the national disasters of war and the mysteries of death. The despair of the mocking-bird in the earlier 'Out of the Cradle' becomes, in the thrush's song of 'When Lilacs Last in the Dooryard Bloom'd', a carol of joy. If the former poem accounts for the inception of poetic power through vicarious suffering, the latter demonstrates the more awesome qualities of wisdom and serenity of soul. Whitman is, I believe, all the greater for the Calamus experience. Without it, *Leaves of Grass* wants essential honesty, Whitman's poetry loses the greatest triumph of his selfhood, and the arc of experience is left broken.

*   *   *

A conscious heir of Whitman in the twentieth century is Hart Crane,[4] who strove so intensely to realise selfhood and purpose in his world. But that world differed from Whitman's. The technological progress with which Whitman had come to terms now seemed monstrous. The search for selfhood became, for this sensitive poet, grim and lonely. No longer, as in Whitman's day, does such a poet as Crane find infinite resources and assurances in the busy, exciting human scene about him. Crane feels like a Rip Van Winkle, come suddenly into a world he never made and demeaned by it. Thrust forward in time,

> . . . *Rip forgot the office hours,*
> > *and he forgot the pay;*
> > *Van Winkle sweeps a tenement*
> > > *way down on Avenue A.*

This is Whitman's same continent of majestic mountains and rivers, but now man has changed all that he touches, until

> *Macadam, gun-grey as the tunny's belt,*
> *Leaps from Far Rockaway to Golden Gate.*

The West offers no escape, for there the demanding signboards follow, with 'the telegraphic night coming on Thomas/a Ediford'. In his need the poet is forced back in history, as Whitman was not, to evoke the archetypal love and compassion of Pocahontas for John Smith—

[4] Cf. Chapter IX, pp. 216-19, below.

Pocahontas, whose beauty for Crane is that of the whole unviolated new world:

> your hand within my hands are deeds;
> my tongue upon your throat—singing
> arms close; eyes wide, undoubtful
>   dark
>   drink the dawn—
> a forest shudders in your hair!

Her counterpart in the latter day has become a repellent burlesque performer:

> Her eyes exist in swivellings of her teats,
> Pearls whip her hips, a drench of whirling strands.
> Her silly snake rings begin to mount, surmount
> Each other—turquoise fakes on tinselled hands.

This is far from the New York of Whitman's day, with 'The glories strung like beads on my smallest sights and hearings, on the walk in the street, and the passage over the river.' That river between the islands flows as before, but Whitman's Brooklyn Ferry is gone, the ferry by whose transit he was carried to a new identity and spiritual realisation. It is no coincidence that Hart Crane goes back to the same spot to make the journey once more, and no surprise to find the journey more difficult. 'Crossing Brooklyn Ferry' becomes *The Bridge*. For Crane there are two means of physical transit—the clanking, swaying subway which dives beneath the river and the soaring bridge of stone and steel which rises above it. The subway and all it represents in modern life he associates with Poe, his symbol of the alienated, riven artist. Here, among the advertisements for toothpaste and dandruff cures, he finds 'Death, aloft,—gigantically down/Probing through you—toward me, O evermore!' Only the useful machine above the river truly bridges the stream of time and awareness man must cross, and only this at once useful and beautiful structure now can express the vision and faith of Whitman, he whom, in our past, we can least afford to lose.

Another vital image and symbol in *The Bridge* is the airship, man's most dramatic machine for soaring. Crane explores this symbol in the 'Cape Hatteras' section—that graveyard of man's ships, yet near Kitty Hawk, the birthplace of the airship. The epigraph comes from Whitman: '*The seas all crossed,/weathered the capes, the voyage done . . .*'—

lines which are at once hopeful and ironic to Crane. The earlier faiths
seem now impossible:

> '—Recorders ages hence'—ah, syllables of faith!
> Walt, tell me, Walt Whitman, if infinity
> Be still the same as when you walked the beach
> Near Paumanok . . .
> O Saunterer on free ways still ahead!
> Not this our empire yet, but labyrinth . . .

The poet, Crane feels, must seek his faith, not to the sound of sea and
cry of birds, but to 'the nasal whine of power' which 'whips a new
universe'—'New verities, new inklings in the velvet hummed/Of
dynamos.' Man's airships lift him to no truths but become instruments
of hideous, impersonal death in the 'Great War' of Crane's day.
Hatteras and the airship presage only despair and ruin. Only the bridge,
as product of man's technical cunning and as expression of his yet
unquenched spirit, only Brooklyn Bridge can image the hope which
Crane seeks desperately to confirm. In Crane's imagination, master
and bridge merge:

> Our Meistersinger, thou set breath in steel;
> And it was thou who on boldest heel
> Stood up and flung the span on even wing
> Of that great Bridge, our Myth, whereof I sing!

The close of *The Bridge* is reminiscent of the final lines of Whitman's
'Passage to India', in cosmic vision, in a unity of West and East, and in
foreseeable victory, though the language is tortured as Whitman's was
not:

> So to thine Everpresence, beyond time,
> Like spears ensanguined of one tolling star
> That bleeds infinity—the orphic strings,
> Sidereal phalanxes, leap and converge:
> —One Song, one Bridge of Fire! Is it Cathay,
> Now pity steeps the grass and rainbows ring
> The serpent with the eagle in the leaves . . .?
> Whispers antiphonal in azure swing.

*   *   *

As a poet Whitman felt little response to the great political events,
the early leaders or the public issues of American history, but within a

year after the Calamus poems appeared as part of the 1860 edition of *Leaves of Grass*, the nation faced the crisis of the century. Whitman, who more and more was coming to consider himself an unofficial American laureate, confronted the brutal and complex forces of history that could not fail to involve him. Events beyond human power threatened Whitman's certainty of man's self-determination and imperilled his confidence in his imminent perfection. How would Whitman respond? It was in the 1860 edition that he published 'I Was Looking for a Long While', where he rejects the fabled past; but here, with war, was present history of such scope that it could not fail to touch him personally (as it did with the wounding of his brother) or fail to move him deeply as a man.

Yet neither before the war nor after it was Whitman drawn to history as such. He wrote no poems comparable to Bryant's 'The Battlefield', or Longfellow's 'Paul Revere's Ride', or Emerson's 'Concord Hymn'. Though fully convinced that America's revolution was a great moment in human history and though he was fond of dating the years of American history, either by 'presidentiads', as he called the terms of American presidents, or by the years that had elapsed since 1776, he has little to say about the country's historical past. The casual reference in 'By Blue Ontario's Shore' is typical: 'The haughty defiance of the Year One, war, peace, the formation of the Constitution.' There is no mention of such men as Franklin or Paine or Patrick Henry. He mentions Jefferson once and though there are a dozen references to Washington, none of them extensive, neither this great American nor others are central in Whitman's poems.

As for the widening split between North and South before hostilities, Whitman was uneasily aware that the nation was drifting towards disunity, a course exactly opposite to that which he foresees in his poetry. Yet his poetry shows little attempt to speak out for human nobility, then under such direct challenge. If he speaks of the selling and enslaving of Negroes, it is seldom and only as details in other contexts. The passage on the fugitive slave in 'Song of Myself' is a vivid one, but it can be considered as an eastern episode to counterbalance a western one. In 'I Sing the Body Electric' the allusions to slavery seem to be references to American realities rather than a condemning of injustices as such. In this poem celebrating the nobility and cleanness of the human body, Whitman speaks of a male and a female slave at auction, but the point here is that this is yet one more instance of the beauty and greatness of the body, this magnificent Negro being worthy to be 'the start of populous states and rich republics'. For a true commitment, one has to turn to such an early piece as 'A Boston Ballad', where the intention is clear and the sense of outrage apparent—fury that the laws and authorities of Massachusetts abet the return of escaped slaves. However, one must then admit that this poem is weak and of a humble imaginative order. In all his poetry there is only one allusion to the liberation of the slaves, a poem called 'Ethiopia Saluting the Colors', written not before or during the war but in 1871. And, again, it is no masterpiece.

In point of fact, the Civil War went surprisingly unregarded in American literature generally; and few writers came close to the conflict. They largely missed it. Lowell pursued his career undisturbed, Henry James had a physical disability, Howells was living in a comfortable consulate in Venice, and Clemens went off to rough it not in Virginia but in Nevada. Melville made a brief visit to the scene of hostilities, but it was chiefly a pleasant outing among hospitable and gentlemanly officers. Whitman saw and felt the ugly realities of the conflict, but as an observer; and even he, with all his capacity for feeling, responded best to the sad lyricism of hospital suffering and dying. (His great elegy on the death of Lincoln, of course, came afterwards and is not a war poem.) The one great novel on the Civil War appeared in 1895, written by a young man born six years after the conflict. Only two volumes are serious candidates for significant war poetry, Whitman's *Drum-Taps* (1865), which is not now in print for the general reader, and Melville's *Battle-Pieces* (1866), which has been reprinted only recently chiefly on account of the current interest in the Civil War centennial; neither is a major work of its author. Clearly the war did not excite American authors to rush into enlistment, nor did it move them to turn that vital moment to immediate literary account. The Civil War had no volunteer Hemingway or conscripted Mailer.

War was spiritually repugnant to Whitman at the same time that it generated conventional patriotic responses. His notable response to it is in action, not words; and much of the poetry and prose which he left is a record of what he saw. The most moving of these accounts is the prose *Memoranda of the War*, in which one can feel the full force of Whitman's compassion as he tenderly ministers to the human casualties of conflict, the sources and issues of that conflict quite unregarded as he moves from bed to bed, giving what comfort lay in his power to rebel and Yankee alike. The ruin of his health in this service attests what the war meant for him.

The poetry in *Drum-Taps* proves bad when Whitman assumes the role of public poet, treating events and not men, recording mass feeling rather than individual response. The introductory poem, 'First O Songs for a Prelude', is one of these—the early excitements and fervour as war broke; and the lines, 'Mannahatta a-march—and it's O to sing it well!/It's O for a manly life in the camp', are typically commonplace. Topical poetry composed under pressure of historical events need not be mediocre, but Whitman could not bring it off. To see the difference, one need only compare 'Song of the Banner at Daybreak' with 'Vigil Strange I Kept on the Field One Night', and it becomes apparent that the larger issues of war excite only surface emotions and poetic excesses, while the silent last vigil for an imagined comrade moves him profoundly. One exclamatory phrase epitomises the war for Whitman. It is a cry from the depths of the heart. It is not 'O my nation's dread peril'; it is, 'O my land's maim'd darlings'.

*   *   *

Looking back upon the course of American letters in the last century, one is struck by the dominance of Whitman in poetry and struck, as well, by the fact that, little as the events of the Civil War touched the imagination of American writers, it stands as the great divide of our literature. The war hastened the age of the machine and all that that was to do to the tone and tenor of American life, but it also showed sensitive Americans the power of doubt and hatred, the irrepressibility of events, and the stern face of the future. Realisations did not come at once, but there were spectres in the house. After the war, Emerson seemed sadly old-fashioned and, alas, by one view of it, was. Not one major writer whose career began after the war thought with Emerson's mind or spoke with his voice. Certainly Hart Crane did not, except for that residuum of irreducible faith in the individual and the nation which he could not forgo.

Surely Robert Frost, in the view of some, happily and providentially brought American poetry back to the verities of rural innocence and fireside virtues; and indeed it is all too easy to pin conventional labels on him—to relate him to the tradition of American humour or regionalism or folk wisdom or the pastoral. The grandfatherly look of the man and the grandfatherly tone of the more popular poems seem to reassure many readers. But to consider Frost as an updated Longfellow is to miss him. In just two lines he forewarns the unwary: 'It takes all sorts of in and outdoor schooling/To get adapted to my kind of fooling.'

Frost is of the tradition of Emerson and Whitman, and independent of it. He does resemble Emerson in his reflective interiority and his sinewy thought and, with an accounting for differences in temperament and personality, he does resemble Whitman in his sense of brotherhood and his faith in American character and purpose. Like them, too, he sounded his individual note from the beginning, with no waste of premature fumbling or juvenility. Surely some of the differences come from the pioneering of Emerson and Whitman. If Frost is less sombre and less prescriptive than Emerson, it is because Emerson had freed the American spirit from enslaving orthodoxies and had asserted the nobility of human nature; and if Frost could more thoughtfully explore the basis of a man's faith today, it is because Whitman published the original manifesto and propounded the doctrine. If in any way he combines the qualities of both it is in merging Emerson's intellectuality and tight poetic form with Whitman's insistent love for men and his poetry of feeling. When Frost does depart from his predecessors, there is often a greater clarity by focus inwards, as the patriotic poems show; though, to be sure, some of the differences are historical (Frost is not a citizen of Young America, as Emerson and Whitman were). In contemplating the nation in his 'Ode' for Independence Day, 1857, Emerson spoke of beating pulses, of God's mandate for the new land, and of the ripeness of 'men of Saxon kind'. Whitman's 'Song of the Exposition,' written for an industrial fair in 1871, is more interesting but no more thoughtful. He addressed the nation as 'protectress absolute', 'generous as God', and concluded, literally, with a strophe of flag waving. On the other hand, Frost is able to enhance the subject with insight and wisdom. In 'The Gift Outright'—'perhaps the best "patriotic" poem ever written about our country', Randall Jarrell has said—Frost addresses himself to the varying forms of possession. 'The land was ours before we were the land's.' In a sense, the land was ours, but

> . . . we were England's, still colonials,
> Possessing what we still were unpossessed by,
> Possessed by what we now no more possessed.

Yet, the real problem is not so much one of political as of spiritual independence and identity—a possession which comes paradoxically from submission:

> Something we were withholding made us weak
> Until we found out that it was ourselves
> We were withholding from our land of living,
> And forthwith found salvation in surrender.

Beyond the severe limits of patriotism and national identity, the land is as much a part of Frost as it is of Whitman. Woods and stars are to Frost what roads and seashores were to Whitman. With them Frost keeps the theme of time before us as man responds physically to the demands of the seasons and spiritually to the mysteries of time and space. For Frost man moves alternately between solitude and brother-hood, between timeless truths and all-too-immediate problems, between doubt and assurance, terror and gaiety. He does not tell us so much as he quietly and incisively reveals.

The images of woods and stars are to be found early in his first volume, just as they can be found in his last; and although he never permits us to forget that we sail through great voids of space among countless globes and suns, it is the image of woods that he takes for the title of his final volume, *In the Clearing*. The dialogue called 'Cabin in the Clearing' employs a metaphor uniquely American, yet clearly Frost speaks for all men as well. We all live at the edge of the wilderness where, as Mist presumes, the sleepers in the house don't know where they are or who they are. 'They've been here long enough,' says Smoke,

> To push the woods back from around the house
> And part them in the middle with a path

a path which, Mist observes with detachment, 'they maintain . . . for . . . the comfort/Of visiting with the equally bewildered'. As Smoke realises, it is basically a matter of identity and of the priority of 'who' over 'where':

> If the day ever comes when they know who
> They are, they may know better where they are.
> But who they are is too much to believe—
> Either for them or the onlooking world.
> They are too sudden to be credible.

The metaphor of wilderness and clearing is made to carry much of the poet's meaning, whether we read the lines psychologically, historically, or spiritually.

In two sections entitled 'Cluster of Faith' and 'Quandary' the volume also indicates the polarities of Frost's thinking that recall Whitman's: stars related to faith and the cosmic (here, in the poem 'Accidentally on Purpose') and woods related to quandary and the personal (here, in 'In Winter in the Woods Alone'). This latter poem, the final piece in the volume, is the exact counterpart of 'Into My Own', the poem that opened Frost's earliest collection, *A Boy's Will*. There he had announced his intention of pressing forward, alone if need be, into 'those dark trees'. Between the two poems Frost lived and wrote at his own pace and to his own purpose, scorning experimental verse—and experimental thought. The often tense insistence of Emerson and Whitman are gone, and with Frost we are persuaded by calm insights—all illumined with a humour that flickers at the rim of sobriety. In his wonderfully varied monologue, 'New Hampshire', Frost moves swiftly from humorous anecdote to sober commitment:

> Lately in converse with a New York alec
> About the new school of the pseudo-phallic,
> I found myself in a close corner where
> I had to make an almost funny choice.
> 'Choose you which you will be—a prude, or puke,
> Mewling and puking in the public arms.'
> 'Me for the hills where I don't have to choose.'
> 'But if you had to choose, which would you be?'
> I wouldn't be a prude afraid of nature.

One can see the smirk on the face of the 'alec' at such a droll preference for living with hills, and feel him dead to the ironies of 'where I don't have to choose'. The choices for Frost have been made again and again, sometimes, as in 'Birches', in terms of faith, sometimes, as in 'Desert Places', in terms of quiet despair. Frost clearly preferred his woods and hills to city streets and crowds, but in that choice there is no hint of evasion. The final poem of his last volume has the sound but not the sense of solitude:

> In winter in the woods alone
> Against the trees I go.

I mark a maple for my own
And lay the maple low.

At four o'clock I shoulder axe
And in the afterglow
I link a line of shadowy tracks
Across the tinted snow.

I see for Nature no defeat
In one tree's overthrow
Or for myself in my retreat
For yet another blow.

★   ★   ★

The Civil War came while Whitman was trying to resolve his own Calamus crisis and surely it must be accounted fortunate that he could lose himself in the larger cause, as he did with such desperate energy in hospital work. But while the ministrations to hundreds of wounded men absorbed his energies, we find him still playing two different roles to the maim'd darlings, that of the lover and that of the father— 'Calamus' and 'Children of Adam' still in conflict in his nature. Whichever force was at work, there can be no doubt that these years were the most momentous of his life. He had seen suffering and death before, but this was overwhelming, quantitatively and emotionally. To many, these would have been Northerners and Southerners, but to Whitman they were men first, and Americans second. There it stopped.

What it came to mean for him we cannot see either in *Drum-Taps* or *Memoranda of the War*, I think. All the deeper emotions of these war years he poured instead into his great poem, 'When Lilacs Last in the Dooryard Bloom'd'. The poems which he had written consciously and publicly to celebrate the historical event of war had failed. This poem succeeds because into it went all that the war meant to Whitman. True, the opening sections have President Lincoln fully in mind, as do the closing lines; but Lincoln is nowhere named and the martyred leader is subsumed in the hundreds of ordinary but noble men whom Whitman had seen dying with serenity. The poem is Whitman's supreme postwar utterance and clearly it is superior to anything he wrote during the war.

As in his earliest important poems, Whitman places his deepest convictions in a dramatic frame. Starting with the ceremonial progress of Lincoln's coffin as it moves westward to final rest, he broadens the scope of his lines when he says,

> Nor for you, for one alone,
> Blossoms and branches green to coffins all I bring,
> For fresh as the morning, thus would I chant a song for you
> O sane and sacred death.

This and the song of the thrush about death bring us, through successive levels of awareness, to a more inclusive perception than we began with. However, unlike some of the early poems, this shows Whitman in full possession of his experience. Whereas in 'Crossing Brooklyn Ferry' he left us with the unspecified possibilities of the many 'dumb, beautiful ministers', he endows us here with certainties. Whereas in 'Out of the Cradle Endlessly Rocking' nature had moved a boy's spirit towards an as yet 'unknown want' or unrealised destiny, here the realisation is achieved.

Nature speaks more eloquently because the poet through his suffering is now ready for complete awareness. Simply and yet subtly Whitman suggests to us the years that have elapsed since the lilacs bloomed by his boyhood dooryard, as now they bloom to a wholly different man. What he has seen and experienced, particularly in the war years just past, makes him fully responsive to the seeming incongruity of springtime renewal and the finality of death. 'I and this mystery here we stand', he had confidently said in 'Song of Myself'. In the thrush's joyful carol of death in this poem is mystery yet, but mystery more meaningful because time and sorrow have quieted the insistent and often disruptive demands of the self and have brought serenity of spirit. Acceptance and submission to the mystery bring true wisdom. The 'western falling star' is nature's conterpart of the grieving poet, bringing human and cosmic into conjunction, as do the promise of hope in the lilac and the thrush. Death, then, is to be beckoned, 'Come lovely and soothing death'; and death takes its place with life to give it meaning. Here, for once, Whitman conjoins his public and his private roles with complete success, writing a magnificent commemorative poem that is also a fine philosophical poem. The loud pronouncement and assertive yawp become quiet assurance and tender lyricism.

Whitman's career did not terminate, as one is tempted to feel it should, with this remarkable poem. Understandably, he could not sustain this level of poetic achievement. His life was by no means over, though his career as a significant poet largely was. From the impressive poetic visions of the early years there is a falling off, with few exceptions, to uninspired verse, ending with several series of valedictory pieces which are largely repetitive poetic peeps.

Perhaps 'Passage to India' best represents the later Whitman, for in this poem he faces the means (if not the full implications of them) by which modern man conquers the physical world. These accomplishments of railroad, cable and canal he accepts and uses as occasion for his call to spiritual conquests. If by machines man unifies his earthly sphere, then surely by perfection of spirit he must regain his soul. The image reflects some measure of the defeat which Whitman senses: man, he feels, must return, move backward to lost perfection, not forward. But the essential vision of attainable perfection remains bright. Whitman concludes the poem with ringing assurances and with imperatives:

> Passage indeed O soul to primal thought . . .
> To realms of budding bibles.
> O soul, repressless, I with thee and thou with me,
> Thy circumnavigation of the world begin,
> Of man, the voyage of his mind's return,
> To reason's early paradise,
> Back, back to wisdom's birth, to innocent intuitions,
> Again with fair creation . . .
> Passage to more than India! . . .
> Sail forth—steer for the deep waters only . . .
> O my brave soul!
> O farther farther sail!
> O daring joy, but safe! are they not all the seas of God?
> O farther, farther, farther sail!

The drama of selfhood and the faltering purpose in 'Calamus' lie far behind. In so far as it could be for Whitman, the Adamic motif of 'Children of Adam' is renewed, but the New Garden by 1871 seems not so immediate as it formerly did. No longer to be had for the looking, under your bootscles, perfection now is distant in time and space, a return in time to recapture the loss, not a triumphal progress to seize it just ahead. What remains constant are the vistas of promise. To this Whitman devoted his being.

Note

Any study of Lowell's work must begin with H. B. Staples, *Robert Lowell: The First Twenty Years* (1962). This book contains a page of biography; five chapters of analyses and interpretations of Lowell's main poems ending with *Life Studies*; a careful bibliography of the poet's works up to the spring of 1961; and many indications of further sources of information about Lowell. The bibliography may be supplemented by Jerome Mazzaro, *The Achievement of Robert Lowell* (1960), which seems especially useful for finding reviews of Lowell's books. An important essay on Lowell's early poems is Randall Jarrell's 'From the Kingdom of Necessity', originally published in *The Nation* (New York), vol. 164 (18 January, 1947), pp. 74–5, and reprinted in Jarrell's *Poetry and the Age* (1953). Still more important is the symposium on 'Skunk Hour' edited by Anthony Ostroff and including contributions by Richard Wilbur, J. F. Nims, John Berryman, and, above all, Lowell himself, and published in *New World Writing 21* (1962).

For biographical information this chapter rests primarily on Frederick Seidel's 'Robert Lowell', an account of a most helpful interview, published in *The Paris Review*, no. 25 (Winter–Spring, 1961); and on '91 Revere Street', an autobiographical essay included in American editions of *Life Studies*. Here and there the author has ventured to paraphrase a few remarks made by Mr. Lowell in the course of informal discussions in a small class at Harvard University in the spring of 1963. Facts about Lowell's ancestors derive from the *Dictionary of American Biography*, and information on Lowell's dealings with his draft board comes mainly from the Boston *Post* of 9 September and 2 October and the Boston *Globe* of 9 September (morning), 1943. Lowell's more recent remark on atomic bombs is from his contribution to a symposium, 'The Cold War and the West', in the *Partisan Review*, XXIX (Winter, 1962), 47. The anecdote about Robert Frost is in Seidel; the references to John Crowe Ransom are mainly based on Ransom's 'A Look Backwards and a Note of Hope', his contribution to the 'Robert Lowell' number of the *Harvard Advocate* (November, 1961), pp. 22–3. The quotation from Louise Bogan comes from her review of *Mills of the Kavanaughs* in the *New Yorker*, 9 June, 1951.

Lowell's poems are quoted from the following editions: *Land of Unlikeness* (Cummington, Massachusetts, 1944); *'Lord Weary's Castle' and 'The Mills of the Kavanaughs'* (New York, 1961); *Life Studies* (New York, 1960); *Imitations* (New York, 1961); and 'Buenos Aires', in *The New York Review of Books*, February 1963, p. 3; 'Eye and Tooth', in *Partisan Review*, XXIX (Winter, 1962), 90–1; and 'Night Sweat', in *Encounter*, XXI (November 1963), 51. The three poems last mentioned are collected in Lowell's most recent book, *For the Union Dead* (New York, 1964), which came out too late to be considered in this chapter.

III

The Age of Lowell

IRVIN EHRENPREIS

★

FOR an age of world wars and prison states, when the Faustian myth of science produces the grotesquerie of fall-out shelters, the decorous emotion seems a fascinated disgust. After outrage has exhausted itself in contempt, after the mind has got the habit of Dallas and South Africa, the shudder of curiosity remains. Every morning we think, something new and insufferable is about to happen: what is it? Among living poets writing in English nobody has expressed this emotion with the force and subtlety of Robert Lowell. In an undergraduate poem Lowell described himself as longing for the life of straightforward beliefs and deeds, of simple lust, conventional faith and boyish sports. But 'sirens sucked me in', he said; and painful, feverish contemplation was his fate:

> On me harsh birches, nursing dew,
> Showered their warm humidity.
>
> ('The Dandelion Girls')

Like Baudelaire, he saw things so disturbing that they almost kept him from making them into poetry.

Yet the confident life of public action might have seemed young Lowell's certain destiny. For his family line ran about as high as an American genealogy could go. His mother was descended from Edward Winslow, a Pilgrim Father who came to America on the *Mayflower*. Edward's son was a mighty Indian killer and a governor of Plymouth Colony. Lowell's mother also traced herself to the New Hampshire frontiersman John Stark, who was made a colonel at Bunker Hill and a general in the Revolutionary War. Lowell's father, though trained as a naval officer, belonged to the intellectual family that produced teachers and clergymen as well as fighters. The original R. T. S. Lowell, five generations ago, was also a naval officer. Another namesake, Lowell's great-grandfather, 'delicate, sensitive, strangely rarefied', was a poet best known for a ballad on the relief of Lucknow, and spent four years as headmaster of St. Mark's, one of the most fashionable boys' schools in the United States. Lowell's great-great-uncle, James Russell Lowell, a Harvard professor and one of the famous poets of his era, became ambassador to the court of St. James's. For most of the memories on which Lowell was bred, Puritan New England, especially Boston, provided the setting; and in the history of the Massachusetts Bay Colony he could find his Tree of Jesse.

It was on these very elements that he was to turn his first great storm of poetic disgust. They supplied the object of a clamorous repudiation. The shape the outburst took, however, depended less on ancestry than on a set of experiences that seem to have determined Lowell's original literary colour: his meeting with the circle of John Crowe Ransom and Allen Tate, his conversion to Roman Catholicism and his dramatic response to the second world war.[1]

At St. Mark's School, Lowell found his interest in poetry encouraged by the poet Richard Eberhart, one of the teachers. He began experimenting with free verse but soon switched to stanzaic forms. As an undergraduate at Harvard he went to see Robert Frost, bearing a 'huge epic' on the First Crusade. The great man perused a page, told the visitor that he lacked 'compression', and read him Collins's 'How Sleep the Brave' as an example of something 'not too long'. For a period Lowell tried to write simple, Imagistic poems like those of W. C. Williams; but the university around him seemed less than a nest of singing birds, and he heeded a recommendation that he should study under John Crowe Ransom. In the middle of his undergraduate career, after a summer spent with Allen Tate, he left Harvard altogether and went to Kenyon College, in rural Ohio, where Ransom was teaching.

For a while now, Lowell even lived in Ransom's house, and later shared lodgings with two other young writers, one of whom, Peter Taylor, has published a short story based on their college friendship ('1939'). During these years, the critic Randall Jarrell taught English at Kenyon, and he too lived a while with the Ransoms. It seems obvious that the network of literary affiliations gave the young student, who had been growing 'morose and solitary' at home, a welcome substitute for blood relations who felt small sympathy with his talent. Lowell often describes himself as belonging to the 'second generation' of the

[1] Cf. Chapter VIII, pp. 186-7, below.

Fugitives; he spent long periods in a quasi-filial or fraternal connection with three or four of the authors he met in the years before the war, and he speaks of them with the sort of loyalty one extends to kin. The conservative politics, strong but orthodox religious faith and high literary standards to which these Southerners were attached must have seemed to him seductive alternatives to the commonplace Republicanism, mechanical church-going and materialist aspirations that characterised a 'Boston' formed (as he saw it) by successive lines of Puritans, Unitarians and low-church Episcopalians. To Lowell the home of his forebears stood for a rootless but immobile sterility.

In 1940, when he took a step towards establishing a family of his own, Lowell not surprisingly married another writer, the novelist Jean Stafford, whose 'flaming insight' he commemorates in a recent poem. He was also converted to Roman Catholicism, the church peculiarly associated in Boston with the large population descended from humble Irish immigrants, natural enemies, in politics and culture, of his own class. But the poet already felt committed to a kind of moral vitality that could for only a limited time be expressed in Roman terms. During the period when his new-found church was something defiant of the Boston he had repudiated, and so long as the language, symbols and ritual represented materials to be conquered and employed for explosive purposes, he could use Catholicism as an ingredient of poetry. But when it was only the faith he had to accept, the church came to seem as oppressive and self-contradictory as the code of his native class.

It was during the years of his first marriage and his adherence to the church that Lowell's earliest books of poetry appeared. Apart from what had come out in an undergraduate magazine, the first poems he published were a pair in the *Kenyon Review* 1939. But years went by before any successors could be seen in print, partly because the few he wrote were rejected when he sent them out. Then in 1943 about a dozen of his poems turned up in the literary quarterlies, to be followed the next year by a collection, *Land of Unlikeness*. This gathering, withholding and sudden releasing of his work is typical of the poet's method; for he labours over his poems continually and plans each collection as a sequence, the opening and closing poems in each making a distinct introduction and conclusion, and the movement between them tending from past to present, from question to resolution, from ambiguous negation to hesitant affirmative.

Above the influences of Ransom and Tate, or the steady use of Catholic religious imagery, or the many motifs drawn from Boston and New England, the most glaring feature of Lowell's two earliest volumes was a preoccupation with the second world war. Not long after the United States joined that war, he committed the most dramatic public act of his life. Characteristically, this act seemed at once violent and passive, and was calculated to make his parents very uncomfortable. In what turned out to be no more than preliminary steps, he twice tried to enlist in the navy but was rejected. Soon, however, the mass bombing of non-combatants shocked his moral principles; and when he was called up under the Selective Service Act, he declared himself a conscientious objector. Rather than simply appear before the responsible board and declare his convictions, he refused to report at all, and thus compelled the authorities to prosecute him.

In order to give his deed the widest possible significance, he released to the press a thousand-word open letter to President Roosevelt. Here Lowell drew repeated attention to the historic eminence of his ancestors. He described himself as belonging to a family that had 'served in all our wars, since the Declaration of Independence'; he told the President that the Lowell family traditions, 'like your own, have always found their fulfillment in maintaining, through responsible participation in both civil and military services, our country's freedom and honor'. He said that he had tried to enlist when the country was in danger of invasion but that this danger was past, and the intention of bombing Japan and Germany into submission went against the nation's established ideals. He could not participate in a war, Lowell said, that might leave Europe and China 'to the mercy of the U.S.S.R., a totalitarian tyranny committed to world revolution'.

Twenty years later he was still signing open letters of protest to newspapers; and although his opinions had altered, their direction had not shifted. 'No nation should possess, use, or retaliate with its bombs', he wrote in a 1962 symposium. 'I believe we should rather die than drop our own bombs.' It is suggestive of the poet's sensibility that he should link suicide with mass murder, as though the way to prevent the second might be to commit the first. The themes of self-destruction and assassination are often joined in his work, the one apparently redeeming or proving the altruism of the other. Yet parricide becomes a mythical, guilt-ridden route to justice and liberty; for by throwing

over the traditional family pieties, the young Lowell seems to have
felt he was destroying his begetters and oppressors.

*   *   *

The poems that appeared in *Land of Unlikeness* (1944) were mostly
written during a year Lowell spent with the Tates after leaving Kenyon
College. In them he devoted himself mainly to a pair of themes reflect-
ing recent history. One was the unchristian character of the Allies' role
in the second world war; the other was the causal connection between
the doctrines of America's founders and the desolate condition, spiritual
and material, of the country in the thirties. Looking back, Lowell saw
in the ideals and motives of his ancestors the same contradictions, the
same denial of a Christ they professed to worship, that made his own
world a land of unlikeness, i.e. a place obliterating the image of
divinity, a culture where the old metaphors that made created beings
recall their creator, no longer operated. Those who had flown from
persecution came here to persecute the red men; those who hated war
made war on nature, plundering whales and neighbours for unspiritual
profit.

In order to dramatise and generalise this view, he drew parallels be-
tween divine and human history: between the war and Doomsday,
between the dust bowl sharecroppers and Cain. And he set up anti-
theses: between profits and mercy, between political slogans and
charity. To the second world war he opposed Christ. In the social and
political theories of the Fugitives, Lowell found support for his ten-
dency to identify degeneracy with the city, the machine and Roosevelt's
centralised democracy, even as he associated true civilisation with
rural, aristocratic society. And since the South itself was yielding to the
rapid movement from one set of conditions to the other, Lowell could
apply his argument to humanity in general, through parallels drawn
from *Genesis* and *Revelation*, from the myth of Troy, and from history.
Thus the advent of cosmopolitan industrialism becomes a sign that
we are all descended from Cain; the first Eden becomes a symbol
of that ante-bellum, ostensibly Augustan society which the North
supposedly destroyed; the fall of Troy becomes the analogue of the
defeat of the South. Since the new war had the effect of speeding
the hated process, it was easily drawn into this aspect of Lowell's
rhetoric.

By the time he composed these poems, Lowell had given up free verse and was writing obscure poems in metre in a style of his own. Most of those in *Land of Unlikeness* are savagely ironical. Besides employing puns or conceits repeatedly and with great earnestness, he brought in hackneyed phrases and common tags of quotations, giving sarcastic new directions to their meaning. He invented grotesque metaphors, such as 'Christ kicks in the womb's hearse'. Although the stanzas of most of the poems are elaborate, the rhythms are heavy, the sounds are cluttered, alliteration occurs often and unsubtly.

Into such verses he pressed enough violence of feeling to stun a sensitive ear. Certain dramatic monologues and visionary pieces on religious themes make the greatest uproar. The tighter the stanza forms, the wilder the bitterness: erratic rhythms, blasphemous images, deliberately hollow rhetoric erupt over the objects of his onslaught. But instead of the tight form providing an ironic contrast or intensifying counterpoint to the violent tone, it seems arbitrary. The mind that follows the form seems cut off from the mouth that screams the sacrilege:

> In Greenwich Village, Christ the Drunkard brews
> Gall, or spiked bone-vat, siphons His bilged blood
> Into weak brain-pans and unseasons wood. . . .
> > ('Christ for Sale')

In another poem the speaker is a slum mother apostrophising the corpse of her baby, who has died on Christmas Day, 1942 (soon after the sinking of the British aircraft carrier *Ark Royal*):

> So, child, unclasp your fists,
> And clap for Freedom and Democracy;
> No matter, child, if Ark Royal lists
> > Into the sea;
> > Soon the Leviathan
> > Will spout American.
> > > ('The Boston Nativity')

In this kind of satire the irony sounds so wild that most readers ignore the poet's meaning while observing his frenzy. The caricature of the nativity scene does not succeed in mocking America's moral pretensions during the war. It only forces upon one's perceptions the distorted religiosity of the writer. After all, by Lowell's own argument, there could be no real heroes in history apart from Christ. As in Tate's 'Aeneas at Washington', the Southern gentleman comes finally to seem less like Hotspur than like Richard II, standing for ideals he did not die to defend.

Yet not every speech is a tantrum. In a few of the poems Lowell's detachment suggests that his churnings, in the others, are an effort to produce a heat wave in a naturally cold climate. Observation, dry and wry commentary, fascinated disgust—these are the marks of his subtler self, and these are what appear, for example, in 'The Park Street Cemetery'. This poem, a survey of the tombstones in a Boston graveyard, has less violence than distaste in its tone. Lowell treats the site as a repository of those Puritan colonists who bequeathed to the America they founded their own confusion of grace with fortune. The form is appropriately relaxed: three stanzas, each of seven unrhymed, irregular lines; and the poet ends not with a scream but a deadnote:

> The graveyard's face is painted with facts
> And filagreed swaths of forget-me-nots.

The positive doctrines of *Land of Unlikeness* seem less significant than the negative directions. Whether Lowell espouses Southern agrarianism or Roman Catholicism, his principles attract him less as ideals of aspiration than as possibilities disdained by his ancestors. Against early New England the real charge he makes is that it failed to meet its own ultimate standards; for Lowell is after all another sober moralist with a Puritan's severity. He scolds Boston as Blake scolded London: for the death of vision and the death of conscience. Nowhere does he imply that dogma bestows serenity, or that, as some Southerners would argue, the integrity of a ceremonious traditionalism outweighs the human misery on which it may rest.

For the poet, finally, the real problem remained unsolved. In most of this volume his best-integrated poems were his understatements; those that showed the highest technical ambition were bathetic. He had to find a style that would reconcile his interest in technique with his interest in justice, that would identify private with public disturbances. For such a style the elements lay not in the regularity of his stanzas, not in the depth of his piety, and not in his political judgments. It lay in Lowell's preoccupation with tone, in his humanitarian conscience, and in his sense of history. When he employed these to enlarge the meaning of an immediate personal experience, he produced the best poems in *Land of Unlikeness*: 'The Park Street Cemetery', 'In Memory of Arthur Winslow', 'Concord' and 'Salem'.

✱   ✱   ✱

Not only the older writers belonging to the circle of Ransom and Tate but also several other critics gave unusual attention to *Land of Unlikeness*. It was praised briefly but intensely by F. W. Dupee and Arthur Mizener. There was a careful review by Blackmur and a eulogy by J. F. Nims. But when Lowell's next book *Lord Weary's Castle* appeared (1946), the critical reception became a thunder of welcome.

As usual, there is a link between the old work and the new. In the last poem of *Land of Unlikeness* the poet had mentioned the curse of 'exile' as the alternative to the blessing of Canaan: God offered Israel the choice, says the poet; and when Israel chose to turn away from God's 'wise fellowship', the outcome was Exile. The opening poem of *Lord Weary's Castle* is called 'The Exile's Return', suggesting a common theme for both books. But the theme has broadened. In the new collection the poet implies that nothing was or could be settled by the war. In rejecting divine leadership, it is moral justice, the creative principle bringing order out of chaos, that we have banished from its self-made home. Thus if the expatriate is taken to mean Christ, the lord still waits for the world he built to pay him his due homage. He still menaces us with the judgment that the war prefigured. As a creator, however, the Exile is also the poet or artist; and in this sense he wants to be paid for the truthful visions with which he has blessed an ungrateful world. For he holds out the threat of a poet's curse, and his isolation remains the mark of society's misdirection. In a private extension of this sense the Exile is Lowell himself, released from jail after serving about five months of the year and a day to which he had been sentenced. Coming back to ordinary routines, he meets in new forms the same moral issues he had wrestled with before his imprisonment.

All these implications are in 'The Exile's Return'. Here, an émigré comes back to his German home after the war, under the protection of American garrisons. But the shattered place looks the opposite of Eden; and if the first springtime brings lilies, it brings as well the agony of responsibility. To suggest the aspect of the neglected artist, Lowell crowds the poem with allusions to Mann's Tonio Kröger, who stood 'between two worlds' without feeling at home among either the bourgeoisie or the artists. To suggest the themes of heaven and hell, he has seasonal references to an infernal winter, a spring of rebirth, the 'fall' of autumn, and the entrance to Dante's hell. For the motifs of imprisonment and release he uses a jail-like hôtel-de-ville, a Yankee 'commandant' and a parcel of 'liberators' who are as yet innocent or 'unseasoned'.

In direct contrast, the closing poem of the book, 'Where the Rainbow Ends', deals with an American city, Boston, that has never been bombed but that faces the dissolution caused by decay of conscience. Not war but winter devastates this city. Not as a refugee but as a voluntary exile from worldliness, the poet-prophet offers his people the alternative to the Judgment prefigured by the cold season:

> What can the dove of Jesus give
> You now but wisdom, exile? Stand and live,
> The dove has brought an olive branch to eat.
> ('Where the Rainbow Ends')

Repeatedly in this book, Lowell shows an understanding of how his elemental powers might be fused, how his unnatural calmness of tone in dealing with horrifying material might be supported by an apparent casualness of style screening a meticulous exactness of underlying structure. His sense of the past justifies ironically the calmness of tone. For to the degree that one considers human misery and cruelty as the reflection of permanent instinct—rather than transient ignorance—one will view one's own corruption and one's neighbour's not with scandalised outbursts but with comprehending calm. Furthermore, through the distancing effect of history, as through the shaping effect of complex form, one can even achieve a coherent grasp of one's own deepest, most secret anguish. With these several powers Lowell also made good use of a set of influences that he had earlier felt only at some remove, as they were present in the work of Tate, Eliot and Ransom. These influences emanate from the great line of French Symbolists and post-Symbolists, to whom the 'modern' experimental movement in poetry owes its origin. When Lowell turned to Rimbaud, Valéry and Rilke for models, he was accepting the cosmopolitan conception of literature that American poets as diverse as Whitman and Pound have worked with.

The defect of *Lord Weary's Castle* is the same as that of *Land of Unlikeness*. In Whitman, Tate and Hart Crane, one cannot help noticing a habit of substituting rhetoric, in the form of self-conscious sublimity, for poetry. If Lowell, their heir, yields to this habit, it is because, like them, he has the highest conception of the poet's task. But the mere posture of soaring, the air of prophecy, does not make a speech either noble or prophetic. In Lowell's most commonly over-praised work, 'The Quaker Graveyard', the use of rhetoric joins with a denseness of symbolism to make a poem that seems more impressive for aspiration than for accomplishment.

Throughout this poem he contrasts two views of saving grace: the idea of a special gift to the elect, and the idea of something that infuses not merely all men but all creatures. The in-group's complacency Lowell attaches to the Protestant sects of colonial New England and to his patriotic cousin, who died at sea for a cause Lowell rejected. As a measure of the limitations of this ethic, which he associates with war-loving capitalism, Lowell invokes the great evolutionary chain of created beings. The world, he keeps saying, exists as a moral order in which separate men are not masters but participants: both the sea slime from which we rose and the whale that we plunder lie beneath the same law that subsumes humanity. To sectarian arrogance he opposes the innocence of the humbler orders of creation, for whom cruelty is an accident of their nature. As the solvent of arrogance he offers the Catholic compassion of Christ embodied in Mary his mother.

In Lowell's usual manner, the end of the poem recalls the beginning. We move back to the Quaker graveyard on Nantucket Island off the coast of Massachusetts. But where the initial scene was of violent death in a great war, the closing gives us the lifeless cemetery of wind and stone and tree. Now the poet glances back to the very start of the evolutionary process and contrasts that moment, when life and death were born together, with the present outlook of a corpse-littered sea. And suddenly the capacious cemetery of the Atlantic becomes a symbolic contrast to the filled graveyard of the Quakers: God has more room than this; the old covenant has given way to the new gospel.

In this fascinating work the failure of the rhetoric grows obvious if we notice the weakness of the poem's penultimate section. Here Lowell puts the snug, familiar salvation that his cousin might aspire to beside the Catholic vision of the universal but quite unknowable God reflected in the image of Our Lady of Walsingham. Though this passage is a deliberate understatement, the effect is not powerful by implication;

rather, it sounds bathetic. Beyond human griefs or joys, says the poet, the Virgin

> knows what God knows,
> Not Calvary's Cross nor crib at Bethlehem
> Now, and the world shall come to Walsingham.

If we compare Lowell's two stanzas, in their attempt to express the inexpressible, with similar passages in Eliot's 'Dry Salvages' (which is, with *Lycidas*, one of the models for this poem), we must admit that there is a posed air, a willed simplicity, in Lowell's lines that never appears in, say, 'Lady, whose shrine stands on the promontory', etc. This forced tone seems the more regrettable because Lowell's passage is meant to deliver the positive alternative to the errors he denounces with such thoroughness. It is in the overcharged stretches of churning sounds, eruptive rhythm, and violent imagery that we seem to hear the authentic voice of the poet:

> In the great ash-pit of Jehoshaphat
> The bones cry for the blood of the white whale,
> The fat flukes arch and whack about its ears. . . .

We cannot help feeling that he enjoys his destructive vision in a way not compatible with his role as prophet, moralist or recipient of wisdom.

In another long poem, 'At the Indian Killer's Grave', Lowell gives a more appropriate display of his powers. The history of its composition reminds us of his habitual alteration of his own work; for much of the poem comes out of the 'Park Street Cemetery', and the closing lines are a magnificent adaptation of verses from another early poem. Moreover, as he transforms these materials, the poet enlarges their meaning. Like the speaker in Tate's 'Ode to the Confederate Dead', the poet here contemplates a graveyard where his direct or spiritual ancestors are buried among their peers. Unlike Tate's speaker, however, he searches for the meaning of their sins, not their virtues. Staring about at the figures carved on the gravestones among the vegetation, he contrasts the Puritan dead with the living Irish who now hold political power in Boston. The sound of a train stopping underground makes him think of time stopping and of the Judgment to come; and he wonders about the fate of the Pilgrims' souls. He imagines the spirit of the Red Indian chief, King Philip, addressing the Puritan Indian-killers and reminding them that all their pretensions to being the chosen of God have left them only the corrupted bodies that now serve as carrion for sea-gulls. He looks at the toothed railing, thinks of dragon's teeth, and ponders the double source, natural (i.e. Cadmean) and spiritual (i.e. Adamic), of our instinct for evil. Then in a sudden, astonishing close, the poet turns from the old law to the new, from Adam to Christ; and he calls on the four evangelists to guide him towards the inclusive faith of the Roman Catholic church, to a vision of salvation that more than admits the Indian chief; for it promises Philip that the blessed Virgin herself will deck out his head with flowers:

> John, Matthew, Luke and Mark,
> Gospel me to the Garden, let me come
> Where Mary twists the warlock with her flowers—
> Her soul a bridal chamber fresh with flowers
> And her whole body an ecstatic womb,
> As through the trellis peers the sudden Bridegroom.

And there, in a fine identification of his private conversion with both the history of Massachusetts and the religious or mythical account of all human history, Lowell brings his poem to a close.

Generally, the poet sounds a tone of self-restraint, of calm but engrossed repugnance, that reminds one of Ransom's poems 'Necrological' and 'Armageddon'. This tone he drops appropriately in two counterbalanced passages: the outburst of Philip, who speaks with a savage violence of sound and image, and the lyric close and climax, when calm is replaced by rapture. The apparently loose-knit free associations rest on a carefully adjusted underpinning. Even the setting of the poet's meditation belongs to his subject, because the Puritan colonists brooded hourly upon death and the grave. They dressed in black and regarded the beauties of animate nature as bad diversions from the proper study of man, viz. death and judgment, heaven and hell. Nevertheless, they proudly gave themselves the title of the elect of God, promoting themselves to Paradise. It is a tremendous historical irony that their haughty Calvinism should have given way, in Boston, to the avowedly humble, Catholic faith of the Irish—to the church that in colonial times proselytised among the Indians instead of beheading them. In effect, the whore of Rome waltzes over the Puritan graves: 'the trollop dances on your skulls'.

A shimmering elaboration of imagery in the Symbolist manner connects the past and the present, the beginning of the poem with the end.

the surface and the meaning. As the poet questions the spectacle before him, he wonders whether the fate of the dead is knowable or whether the pagan idea of vengeance may not be carried out, so that Philip may eternally scalp the self-styled righteous men (Blake's 'just man') who killed his people. This scalp-head-skull image appears again and again in the poem, reaching its most brilliant transformation at the end, when the Virgin is pictured as twisting Philip's 'warlock' or pigtail with flowers. Between these points the head becomes the English crown, responsible for building King's Chapel—a motif that opposes King Charles to King Philip. It then turns into the 'dome' of the State-house that replaced the royal authority. Next, Philip's head reappears on a 'platter' or gravestone. The phrasing recalls St. John and therefore the apostle or evangelist Philip. As a prophet now, the Indian can address his damned enemies and point out that the Catholics are raised over their heads. The dome becomes a globe that is the natural world, rejected (so says the poet) by the Puritans as they 'hurled/Anathemas at nature'. The head reappears in the headstones of the graves and finally in Mary's handling of Philip's head.

Parallel to these metamorphoses move the images of the garden. We start in the desolate garden of the cemetery, which the Puritans have reached in place of Paradise. Shrubs and sculpture remind one of similar scenes. So the view expands into both the Public Garden, where the Beacon Hill brahmins walked, and the Boston Common, which was more likely the playground of the Irish. Lowell toys with the ironies implicit in 'garden' and 'common', and with the further irony that though fashionable Beacon Hill is where his own class live, it is topped by the Statehouse that in effect belongs to the Irish. Under the Common, meanwhile, runs the subway, analogue of hell, with its serpentine green trains, symbolic of time. Easily enough, the Garden and the Common expand into the whole 'land' that the Puritans denounced and despoiled. This contracts at once into the mud that buries them now. The buildings around the Common are like palisades around the early settlements, intended, however, not to keep the wilderness from swallowing the villages but to keep, as it were, the remnant of natural ground from spreading. Finally, the motif reminds the poet of the ground in which Cadmus sowed the dragon's teeth, emblematic of original sin.

★　　★　　★

It seems remarkable that while some of the best poems in *Lord Weary's Castle* were imitations, or free English versions, of works in other languages, some of the least effective were dramatic monologues. In a poem like 'The Ghost', based upon Sextus Propertius, Lowell performed a superb job of giving his own voice to another poet. But in the double-monologue 'The Death of the Sheriff', the structure of which depends upon changes of voice and shifts in point of view, the speaker's smothered, crowded, dull murmur hardly alters from beginning to end. It's as though Lowell had too much to say to be able to submerge himself in an imaginary personality, and for that very reason found it easy to submerge a sympathetic author's character in his own.

His next book, *Mills of the Kavanaughs* (1951), brought these complementary tendencies to a crisis. The unqualified successes in it are a dazzling pastiche of Virgil and an adaptation of Werfel. But the longest and most ambitious works are five attempts at narrative dramatised through monologue. In four of these one feels that the poet has contrived situations offering the greatest opportunities for allusiveness and symbolism, and has sacrificed to such opportunities the absolutely essential narrative line upon which any dramatic monologue depends. He had obviously worked with immense pains over the title poem, running to more than five hundred lines, many of them beautiful evocations of the Maine landscape that gives the piece its setting. Nevertheless, although the plot would sound irresistibly sensational in summary—dealing with the madness and suicide of a patrician Catholic who married his sister by adoption—the poem is so hemmed in by cross-references and correspondences as to be wholly static. At one point Lowell goes so far as to match the number of a figure on a bird guide, once memorised by the protagonist, to the number of the stanza in which the man tries to recall the bird's name. The same substitution of arbitrary parallelism for narrative drama almost makes an impasse out of the last poem in the book, 'Thanksgiving's Over'. Here Lowell sends his main characters to a church on Thirty-First Street in New York, and situates their home next to the Third Avenue elevated train ('El'), in order to supply allusions to the Trinity.

Yet 'Thanksgiving's Over' is one of the most revealing of Lowell's poems. Published two years after his divorce from Jean Stafford and the year after his marriage to the essayist Elizabeth Hardwick, it comes from a time when he no longer felt buoyed up by the church. Louise Bogan called the book *Mills of the Kavanaughs* a 'dark midpoint' in his development, 'which must in some way be transcended'. In this closing poem Lowell shows that he was passing the midpoint and going on. All the ingredients of his false rhetorical style are here: the monologue, the nightmare, madness, murder, suicide and blasphemy. But the implications are not the old ones.

To the speaker of the poem Lowell gives the voice of a man who has lost the struggle to maintain his Christian faith and now ponders the events that culminated in his failure. He is a Roman Catholic, a New Yorker and a widower, whose young, demented wife had believed herself impregnated by the Holy Ghost. After she tried to kill herself by jumping from a window, he sent her to a sanatorium in the mountains of Vermont, where she died. It is now Thanksgiving Day, 1942, and Michael the widower half remembers, half dreams of his dead wife. As he tries to make sense out of the monstrous experiences, he thinks he hears her talking.

The themes of the wife's increasingly disconnected chatter are love and peace, her assumption being that these are united in the church. But as her incoherence deepens, it becomes clear that the serenity she offers is available only to those who are as credulous as children. Within the wife's character, therefore, the themes are split so as to suggest the opposition between religious doctrines and human nature. She would like to feel love as spiritual charity, and therefore denies her passionate impulses. She would like morality to issue from the passive acceptance of authority, and so she denies the need for a struggle between the good and evil in our constitution. Through suppression, her hidden passions become adulterous lusts projected on other persons. Towards Michael her affection turns to jealousy, and she feels like killing him. When this wish is thwarted, the hate turns inward, and she tries to kill herself.

The poet implies that by giving up religion one might resolve some of these conflicts, but one would then have to face the pain of a life without ultimate meaning. Michael must choose between abandoning God and abandoning his rational conscience. As the peculiarly shocking symbol of his dilemma the poet focuses on the doctrine of the Trinity. Thus the action of the poem is set at the very end of the Trinity season, the week before Advent Sunday. Since the third person of the Trinity appears iconographically as a dove, there is a profusion of sacrilegious bird imagery. In order to involve other aspects of doctrine or ritual, the poet complicates the central theme with allusions to the Eucharist (etymologically 'thanksgiving'), the Incarnation (as enacted

in the Annunciation), and so forth. As a kind of parody of each, he pro-
duces natural analogues. Within the fantasy of the girl's unconscious
the Trinity takes the form of a love triangle. She confuses the Dove with
a celluloid parrot and imagines herself pregnant with birds. Since the
conventional dish at an American Thanksgiving dinner is a turkey, the
poet can introduce grotesque ambiguities signifying the sterility of the
Holy Ghost or the end of Michael's belief: 'My fowl was soupbones.'

In flying from adultery to death, the girl was impelled by a guilt due
to religion. So against the ideal of sexless conception displayed in
paintings of the Annunciation, the poet sets the pagan fertility of 'St.
Venus' in Botticelli's Primavera. Against the child's sexless world of
faith (evoked by allusions to Mother Goose rhymes, nursery tales and
Peter Pan) he sets the world of parenthood. In a distortion of phrases
from the *Messiah* we hear the solution that Michael cannot yet accept:
birds singing, 'Come unto us, our burden's light'—not the Dove but the
birds of nature, of light and Lucifer and reason.

Over such themes the poet builds his characteristic sort of towering
edifice; for the poem stands on an amazing reticulation of allusions.
Paradise Lost, for obvious reasons, is continually evoked. The wretched
couple are identified with Faust and Gretchen or with Hamlet and
Ophelia. From her asylum window the wife sees the harpies of
Baudelaire's 'Cythère'. Yet the essential image and meaning of the poem
do not hinge on such clues. Michael sits and listens at the end of the
poem, but he does not pray or receive a sign. It seems certain that when
he boards a train, it will take him away from 'this deaf and dumb/
Breadline for children'—as the wife unintentionally describes Roman
Catholicism for the poet.

In Michael we confront again those linked themes of passive obser-
vation and wild impulse to travel that underlie so much of the night-
mare violence in Lowell's poems. The wife's confinement in a cell
reflects Michael's emotional seclusion. For the faithful Christian, life is a
cage from which he escapes to Life; for the fallen Christian the limits
of mere life make another kind of cage. Afraid to stir, for fear of wreck-
ing the object of his stirring, the poet repeatedly speaks as a walled-off
voyeur frantically watching the lives of others. Like a traveller in a
sealed railway car, he passes over the earth, looking but never doing,
always on the move and never in motion: he has replaced action by
vision.

*   *   *

Lowell has said it was hard for him to find a subject and a language of his own. He can describe himself as writing a rather formal style coming out of Tate, Hart Crane, Ransom and Eliot. But when he composed the brilliant, influential poems that were collected in *Life Studies* (1959), he took a line less reminiscent of those masters than of Pound. At last he had discovered his language and subject.

By the time this book appeared, Lowell had received enough prizes and awards to ease most men's desire for public recognition. He was the father of an infant daughter (born January, 1957); he was a member of the Boston University Department of English; and he held the honorary degree of Doctor of Letters. Yet he had suffered a deeply disturbing experience when his mother died (February, 1954); and the emotional pressures evident in his poetry had undermined his health until he was forced to turn for aid to hospital treatments.

The continuance of the emotional strains, tempered by domestic amenities and balanced by extraordinary marks of success in his career, seem to have enabled Lowell to discover the best uses for his talent. Superficially the transformation appeared in the lightening of his style. Lowell has said that soon after the *Mills of the Kavanaughs* came out, the pace of his writing slowed almost to a halt, and his allusive, rhetorical manner came to seem 'distant, symbol-ridden and wilfully difficult'. He felt that his old poems too often hid what they were about, presenting a 'stiff, humourless and even impenetrable surface'. So he began paraphrasing Latin quotations when he used them, and adding extra syllables to lines in order to make them clearer or more colloquial. With such a poem as the short, perfect 'In the Cage' (1946)—a tetrameter sonnet recapturing the grimness of the months he spent in jail— he had already shown the strength of a comparatively unadorned language, free from obscurities but suffused with irony. This manner now became not the exception but the rule. Line after line, in poem after poem, reads like a well-turned but easily spoken remark made by a fastidious, self-critical speaker who is at home with slang.

But the ease of language was only the outer sign of Lowell's new attitude towards his own nature. Without losing the tone of fascinated disgust, he now found it possible not only to treat himself as part of history but to treat history as part of himself. The course of his life became the analogue of the life of his era; the sufferings of the poet became a mirror of the sufferings of whole classes and nations. It was not as a judge that he now claimed his authority: it was as the heroic artist, the man capable of turning vision into act. Through the title of his book Lowell gave himself the status of a craftsman who reveals life in general by the rendering of his own life.

Appropriately enough, *Life Studies* opens with a train journey from the city of priests to the city of artists, Rome to Paris. But the speaker is neither a character in a dramatic monologue nor an impersonal commentator. He is the poet talking about his own experiences. Here as generally in the book, Lowell has of course invented facts and altered truths. Yet the reader feels himself in touch with the real author and not with a mask. Similarly, the entrance into the poem is deliberately casual, with what look like random associations suggesting the real flow of a unique consciousness.

If the formal frame is thus a common earthly journey, the object presented is a miraculous one: the bodily assumption of the Virgin, proclaimed as dogma in the jubilee year 1950. So the title 'Beyond the Alps' means not only a trip towards France but also its opposite, 'ultramontane', or the old epithet for supporters of papal infallibility. Lowell is using that doctrine, which the proclamation of the new dogma pressed to a record-breaking extreme, as the emblem of vulgar human credulity—the decay of imagination into superstition—a principle embodied in the pope. To escape from such tempting corruptions, the poet struggles within himself, during the night of his train journey, emerging at dawn into a sense of rebirth, a commitment to the creative imagination. Turning towards the intellect and the arts—towards Athene and Apollo—he rejects Mary and Pius. The pope is depicted, with grotesque irony, between a purring electric razor in one hand (the cat of rational science) and a canary in the other (the dove of faith).

In keeping with the opposition between religion and art, Lowell treats the mountains that appear in his poem as versions of Parnassus. So the journey recalls the celebrated simile, in Pope's *Essay on Criticism*, comparing the Alps to the challenge that art sets before the ambition of genius: 'Hills peep o'er hills, and Alps on Alps arise.' It is thus appropriate that at the time the poem opens, the inartistic Swiss should just have failed to climb Everest.

Violence, as usual in Lowell's work, accompanies the polarity of stillness and movement. By mentioning the Swiss (historic mercenary soldiers), the poet hints at the third principle of human nature which the poem deals with, i.e. destructive violence, personified by the warrior-king. The success of Caesarean terror in chaining the mind differs only in mode from the success of the magician-priest: Mussolini is as Roman as Pius. For an ideal culture, that could make violence, magic, and reason work together, Lowell offers not Rome but inimitable Hellas; and while the morning sun, like the imagination, transforms the bleak moonlit peaks into dazzling Parthenons, the reborn poet thinks of another traveller, Odysseus, escaping symbolically from the dark cave of Polyphemus by blinding the cyclops with a dazzling firebrand. Athene, the guide of Odysseus, easily united in herself all the roles to which popes and dictators aspire; the reader recalls that she was also *parthenos* or virgin, born miraculously without a mother, inspirer of a temple outshining St. Peter's; and Lowell reminds us that she sprang not from the flesh but from the intellect of Jove. To this white height the poet dare not attempt to climb. Only Paris is left, the 'black classic' city of our own disintegrating culture; for our age seems unable to give direction and purpose to the primeval, irrational violence of human nature.

The intellectual design of this exhilarating poem has little system about it. Yet the texture, phrasing and versification offer immediate pleasures to the ear. It consists of three sonnets with slightly irregular rhyme schemes, the last of the three ending in a couplet that also serves as epigrammatic close to the whole work.[2] This pattern is enriched by a fullness of alliteration, assonance and internal rhyme that, so far from obtruding upon the offhand casualness of phrasing, only seems to deliver an ironical counter-thrust to it. Puns and other witticisms supply an elegant distance from which the poet can regard his own discomfort:

> I envy the conspicuous
> waste of our grandparents on their grand tours—
> long-haired Victorian sages accepted the universe,
> while breezing on their trust funds through the world.

The imagery has the same sort of forceful inconsequence: mountains and birds, tyrants and feet reappear in startling transformations as the wonderfully managed tone deepens from humour to bitterness to sublimity. The elaborate manipulations of height and depth, white and black, the four elements, are old habits of the poet. But the similar treatment of tiny details turns accidents into beauties. Thus the train

---

[2] When Lowell revised this poem for his most recent collection, he also restored a fourth stanza which was judiciously omitted from the text in *Life Studies*.

stewards' tiptoe walk (while they ritually bang on their dinner gongs in a startling allusion to the Mass) becomes, in the second stanza, the toe of St. Peter, superstitiously kissed by pilgrims; and then, in the third, the splendour of the dawn of our culture as the poet sees

> Apollo plant his heels
> on terra firma through the morning's thigh.

It is not easy to overpraise *Life Studies*. I suppose the most startling ingredient in the book was the new direction taken by the poet's conscience. In place of either direct protest or the fusion of his own morality with that of a Christian community, Lowell attached himself to several classes of heroic victims: children, artists, imprisoned criminals, and the mentally ill. Though these have always been linked in the Romantic tradition, most poets dealing with them risk the dangers of posturing and sentimentality. Precisely through making his own case the central case, Lowell avoids either fault. Instead of merely seeing him, we see his view of his peers.

Thus by reviewing his early memories not as they point inward but as they revolve about this or that pathetic adult, he gives a toughening perspective to the sufferings of the child; for these are balanced by the sufferings the child either causes or ironically ignores in the adult. Dealing with poets, he secures a similar distance by balancing the ignominies of the external life against the victories of the imagination. When he handles his most recalcitrant material, the humiliating lives of psychotics, he can allow himself a comical irony that would sound intolerable coming from anyone but the inmate of an institution:

> There are no Mayflower
> screwballs in the Catholic Church.
>   ('Waking in the Blue')

Of course, each of these figures also stands as a measure of the disorder in society: the unrewarded artist, the corrupted child, the madhouse that mirrors the world. Each further becomes an extension of the past: thanks in part to the mere movement of decades, Lowell can bestow on personal recollections the dignity of history:

> These are the tranquillized *Fifties*,
> and I am forty.
>   ('Memories of West Street')

Not through the public aspect of his ancestry but through the independent private experiences of the struggling poet, he can serve as the record of his age, and connect that age with the sweep of earlier epochs.

In all these accomplishments the controlling factor is a matter of tone. If Lowell had not managed to infuse the despair of his disgust with the humour of his irony, he could not have established the framework that screens the reader from the simple pathos of most confessional verse. In the production of this tone, the use of slang, re-sharpened clichés and witticisms is crucial: instead of straining, as in Lowell's earlier work, to give the banalities of life a moral urgency (often without succeeding), they now suggest the speaker's mastery of his experience. It is this saving irony, energised by disgust, that carries him across his most difficult, self-destructive nights. When he emerges from the darkness of 'Skunk Hour', the penultimate (originally the last) and almost the finest poem in this almost uniformly splendid book, what supports him and us is surely the power of his tolerance and humour, shoved smack up against a hideous crisis.

★   ★   ★

In tracing Lowell's career up to 1960, one may describe it as following two successive motions. When he wrote his earlier works, the poet tried to give them importance by starting from the great moral issues or crises of history and then matching those with themes derived from his private ordeals. After *Mills of the Kavanaughs*, however, he was willing to start from his private experiences and project these upon history and public life. Since the effect of the change was a fresh and distinctive kind of poetry, Lowell seems to have felt impelled to push his explorations further. Preoccupied as he was with the continuity of his own work, and educated as he was in Eliot's idea of literature as a body of classics that the innovator alters and enlarges, Lowell naturally looked around among established masters to find either foreshadowings of his discoveries or parallels to his themes and tone.

From the very beginning he had in a sense been doing this. When he incorporated other men's lines into his own verses, when he made a Latin, French or German author's words the basis for a new poem in American English, he was suggesting that at least in certain corners of their *œuvre* the strangers shared his moods. As if to show there were no limits to his ambition, Lowell now set about discovering his own qualities in the whole range of European literature. Having projected his experiences as a human being upon the history of the twentieth century, he now projected his identity as an artist upon the meaning of 'poetry'; for he began producing free adaptations or 'imitations' of the work of a dozen and a half poets from Homer to Montale. Even before they were reprinted in the collection entitled *Imitations* (1961), these poems were received with a surprising degree of incomprehension, which was aggravated rather than lightened when the whole book came out. Only the rare reader either observed that the arrangement of the book was not chronological, or accepted the author's statement that the contents were a sequence rather than a miscellaneous collection.

In fact, of course, *Imitations* is Lowell's attempt to find his voice in the high places of literature, to fashion retrospectively a tradition for his accomplishment. He is legitimising his progeny, replacing the Lowells and Winslows by Baudelaire, Rimbaud and Rilke. In drawing up such a genealogical tree, Lowell again implies that he has found his essential identity not in a social class or in a religious communion but in his character as a writer. So it seems appropriate that the bulk of the models belong to the Symbolist tradition. For Symbolism is the movement that defined the creative mind as the supreme object of poetic contemplation.

Once again, the opening and closing poems have special significance. Lowell begins with a startling extract from the *Iliad*, which picks up the motif of his 'For the Union Dead'—the last poem (under a different title) in the revised edition of *Life Studies*. 'For the Union Dead' had dealt with the mystery of heroism, in which a human life reaches nobility by the manner of death: 'man's lovely/peculiar power to choose life and die'. To open *Imitations*, Lowell gives us 'The Killing of Lykaon'. Suddenly Homer is not the Olympian whose view shifts with dignified ease from Greek side to Trojan, or from man to God; but he is the singer of the 'mania' of Achilles. 'Mania' rather than the conventional 'wrath', says Lowell in his version of the epic invocation. No doubt he is punning on *ménin*, the first word in the first of all our poems. However, he is also, and quite fairly, discovering in the ancient poet his own tendency to regard any irresistible passion as a sort of madness. The extract that follows the bit from the invocation comes from Book XXI of the *Iliad*, and contrasts heroic murder with ignominious death: Achilles insists on despatching the vanquished Lykaon and spurns his victim with a tirade on the killing of Trojans. The hero, foreseeing the dissolution of his enemies' corpses, suggests that the reduction to nothingness eliminates their value as persons. Lowell makes the speech

his own by infusing it with a love-hate hysteria that sounds feverish
and self-conscious but possesses a marvellously nervous vitality:

> You too must die, my dear. Why do you care?
>
>   .   .   .   .   .   .
>
>   the dark shadows of the fish will shiver,
>   lunging to snap Lykaon's silver fat.

The answer to Achilles' debasement of the human spirit is the final
work in *Imitations*, 'The Pigeons', from Rilke. In the middle of this
poem we meet a band of Greek warriors about to die. But here they
personify the poet's army of creative impulses, destroyed through being
realised. The word 'mania' appears too, in the last line of the poem
and the book. Yet it is no longer Achilles' rage to annihilate; it is now
the resistance of reality to the artist's drive towards perfection; for the
imagination of course opposes itself to nothingness and aspires to
eternity. So the metaphor changes, and a poem becomes a ball flung
from 'all-being' towards eternity, 'almost out of bounds', but gaining a
tragic intensity, or 'body and gravity', from the pull that draws it back
towards non-existence. In the exquisitely phrased first half of this fine
work, Lowell-Rilke employs not a ball or an army but the flight and
return of pigeons as a metaphor for the artist's impulses. Each bird is
like a creative vision seeking independent life. So the most beautiful
pigeon is always the one that has never left the coop, the pure concep-
tion not yet embodied; for to be fixed is to be finished. Nevertheless,
says Lowell,

>   only by suffering the rat-race in the arena
>   can the heart learn to beat.

The soaring unity, in such lines, of slang, passion and insight reveals
the strength of Lowell's talent.

The progress from the death-bounded battles of Achilles to the tragic
campaigns of the artist reaches its peripety in the poems from Baudelaire,
placed ironically after Hugo's tributes to the defeated warrior Napoleon
and the dead artist Gautier. In Baudelaire the great themes of *Imitations*
surge together: death, love and art. Lowell has selected poems that
carry us from the revulsion of the artist against passion to the welcome
the artist gives death. If his style sounds drier than Baudelaire's and less
felicitous in rhythm than Pound's, it has a decorous violence of lan-
guage and imagery that no other American poet can produce. Yet not
intensity of expression alone but strength of intellect, the consciousness

enveloping the intensity, draws the disruptive forces together. Lowell's confident metres, the bold, catchy phrases, express not simply what Baudelaire felt but what we still want: a power to transcend lust and decay by the imagination that digests them:

> reptilian Circe with her junk and wand. . . .
> Desire, that great elm fertilized by lust. . . .
> It's time. Old Captain, Death, lift anchor, sink!

If in artistic sensibility Lowell seems peculiarly at home with Baudelaire, he seems as a person still more at ease with Rimbaud, whose work is placed at 'the exact centre of the book. With both poets he finds continual opportunities for employing his own tone and his imagery of passivity eager for motion. But Rimbaud brings out attitudes towards childhood and corrupted innocence that remind us at once of *Life Studies*. Mme. Rimbaud as 'Mother' inexorably recalls Mrs. Lowell:

> she thought they were losing caste. This was good—
> she had the true blue look that lied.

So also the isolated 'poète de sept ans' brings back the 'last afternoon with Uncle Devereux Winslow'. Yet in revealing what he shares with Rimbaud, Lowell also reveals what the rest of us share with them both. The double image here has the distancing but clarifying effect that irony produces in *Life Studies*. When he gives us his amazingly fresh, rich version of 'The Lice-Hunters'—with its symmetry of disgusting perceptions, its complexity of assonance or rhyme, and its steadiness of rhythm—Lowell evokes the whole tendency of our nagging generation to inspect, regret, and enjoy emotional crises:

> He heard their eyebrows beating in the dark
> whenever an electric finger struck to crush
> a bloated louse, and blood would pop and mark
> the indolence of their disdainful touch.

*   *   *

From a glance at Lowell's most recent work, coming out in periodicals, one can prophesy that his next book will establish his name as that normally thought of for 'the' American poet. It will be a wide shift from the fame of Robert Frost, whom so many non-readers of poetry were able to admire along with the literary audience. Frost did many things that Lowell does not. Though unsuccessful as a farmer, he could celebrate aspects of rural life that Lowell never touches. He knew how to tell a story. He was the last important American poet to use the old forms and the old language convincingly. If Frost endured, in the fate of his family, more frightful disasters than Lowell, he was blessed with the power of maintaining his ego against them. Yet he stood for few extraordinary or wayward ideas. His connection with literature outside the conventional English and American models was slight. It is remarkable how often his early poems are indistinguishable from the early poems of Graves or Ransom. He opened few roads that other writers could travel. No one could call Frost a poet's poet.

Lowell, on the contrary, seems determined to maintain his intellectual distinction, his subtlety, his rigorous complexity of form. What appears most astonishing about the recent work is the way old motifs persist in new transformations with deepening significance. There are the city garden, the parallels of beast with man, the bitter pathos of memory working on the fixed character. But in the new poems of private recollection Lowell inclines to emphasise the hold that history has on the present, the powerlessness of the self to resist the determination of open or hidden memories. The insatiable consciousness of the poet comments sardonically on the very self-censuring auto-analysis that produced *Life Studies*.

At the opposite extreme from the private self the poet can now draw human as well as Symbolist analogies between the terrible numbers of suffering people and his own unique experiences. 'Buenos Aires', one of his finest new 'public' poems, has the wit and clever phrasing that make lines attractive on a first reading: 'old men denied apotheosis' (i.e. equestrian statues of defunct dictators); 'Peron,/the nymphets' Don Giovanni'. The poet's games with expressive sound have unusual vigour—for example, a crescendo of echoes of 'air' towards the end, preparing for the name of the city that is the subject of the poem. This 'air' becomes a sarcastic pun; for foul air, miasma, 'hot air', cold fog, emptiness, seem what the place betokens. In the final line the last word, 'crowds', echoes the last word of the first stanza, 'herds', and reminds one of the likeness drawn throughout the poem between cattle and people; for it is the suffering and passivity of the humblest class that connect them with the author.

As usual, the images are what make the poem work. This time they depend on the old partners, love and war, Venus and Mars, united here by means of Peron's name *Juan*, which suggests the Don Juan legend. Lowell, disgusted by the official façade of the city, treats it as a depopulated, over-furnished opera set, which he contrasts with the off-stage crowds of the real Argentina. The opera is of course *Don Giovanni*; and the centre of the poem recapitulates history with dead generals in white marble recalling Mozart's Commendatore. Instead of the file of Don Juan's abandoned mistresses, we meet marble goddesses mourning deceased heroes; or sex and death joined in a skull-like obelisk. Instead of the great lover in hell, we hear Peron bellowing from exile, the seducer of his people.

Among these scenes the poet moves on foot in a circular path, as spectator or sufferer. He starts from and returns to his hotel, caressing inanimate statues (his muses) en route but speaking to nobody. Instead of virile love, he encounters homosexuals in a park; but like Donna Anna, though unlike Argentina, he fights off seduction. Fascinated as so often by what repels him, he sees the truth behind the scrim and delivers it to us by way of his conscience.

A similar solidity of structure and depth of implication pervade the best of the new poems of introspection, 'Eye and Tooth' and the superb tribute to his wife, 'Night Sweat'. 'Eye and Tooth', a skilful extraction of humour from despair, illustrates a truism about middle age: viz. that so far from bringing us serenity, the years leave us naked; only we learn, not without some disgust, that the self can survive even the shabbiest humiliation. The poem depends on a brilliant use of the *eye-I* pun. Treating vision as memory or id, Lowell presents the voyeur poet's eye as an unwreckable showcase of displeasing memories that both shape and torment the person. The dominating metaphor is, so to speak, 'I've got something in my I and can't get it out.' Towards the end Lowell neatly ties the public to the domestic by implying that just as his readers observe his gestures with the unease provoked by their own recollections, so his familiars must in the routines of living find his condition hardly more bearable than he does:

> Nothing! No oil
> for the eye, nothing to pour
> on those waters or flames.
> I am tired. Everyone's tired of my turmoil.

Ransom once played with the idea of Lowell's becoming the Ovid or Virgil of America. But if Lowell feels drawn to themes of epic scope, his mode is neither narrative nor celebratory. For a closer parallel we must look at another epoch in another nation, at the difficult life and disquieting art of Baudelaire. Besides the fundamental similarities of their childhoods, Baudelaire during adolescence inclined like Lowell to a lonely, morose disposition; and it was in the community of artists that he found a lasting family. He was attracted to painting but not to music. As an adult he responded more intensely to city scenes than to country landscapes. In his personality he combined deep passivity with an eagerness to keep working and moving. Though he had begun writing poetry while at school, he always procrastinated about publication, working over his poems with perfectionist ardour. When he produced a book, it was no miscellaneous gathering but an organisation of separate poems into a general scheme reflecting his peculiar outlook.

Still more persuasive are the similarities in the works. Both men have the posture of a fallen Christian. Both deal rather with the horrors of passion than the pleasures of love, and treat death as more seductive than frightening. For both of them, art emerges from profound intellection, from labour, suffering, self-disgust. They build their best poems around complex images linked by connotation, and not around arguments or events. They introduce coarse, distasteful words into a style that is rich and serious. Their poems follow circular movements, with the end touching the beginning.

Their differences are obvious. Lowell's use of history is deliberate; Baudelaire clings to immediate reality. The development of Lowell's characteristic successes depends on an impression of haphazardness at the start turning into a highly wrought climax, whereas Baudelaire's surface has elegance of workmanship throughout. Lowell relies overwhelmingly on visual imagery, whereas Baudelaire appeals elaborately to sounds, and is remarkable for a synaesthetic use of smells. Rhythmically, Lowell sounds less interesting than Baudelaire.

Yet if we search still further, if we place 'Le Cygne' beside 'For the Union Dead', the two sensibilities reveal still more intimate kinship. There is the same sympathy with the wretched, the same disgust with the life that imposes wretchedness upon them, the same transformation of the city-pent poet into an emblem of the human spirit exiled from its original home. Finally, it seems important that Lowell and Baudelaire take so much of the matter of their poems from the most secret rooms of their private lives; for the true biography of them both emerges not from a tale of their friendships or families or external careers but from their works alone. The real Lowell, like the real Baudelaire, is met with in the poetry to which he has given himself altogether.

Note

Biographies. *Emily Dickinson* (1830–86) was born in Amherst, Massachusetts, lived all her life in her father's house; he was a lawyer and at one time a Congressman. Only seven of her 1,775 poems were published in her lifetime.

Marianne Moore (1887–) was born in St. Louis, Missouri, and moved to New York to work in the Public Library; she acted as editor of *The Dial* (1926–9).

Ezra Pound (1885–) born in Idaho, attended the University of Pennsylvania. After a brief episode as language teacher at Wabash College, Indiana, he went to London (1907). Between the two world wars he lived first in Paris and then in Italy. For treasonable radio talks against the Allies during the second world war, he was brought back to the United States; but his case never came to trial, and after a prolonged stay in a mental hospital he returned to Italy (1958).

Publications and Criticism. *The Poems of Emily Dickinson*, ed. T. H. Johnson (1955) and *The Letters*, ed. Johnson (1958) are the fully authoritative editions; he has also written a biography (1955). G. F. Whicher's *This was a Poet* (1938) is still worth reading. R. P. Blackmur's essay is in his *Language as Gesture* (1954) and Allen Tate's in his *Collected Essays* (1959).

There is a selection of the poems with an introduction by J. Reeves (1959).

Marianne Moore's first volume, *Poems*, appeared in 1921. For the London edition of *Selected Poems* (1935), T. S. Eliot wrote an important Introduction. Other volumes include *Collected Poems* (1951) and *Like a Bulwark* (1957).

R. P. Blackmur's essay is reprinted in *The Double Agent* (1935) and two by Randall Jarrell are in his *Poetry and the Age* (1953). W. H. Auden included a study in *The Dyer's Hand and Other Essays* (1962).

Ezra Pound has published voluminously, beginning with limited editions of *A Lume Spento* (Venice, 1908) and *A Quinzaine for this Yule* (London, 1908); important volumes of verse are *Hugh Selwyn Mauberley* (1920), two editions of *Personae: The Collected Poems* (1926 and 1950). There is a *Selected Poems* (London, 1926) including some poems not in the *Collected Poems* of the same year and provided with an Introduction by T. S. Eliot. Pound's *Cantos* have been published in sections, collected in 1949, 1950 and 1954. Later publications have been *Section Rock-Drill* (1956) and *Thrones* (1960).

Pound's other writings include *ABC of Economics* (1933), *ABC of Reading* (1934), *Literary Essays* (1954) and *Letters*, ed. D. D. Paige (1950).

There is an admirably comprehensive but short book, *Ezra Pound*, by G. S. Fraser (1960); F. R. Leavis's essay is in *New Bearings in English Poetry* (1932; revised ed., 1950) and one by A. Alvarez in *The Shaping Spirit* (1958).

IV

Idea and Expression in Emily Dickinson, Marianne Moore and Ezra Pound

ELIZABETH JENNINGS

*

EMILY DICKINSON seems to have been one of those poets who have extracted the largest possible amount of material from the most out-wardly meagre and restricted personal experience. Yet she constructed neither a world of pure fantasy nor a series of exquisite objects which, in the manner of Marianne Moore, might be loaded with agitating emotions or pressed into an ecstatic stillness which poetry surrounds but seldom penetrates. Limited in subject-matter and in metrical cadence though they are, her poems somehow give the effect of largeness, of reverberations. The simple quatrains which Emily Dickinson usually employs seem to be not merely neat, box-like forms holding and sus-taining poetic *trouvailles*, but rather delicate poetic structures which have the power of suggesting shadows or, to change the metaphor, produce momentous and memorable echoes.

But her skill—and it is great—is not the most noticeable thing about Emily Dickinson's poetic *œuvre*. She is one of those poets who depend finally on personal honesty, on the faithful re-creation of a unique experience and lays that experience, with all the nerves exposed, before her readers.

Her subjects are few and constantly repeated—death, love, frustra-tion, self-questioning, loneliness—but they are presented completely, entirely accessible to the reader. Emily Dickinson is also, in a very real sense, a voice rather than simply a person, and it is for this reason that she can describe experiences which might, in the hands of less pains-takingly honest poets, be self-pitying or mawkish. She works at that heightened level where passion is so undiluted that it can become almost something impersonal. It is not surprising that she was a prolific poet, one who worked at white-heat, continually examining and presenting

97

the same subjects, the same obsessions. At the very centre of her work, herself both the subject and object of her poems, she wrought, out of her own highly individual and nervous self-analyses, a poetry which, paradoxically, generates a universal not a merely personal or particular passion. It is this power which places her among the major American poets.

As R. P. Blackmur has said in his study of Emily Dickinson:

> The greatness of Emily Dickinson is not . . . going to be found in anybody's idea of greatness, or of Goethe, or intensity, or mysticism, or historical fatality. It is going to be found in the words she used and in the way she put them together. (p. 34)

And, while commenting on a particular poem, he continues, 'There is no forensic here, nor eloquence, nor justness; it is a bare statement amounting to vision—vision being a kind of observation of the ideal' (p. 35). This is fine, sensitive criticism but I would quarrel with two further comments which Blackmur has made on this poet. One is the remark, 'It [one of her poems] has nothing to do with wisdom, there is no thinking in it', and the other is 'Success was by accident, by the mere momentum of sensibility'. Now the first statement quoted above seems to be everywhere disproved in the poems themselves. They are full of 'thinking' but the thinking is poetic not philosophical, intuitive not organised or discursive. As for Blackmur's remark about Emily Dickinson's accidental successes—this is a criticism which might fairly be levelled against any lyric poet. Blackmur is, I believe, here confusing accident with intuition, chance with the suddenly discovered and surprising truth or felicity. And, furthermore, to use the word 'mere' to qualify the fine phrase 'momentum of sensibility' is surely to belittle all lyric poetry which works by the exercise of concentrated energy in order to find the right word, the fitting cadence. In this sense, *all* lyrical poems are happy accidents but 'accident', in this context, does not seem either a useful or proximate critical term; it obscures far more than it enlightens.

Nevertheless, Blackmur's study is one of the finest introductions to Emily Dickinson's poetry, largely because he is a critic who is entirely at the disposal of the poems he examines. If he blames the state of literature and religion in Emily Dickinson's own time for being the chief cause of her literary limitations, this is at least a generous judgment even

if it is not one to which the co-operative reader of the poems is likely
to give his full assent.

It is interesting to see, therefore, that another fine American critic,
Allen Tate, approaches Emily Dickinson in a way entirely opposed to
that of R. P. Blackmur. He sees the religious climate in which she lived
—that of a 'puritan theocracy'—as the atmosphere in which her parti-
cular kind of poetry could function most effectively. Thus he declares,
'It gave an heroic proportion and a tragic mode to the experience of the
individual . . . it had an immense, incalculable value for literature: it
dramatized the human soul'.

These are large words and perhaps they overstate their case; yet at
least they gave a plausible reason why Emily Dickinson's sort of poetry
could be written in the latter half of the nineteenth century in America.
Such general observations about society and religion are not value
judgments, they neither clarify nor annotate the poems themselves.
They are, in fact, extra-literary reflections, useful scaffoldings, not
pathways into the poetry. But they do clear the ground round the
poems and enable the reader to examine them on their own terms.

It has been suggested already that Emily Dickinson's poems are
notable for their nakedness, for their fearless presentation of experiences
which are deeply, and often painfully, personal. But this poet was such
a finely adjusted instrument for recording experience that the findings
of vision, pain or pleasure which appear in her verse often have a
universal application. And it is, oddly enough, sometimes a kind of wry
wit which makes this generalising power so effective, as in the following
short poem:

> To hang our head ostensibly,
> And subsequent, to find
> That such was not the posture
> Of our immortal mind
>
> Affords the sly presumption
> That in so dense a fuzz
> You too take cobweb attitudes
> Upon a plane of gauze.

It is difficult, I think, to see how any critic could claim that Emily
Dickinson had no *thinking* power when they have the evidence of such
a poem as this before them.

If Emily Dickinson often seems epigrammatic, even aphoristic, her ideas and her wit are not reproving or admonishing. She is, in one sense, always speaking to herself. It is as if we, her readers, were privileged to overhear her meditations and her arguments with herself. This is intense poetry in the very best sense, taut and vibrant not with emotions and ideas which the poet has already formulated outside the poems, but alive with the very process of thought and feeling. A vision is thus caught on the wing, not trapped but held and halted momentarily, just long enough for the poem to be written.

James Reeves, in his sensitive introduction to a selection of the poems, goes far towards explaining the nervous honesty of Emily Dickinson's work when he says:

> She did not withdraw from the world because she hated it: there was nothing in her of the grand romantic manner, rejecting society because the palate had become jaded. Her isolation was a calculated choice, the loss weighed against the gain, with a clear conviction of the necessity and worth of what she had to do.

Reeves is also eager to point out that there was nothing escapist about Emily Dickinson's attitude to life. On the contrary; if she appears to have been retiring and almost eremitical, it was because such an existence enabled her to live more fully, to face her personal predicaments with more dedication and more fearlessness. For her, language was what prayer is to the religious contemplative. She has indicated this in the following eight-line poem:

> The soul unto itself
> Is an imperial friend,
> Or the most agonising spy
> An enemy could send.
>
> Secure against its own,
> No treason it can fear.
> Itself its sovereign, of itself
> The soul should stand in awe.

Emily Dickinson usually restricts herself to the quatrain or the six-line stanza, but if she thus severely limits herself in the matter of form, she compensates for this limitation by her extremely skilful use of half- and quarter-rhymes and also by her extraordinarily apt and original handling of language. Her poems are fresh not simply because they are quite unlike anyone else's but because they seem to have appropriated a poetic speech and vocabulary hitherto unknown in American or

English verse. She has a complete mastery of both sensuous and abstract words, and the success of her best lyrics is often due to a cunning juxtaposition of these two modes of language. She is one of the very few poets who can shock and delight as easily and directly by her handling of abstractions as by the justness and decorum of her concrete imagery. Let me give an example of what I mean by quoting one of her poems:

> Exultation is the going
> Of an inland soul to sea,
> Past the houses, past the headlands,
> Into deep eternity.
>
> Bred as we, among the mountains,
> Can the sailor understand
> The divine intoxication
> Of the first league out from land?

Death is the subject of many of Emily Dickinson's poems, and death for her is as near, as familiar, as commonplace even, as love-affairs are in the poems of less self-sufficient poets. Yet she is not a domestic poet, not a writer who has found a comfortable niche among matters and subjects which are usually thought to be the special province of women poets. Her poems are as bare as Emily Brontë's, as ecstatic as some of Blake's shorter lyrics. If her poems are short, if she is economical and extremely severe with herself, this is because her subjects are so large that they are more effectively presented, more resonant, if they are only hinted at rather than considered at length or extended into long meditations. Her visions are so elusive that to be truthful to them, to suggest the momentariness of their coming and going, she too must be brief but also precise. So in the following twelve-line poem, she tells us more about the questing, visionary mind than many other poets have succeeded in doing in a complete *œuvre*:

> The soul selects her own society,
> Then shuts the door.
> To her divine majority
> Present no more.
>
> Unmoved she notes the chariots pausing
> At her low gate;
> Unmoved, an Emperor be kneeling
> Upon her mat.

> I've known her from an ample nation
> Choose one,
> Then close the valves of her attention
> Like stone.

Allen Tate has some useful things to say about this power of Emily Dickinson's to ensnare and hold an elusive idea:

> It is a poetry of ideas [he says]; and it demands of the reader a point of view—not an opinion of the New Deal or of the League of Nations, but an ingrained philosophy that is fundamental, a settled attitude that is almost extinct in this eclectic age. Yet it is not the sort of poetry of ideas which, like Pope's, requires a point of view only. . . . (p. 197)

Thus Emily Dickinson's poems would seem to demand not only an open sympathy from the reader but also the deepest and most sensitive kind of poetic response. She asks for a total engagement, not necessarily a complete surrender but certainly an acquiescence of the mind and an alertness of the senses. As has been said already, this is a poet who extorted the largest possible amount of poetic material from the most apparently meagre personal experience. The explanation of this phenomenon is, of course, that Emily Dickinson had an intensely rich inner life. One might almost say that what mountains were to Wordsworth and what social life was to Pope, the movements of her own mind and heart were to Emily Dickinson.

*   *   *

In her poem called simply 'Poetry', Marianne Moore wrote,

> . . . there are things that are important beyond all this fiddle.

though she went on to add,

> . . . if you demand on the one hand,
>   the raw material of poetry in
>   all its rawness and
>   that which is on the other hand
>   genuine, then you are interested in poetry.

She appears to have been claiming no more for poetry than a position where it should rightfully be considered seriously. She is neither an upholder of 'art for art's sake', on the one hand, nor a social writer, on the other. She is that anomaly—a poet who uses animals, plants and *objets d'art* to state a moral position. Marianne Moore is, above all, concerned with the question of nobility, courage and restraint. She makes this clear when she writes, in 'The Hero', from *Part of a Novel, Part of a Poem, Part of a Play*,

> . . . He's not out
> seeing a sight but the rock
> crystal thing to see—the startling El Greco
> brimming with inner light—that
> covets nothing that it has let go. This then you may know
> as the hero.

At first sight, Marianne Moore's poetic world seems cluttered with *bric-à-brac*. It bears a close resemblance to a junk shop through which exotic animals wander peaceably. Yet to view her poems as either 'quaint' or 'weird' would be to miss their significance totally. Her objects and animals are detailed, solid, actual, yes, but they are parts of a moral world, not merely lovingly collected, and coveted things. On the other hand, Miss Moore is not a symbolic poet; if she uses her objects to tell a story or illustrate a theme, those objects are not simply ciphers or counters; they have their own powerful and necessary existence. As Eliot has pointed out in his Introduction to the 1935 volume of the *Selected Poems*,

> Some of Miss Moore's poems . . . have a very wide spread of association. It would be difficult to say what is the 'subject-matter' of 'The Jerboa'. For a mind of such agility, and for a sensibility so reticent, the minor subject, such as a pleasant little sand-coloured skipping animal, may be the best release for the major emotions. . . . We all have to choose whatever subject-matter allows us the most powerful and most secret release; and that is a personal affair. (p. 9)

It has been said that Miss Moore is a moralist, a vivid illustrator, a painter of pictures; it should be stressed that she is also an extremely emotional poet, though her feelings are always held on a firm leash. R. P. Blackmur has said, in his essay 'The Method of Marianne Moore': 'The whole flux of experience and interpretation is appropriate subject matter to an imagination *literal* enough to see the poetry in it . . .' (p. 149), and again, 'Much of her verse has the peculiar, unassignable, indestructible authority of speech overheard . . .' (p. 157).

Miss Moore is a moralist who allows intellect, emotion and imagination to play equal parts in the making of a poem; she looks at her objects and animals with a loving observation or almost microscopic care, but she also looks beyond them to their further significance and their meaning in a larger world. The pure symbolist looks, as it were, directly at his symbols and is concerned only with what they represent or signify. The poet who is primarily interested in imagery is more concerned with the meaning than with the autonomous life of his images. Miss Moore, on the other hand, displays her objects in all their burning and fierce life and only after she has done this does she meditate on their wider meaning, or else hint to us what moral viewpoint they bring to her mind. It is worth giving a few examples to show precisely what I mean by these assertions:

> I remember a swan under the willows in Oxford,
>   with flamingo-coloured, maple-
>   leaflike feet. It reconnoitred like a battle-
>   ship. Disbelief and conscious fastidiousness were the
>   staple ingredients in its
>   disinclination to move. . . .
>   ('Critics and Connoisseurs')

> They answer one's questions,
> a deal table compact with the wall;
> in this dried bone of arrangement
> one's 'natural promptness' is compressed, not crowded out;
> one's style is not lost in such simplicity.
>   ('People's Surroundings')

> Not brittle but
> Intense—the spectrum, that
>   Spectacular and nimble animal the fish,
>   Whose scales turn aside the sun's sword with their polish.
>   ('An Egyptian Pulled Glass Bottle in the Shape of a Fish')

W. H. Auden, in *The Dyer's Hand*, has compared Marianne Moore's world of beasts with that of D. H. Lawrence. He has some interesting things to say about Miss Moore's use of animals as 'emblems'. Thus he writes:

The approach of her poetry is that of a naturalist but, really, their theme is almost always the Good Life. Sometimes, as in the bestiaries, she sees an animal as an emblem—the devil-fish, so frightening to look at, because of the care she takes of her eggs becomes an emblem of charity, . . . the jerboa-rat an emblem of true freedom as con-

trasted with the false freedom of the conqueror-tyrant—and some-
times, as in the beast fable, the behavior of animals is presented as a
moral paradigm. Occasionally, as in 'Elephants', the moral is direct,
but, as a rule, the reader has to perceive it for himself. (pp. 304-5)

It is true that Marianne Moore's beasts seldom bear one simple, single
meaning as they do in medieval bestiaries. Yet her moral conclusions
often appear very direct and apparently even naïve, as when she says in
'In Distrust of Merits', 'there never was a war that was/not inward'. In
fact, however, she works very hard for her summings-up and inter-
pretations; her simplicities are hardly won out of great complexities
and she only proffers them to us when she is herself satisfied that they
are really valid. It is not surprising, then, that in her translations of La
Fontaine's *Fables*, she sometimes makes the French poet's conclusions
sound remarkably like her own. One thinks particularly of the end of
'The Mountain in Labour':

> . . . 'Here is an exposition
> Of Mars terrorized by the Titans' war.'
> One is promised marvels and finds one's hurricane
>   A fan.

Miss Moore's versification presents fascinating problems. She is
almost certainly one of the hardest modern poets to read aloud. Prac-
tically every poem she writes is an intricately devised metrical system, a
system which often has a complex rhyme scheme and a carefully con-
trasted method of scansion. Her rhythms are almost always subtle and
sometimes remind one of those high notes which musicians play for the
ears of the *cognoscenti* only. Eliot says: 'Of the *light* rhyme Miss Moore
is the greatest living master . . .' (p. 11). And, indeed, she is continually
making subtle experiments with it. Her poetic *forms*, also, are anything
but free; their patterns may be elusive and sometimes difficult to grasp,
but they are always present. Much of the pleasure she gives us is the
sudden discovery of an elusive music.

Most people would agree, I think, that these poems are best read on
the page. Indeed the pattern of their lay-out, the arrangement of each
line and word is devised by the poet in order to ensure that the reader
shall comprehend the given poem totally. The visual arrangement of
the poem is not only part of its effect, but an essential element in its
raison d'être. The poems need to be read carefully and slowly; due weight
has to be given to every stressed and unstressed syllable. Nothing is

accidental in Marianne Moore; she plays no tricks with chance. She is a formalist, a designer of intricate patterns. A superficial reading of her work might suggest, indeed, that she is an exponent of 'art for art's sake'. As we have already seen to some extent, however, she is really a moralist, a poet who uses exquisite objects and animals to reverberate with meaning. Randall Jarrell puts this very well when he says,

> Her forms . . . are like the aria of the Queen of the Night: the intricate and artificial elaboration not only does not conflict with the emotion but is its vehicle. And her machinery—bestiary, rather—fits both the form and final content of her poems as precisely as if all three were pieces of some extraordinary puzzle. Another of the finest American poets, Wallace Stevens, is as addicted to exotic properties; but his often get in the way of what he has to say, or hide from him the fact that he does not this time, care to say anything much. (p. 163)

Mr. Jarrell goes on to discuss what is perhaps the most vital element in Marianne Moore's poetry—its real content. Much has been said of her fastidiousness, her powers of observation and her love of old things. What is too easily ignored and forgotten is the fact that she is also deeply emotional, and that there are certain qualities for which she has an immense and continuous admiration. Mr. Jarrell expresses this when he writes,

> Patience, honesty, the courage that is never conscious of itself because it has always taken itself for granted—all the qualities she distils from, or infuses into, the real pastoral of natural history books, she is at last able to permit even to man, looking at him . . . as equably, carefully, and affectionately as she ever looked at any animal. (p. 164)

It seems, then, that Marianne Moore is, at the last resort, an admirer, a celebrator of life, and particularly of nature. Her stuffed animals, her finely-blown glass, all her man-made objects are bursting with vigour. Their formal design, even their stillness, restrains them from entering chaos. Order is preserved because, for Miss Moore, restraint is a quality which man must both preserve and practise.

*   *   *

Recently, fresh controversy has arisen around the name of Ezra

Pound. It was started by Robert Conquest in *The London Magazine* when he questioned the whole validity and worth of Pound's work, and made the suggestion that the *Cantos* and the earlier poems were derivative, yet not true translations. He also stated that the odd, felicitous phrase or passage was not sufficient to permit him to be regarded as a major modern poet. This attack was challenged by many other critics, both in the columns of *The London Magazine* and on the Third Programme; it became, in fact, a literary talking point for some weeks.

Thirty-one years ago, F. R. Leavis remarked that though *Hugh Selwyn Mauberley* was a 'great poem',

> the *Cantos* appear to be little more than a game—a game serious with the seriousness of pedantry. We may recognise what Mr. Pound's counters stand for, but they remain counters; and his patterns are not very interesting, even as schematic design, since, in the nature of the game, . . . they lack definition and salience. (pp. 155–6)

Perhaps it is as well to remind ourselves at this point of the high praise which Eliot has always accorded to Pound. He called him in the dedication to *The Waste Land*, 'il miglior fabbro', and he has always paid high tribute to Pound's visual and aural gifts. There do seem, then, to be two quite separate and mutually antagonistic schools of thought. One sees him as an unoriginal poet, a rather poor echo of other men's works, while the other sees him as a great innovator, a master of modern verse. Some critics, such as Miss Christine Brooke-Rose, have demonstrated that his *Cantos* (particularly the later ones in *Rock-Drill* and *Thrones*) can be closely and helpfully analysed, while others see him as the creator of lovely fragments merely, the maker of the anthology piece, the poet of the sudden happy discovery, rather than of the long, substantial passage.

I am inclined to place myself with those who represent the second school of thought. Pound appears to me to be the sort of writer who squeezes every possible ounce of value out of other men's work and then makes something new of his own from it. He relies very much on other literatures, whether these be English, Provençal, Latin or Chinese. He is not a poet who stands by himself. Yet in his own odd way he *is* original simply because he does this. And he is original too in his complete mastery of visual *montage*. I can think of no other American or English poet who has such power to evoke landscape or to summon

up a particular period of history; one recalls the following passage from
'Canto 21':

> The tree-spheres half dark against sea
>   half clear against sunset,
> The sun's keel freighted with cloud,
> And after that hour, dry darkness
> Floating flame in the air, gonads in organdy,
> Dry flamelet, a petal borne in the wind.

As a descriptive writer, Pound is unequalled among contemporary
poets writing in English. But his descriptions always serve a purpose.
They are seldom relished for their own sake. Rather they are used for
'placing' a person or a period. They almost become attributes—of
history itself.

Robert Conquest is not the only critic who has attacked Pound.
Indeed, Pound seems to be the kind of poet who is peculiarly open to
a particular type of accusation—namely, to put it at its best, lack of
originality, and, at its worst, sheer plagiarism. We all know that
Pound owes much to foreign literatures; as A. Alvarez has said:

> Pound on his own, in fact, is not particularly full. Pound working
> through other literature is. He needs the framework of translation.
> It keeps his intellect and imagination at full stretch by providing for
> all the technical business whilst he sustains his understanding of the
> poem and the poet. (p. 59)

And of *Homage to Sextus Propertius*, G. S. Fraser explains Pound's
method by stating:

> . . . for his own purposes, he is 'pointing up' that sense [of the
> Latin]. But he is not using Propertius as a *mere* stalking-horse. He is,
> . . . striving by a slight distortion of the literal sense of his original
> to bring over more fully than Butler what he guesses to be its tone
> and feeling. (p. 65)

Homage to Sextus Propertius makes an excellent introduction to the
Cantos; all Pound's best qualities are manifested in it—his sensuousness,
his feeling for the past and for history, his ability to sum up in a line or a
phrase a whole way of thought, a complete attitude towards human
emotion. A few quotations will illustrate what I mean:

> It is noble to die of love, and honourable to remain
>   uncuckolded for a season,

> And she speaks ill of light women
> and will not praise Homer
> Because Helen's conduct is 'unsuitable'.

. . . . . .

> You will say that you succumbed to a danger identical,
> charmingly identical, with Semele's,
> And believe it, and she also will believe it,
> being expert from experience,
> And amid all the gloried and storied beauties of Maeonia
> There shall be none in a better seat, not
> one denying your prestige.

. . . . . .

> A Trojan and adulterous person came to Menelaus under
> the rites of hospitium,
> And there was a case in Colchis, Jason, and that woman
> in Colchis.

With Pound, the past no longer seems like the past; it acquires the immediacy and relevance of the present. And perhaps this is the best answer to those who accuse him either of being an inaccurate translator or else of being a plagiarist. The fact is that he uses other men's writings as most poets use their own emotions and experiences. He loots them and sacks them for all that they have to offer. And not only this: he also transforms them. What with him appear to be comments on history are in fact re-creations of history. Poetry pervades the humdrum event and makes it live before us now and here.

One needs to stress too Pound's powerful visual sense, something that he acquired originally from the Imagists perhaps but a gift which he has certainly made entirely his own. Even in *Thrones*, the latest and most complex collection of *Cantos*, this gift flashes out vividly, if often only fitfully, as in the following quotations:

> A memorial to archivists and librarians:
> Bernicoli in Ravenna, and that stuffed
> shirt who
> wrote such an elegant postcard.
> Some sort of embargo, Theodora died on
> the 19th Justinian.
>
> ('Canto 96')

Unsifted hot words, at first merely to flatter
as an animal his eye eating light
        or run to rat holes
Laws must be for general good,
        for the people's uprightness,
            their moral uprightness.

('Canto 99')

But I suppose the most crucial and controversial aspects of Pound are his obsession with usury, anti-Semitism and Fascism, and his tendency towards archaism. Both these aspects of him are well touched on by Fraser when he declares,

He mistook the violence of Fascist dictatorship for power, for something to build on; it was not. And seeing many of the faults and failings of English and American democracy throughout his lifetime he mistook that either for ochlocracy, mob rule, the weak conspiring against the strong, greed and envy conspiring against creative talent, or for a thin mask of ochlocracy, only half-concealing the rule, a soulless rule, of money. Again, he was wrong. (p. 9)

And again, Fraser comments that, in the Cantos, Pound's 'central intuition' is 'beautifully' expressed—namely, his awareness of 'the human need for the permanence of the human artifact, the memorial, so that there shall continue to be remembrance of things that are to come with those that shall come after'.

As Fraser points out elsewhere, Pound began as an aesthetic poet and appears to end as a didactic one. If some of the lessons he has tried to teach are distasteful, even repugnant, to us, he is not alone in this among English and American poets. What remains sure and permanent is his excited sense of history, his pictorial view of the past. His early poems were exquisite but often static. The Cantos are dynamic, largely because they represent one man's continually changing view of life and politics; that eye is a camera, yes, but it is also an assessor. Pound's obsession with the theme of usury has enabled him to write some of his finest poetry, because his loathing of usury is an integral part of his whole sense of values. What he does value most highly is very plain if we read the following extracts from the Cantos:

He is not vertu but cometh of that perfection
Which is so postulate not by the reason
But 'tis felt, I say.

Beyond salvation, holdeth his judging force
Deeming intention to be reason's peer and mate,
Poor is discernment, being thus weakness' friend

Often his power cometh on death in the end,
Be it withstayed
                    and so swinging counterweight
Not that it were natural opposite but only

Wry'd a bit from the perfect,
Let no man say love cometh from chance
Or hath not established lordship
Holding his power even though
            Memory hath him no more.

                                             ('Canto 36')

'Nothing we made, we set nothing in order,
'Neither house nor the carving,
'And what we thought had been thought for too long;
'Our opinion not opinion in evil
'But opinion borne for too long.
'We have gathered a sieve full of water.'

                                             ('Canto 25')

Leaf over leaf, dawn-branch in the sky
And the sea dark, under wind
The boat's sails hung loose at the mooring,
            Cloud like a sail inverted,
And the men dumping sand by the sea-wall
Olive trees there on the hill
            Where a man might carry his oar up.

                                             ('Canto 23')

These passages display not only Pound's remarkable visual sense, but
also his marvellous ear, his sense of cadence, balance, melody. The early
Cantos are far more fluent, musical and lucid than the later. In the latter,
one feels that Pound is sometimes too urgently trying to find a lan-
guage and a verse-form, for his ideas; everything is compressed, and this
often makes for obscurity. His increasing use of Chinese symbols also
means that it is sometimes very difficult for the Western reader to
extract his full message.

Of course, as well as an aural poet, Pound is very much a visual one.
How his lines are laid out on the page is as vital to him as it is to
Marianne Moore. And the Chinese emblems he uses are, I think,

present as much for their symmetry and harmony as for their actual intrinsic meaning.

What has been Pound's influence on the younger poets during the last few years? On the whole, I would say that it has been a fugitive one. He is not felt in practically all the poets at present writing as Eliot, for example, is, because Eliot not only changed an English poetic language but also provided us with a fresh subject-matter. No, Pound has not been an innovator in this way. What he has done is to recover the sense of the past for us, to hand back, renewed and revitalised, the forms and metres of other countries and other literatures. His influence has only been specific—in the sense that one can actually hear his particular tone of voice—in the work of a rather unusual young poet such as Charles Tomlinson; Tomlinson is a writer who has taken over a good deal of the Imagist technique and method. Apart from him, I can think of few young English poets of whom it could be said 'This man has read and assimilated Pound. One can sense it in his work.' And Robert Graves, of course, in one of his Clark lectures, has attacked Pound fairly fiercely on much the same grounds as Robert Conquest has done.

Pound is also perhaps a little out of fashion at present because the intellectual content of his work has been reduced to a minimum. He has not, as a result, been of much use to those many poets of the 'fifties who made thought one of the essential ingredients in their work. As R. P. Blackmur has said:

> Mr. Pound is explicit; he is all surface and articulation. For us, everything is on the outsides of his words—of which there is excellent testimony in the fact that his best work is his best translation [I would not myself agree with this particular point]. In reading even his most difficult verse, such as the *Cantos*, there should never be any intellectual problem of interpretation. (p. 125)

*   *   *

Emily Dickinson, Marianne Moore, Ezra Pound—these are three very different American poets. It is hard indeed to believe that they belong to the same race or are all using poetry as their means of artistic expression. Yet, when one examines them more closely, one realises that what they share is a contemplative attitude towards men and affairs; they all look, appraise, annotate and re-create. Pound is clearly a more passionate participator in life than the other two poets, but I would say that even his prevailing attitude is a watchful, observant one. This may sound like a paradox, but it is no more a paradox than the fact that the apparently private worlds of Emily Dickinson and Marianne Moore are really extremely public ones. If we are honest we must all admit that such worlds are places which we all have to inhabit and endure. Poetry can render these worlds less painful, but not less dynamic and real.

Note

Publications. Early Imagist poems appeared in *Des Imagistes: An Anthology*, ed.
E. Pound (1914) and *Some Imagist Poets*, ed. Amy Lowell (Boston, 1915, 1916,
1917); 'The Complete Poetical Works of T. E. Hulme' was published as an
appendix to a volume of poems, *Ripostes*, by Ezra Pound (1912).
Besides Pound's advocacy, Imagism was presented by F. S. Flint, 'The History of
Imagism', *The Egoist*, II (1 May, 1915), and 'Imagism', *Poetry*, I (January, 1913).
T. E. Hulme's *Speculations*, ed. H. Read, was published in 1924.

Scholarship. The Life and Opinions of T. E. Hulme (1960) by A. R. Jones includes
the text of all his poems and of 'A Tory Philosophy' and 'A Personal Impression
of Bergson'.
Imagism is considered further in S. K. Coffman, *Imagism: a Chapter for the History
of Modern Poetry* (1951); G. Hughes, *Imagism and the Imagists: a Study in Modern
Poetry* (1931); A. R. Jones, 'Notes toward a History of Imagism', *South Atlantic
Quarterly*, LX (1961); René Taupin, *L'Influence du Symbolisme français sur la
Poésie américaine (de 1910 à 1920)* (1929); and H. Kenner, 'Why Imagism?',
The Poetry of Ezra Pound (1950).

V

Imagism: A Unity of Gesture

A. R. JONES

★

THERE is no reason to doubt F. S. Flint's brief account of the founding of Imagism which appeared in *The Egoist* in May, 1915:

> Somewhere in the gloom of the year 1908, Mr. T. E. Hulme . . . proposed to a companion that they should found a Poets' Club. The thing was done there and then. The Club began to dine; and its members to read their verses. At the end of the year they published a small plaquette of them, called 'For Christmas MDCCCCVIII'. In this plaquette was printed one of the first 'Imagist' poems by T. E. Hulme, 'Autumn' . . .
> I think what brought the real nucleus of this group (1909 group) together was a dissatisfaction with English poetry as it was then (and still is alas!) being written. We proposed at various times to replace it by pure *vers libre*; by the Japanese *tanka* and *haikai*; we all wrote dozens of the latter as an amusement; by poems in a sacred Hebrew form; . . . by rimeless poems like Hulme's 'Autumn', and so on. In all this Hulme was ringleader. He insisted too on absolutely accurate presentation and no verbiage . . . There was also a lot of talk and practice among us, Storer leading it chiefly, of what we called the Image. We were very much influenced by modern French symbolist poetry . . .
> Pound collected together a number of poems of different writers . . . and in February–March, 1914, they were published in America and England as *Des Imagistes: An Anthology* which though it did not set the Thames seems to have set America on fire . . . There is no difference, except that which springs from difference of temperament and talent, between an imagist poem of today and those written by Edward Storer and T. E. Hulme.

F. S. Flint describes three distinct phases in the formal history of the movement; the Poets' Club of 1908, what Ezra Pound describes as 'the forgotten School of Images' of 1909, and the 'Imagistes' whose anthology edited by Ezra Pound appeared in 1914. To this must be added a fourth period best described by Pound as the 'Amygists' whose work appeared in the three anthologies edited by Amy Lowell in 1915, 1916 and 1917.

*   *   *

T. E. Hulme having quarrelled with his family followed the traditional course of seeking to restore his fortunes in the colonies. He took a cargo boat to Canada in July, 1906, and worked his way from job to job across the continent. Although he did not make his fortune, it was during this period that he first began to concern himself seriously with aesthetics and with poetry and came to certain conclusions concerning the nature of poetic language and the supremacy of the image. At this time he wrote to Miss A. M. Pattinson to say, 'I have got some ideas and experiences and am very glad I came, even if it were only for a suitable image I thought of one day working in the railway'. He began to write down these images which were centred on his feelings in fact of the vast spaces of Canada, the huge sky and the flat, rolling grass lands. 'The first time I ever felt the necessity or inevitableness of verse', he said later, 'was in the desire to reproduce the peculiar quality of feeling which is induced by the flat spaces and wide horizons of the virgin prairie of Western Canada.' In effect, Hulme suffered from that 'space-shyness' that he later wrote of in connection with Worringer as the basis of all classical, geometric art. 'The flats of Canada', he wrote, 'are incomprehensible on any single theory' and he sought tentatively to encompass this incomprehensibility within the image.

When he returned from Canada in the spring of 1907 he began a study of French aesthetics, particularly of Jules de Gaultier, Rémy de Gourmont, and began what Pound called his 'shopping round with Bergson'. He found he could use (or misuse) Bergson's ideas in order to provide himself with a suitable language in which to express his conception of poetry. Bergson had said that there are two distinct ways of 'knowing' reality; intellectually by means of the analytic method, and instinctively by means of the intuition. Hulme assumes that these are two distinct kinds of language; prose which is a counter language, a practical but blunt instrument of communication, and poetry which is, or at least can be, a sensitive and individual instrument for communicating the unique, imaginative insights of the poet. Prose is the language of the intellect, a concept language; poetry is the language of intuition, an imagistic language. Only the language of poetry can embody intuitions of the intensive reality of experience. 'No image', said Bergson, 'can replace the intuition of duration', but 'many diverse images, borrowed from very different orders of things, may, by the convergence of their action, direct consciousness to the precise point where there is a certain intuition to be seized'. Moreover, as Bergson pointed out, 'the image has at least this advantage, that it keeps us in the concrete'. In Bergson's metaphysics, Hulme found a congenial language in which to clothe his poetic theory as well as justification for asserting the primary importance in poetry of the image.

But Hulme is nothing if not eclectic and he was probably the first Englishman to profit from Rémy de Gourmont's influential *Problème du Style*.[1] Gourmont for twenty-five years, between 1890 and 1915, was an editor of *Mercure de France* and his influence on English poetry at the beginning of the century was in many ways decisive. T. S. Eliot describes him as 'the critical conscience of his generation', and as combining 'sensitiveness, erudition, sense of fact and sense of history, and generalising power' to a degree that elicits a comparison with Aristotle. (Preface to 1928 edition *The Sacred Wood*.) Hulme was quick to seize on Gourmont's emphasis on visual imagery, on the fact that vision is the basis of all art, that style must not evoke but present the objects of reality as physically as possible, that subject and style cannot be differentiated: 'Nous écrivons, comme nous sentons, comme nous pensons, avec notre corps entier. L'intelligence n'est qu'une des manières d'être de la sensibilité, et non pas la plus stable, encore moins la plus volontaire.' Poetry involved the total sensibility, Gourmont considered, but first it was necessary to the life of poetry to find new images in order to resuscitate the language which was always on the point of dying:

> La métaphore nous est indispensable; ceux qui, par la constitution de leur cerveau, sont inaptes à en créer de nouvelles, usent de celles qui ont cours. Tout cliché fut une métaphore neuve et reste une métaphore banale. Le cliché est une monnaie jetée dans la circulation; la métaphore est le premier exemplaire de cette monnaie; il retournera à la foule, entrera en quelque collection de raretés, ou bien il sera

---

[1] With Rémy de Gourmont as co-editor, Alfred Jarry founded in October, 1894, a review called significantly *L'Imagier*.

tiré à des millions et deviendra si vulgaire que nul ne songera jamais à considérer sa face.

Gourmont returned the responsibility for the life of language directly to the poet. The business of the poet was to coin new images, for only by the fusion of images could he present the object of his vision faithfully:

> Non seulement l'usage complémentaire est intimement intriqué dans l'usage fondamental, mais les deux images, réagissant l'une sur l'autre, se sont fondues en une troisième absolument inattendue; cette fusion, art suprême, est obtenue en passant sous silence l'objet même qui sert de point de comparaison; mais cet objet, qui n'est pas nommé, il était inutile de le nommer.

In the same way that an electric current will be seen passing from one pole to another, so a poem can exist in the tension existing between two images. By the juxtapositioning of two images the mind is surprised out of its habitual responses and creates a third image which is the 'meaning' of the poem.

Hulme vigorously publicised his views about poetry in London's literary clubs and became friendly with a number of poets. Early in 1908 he founded, together with Henry Simpson, the 'Poets' Club' and became its first secretary. The Club dined together monthly and read and discussed poetry and, belatedly, in January, 1909, printed the volume of poetry entitled *For Christmas MDCCCCVIII*. This contained poems by Selwyn Image, Lady Margaret Sackville, Henry Simpson, Mrs. Marion Cran, F. W. Tancred and Dermot Fryer. Hulme contributed two poems, 'A City Sunset', and 'Autumn', both of which demonstrate the maturity to which he had already brought his practice of Imagism. The Poets' Club had at least become prominent enough to be singled out for attack, curiously by F. S. Flint as poetry reviewer of A. R. Orage's *New Age*:

> I think of this club and its after dinner ratiocinations, its tea-parties in suave South Audley Street; and then of Verlaine at the Hôtel de Ville, with his hat on the peg, as a proof of his presence, but he himself in a café hard by with other poets, conning feverishly and excitedly the mysteries of their craft—and I laugh.[2]

Clearly, F. S. Flint's attack is really mainly directed against the upper-class, dilettante character of the club. As secretary, Hulme replied to

[2] *New Age*, V, 14, 5 August, 1909.

this attack on the Club's behalf and pointed out, reasonably enough, that there is no necessary connection between obscure cafés and good poetry, nor is there any reason to suppose that poets must be addicted to 'Circean excesses' and 'discoloured linen'. Flint's nostalgia for the Bohemian life gave Hulme his excuse for attacking him as a 'belated Romantic', and thus demonstrating that even at this time not only his Imagism but also his anti-Romanticism was fully developed. This clash with Flint soon led to a firm friendship between them from which they both profited in a number of ways. Hulme continued to regard the elegant meetings of the Poets' Club as essentially civilised and classical, and the verses that the Club nourished as cultivated exercises in the new classicism which he was ushering in; and although he ceased to act as secretary, he continued to take an active part in its activities. Indeed he proposed both F. S. Flint and Ezra Pound to election as members and at Christmas, 1909, he published two further poems, 'A Conversion' and 'The Embankment' in their volume, *The Book of the Poets' Club*, to which F. S. Flint and Ezra Pound also contributed.

★   ★   ★

It was through Flint that Hulme was introduced to French Symbolist poetry and Hulme was quick to see how the example of the contemporary French poetry could help him and his fellow-poets achieve that hardness, clarity and restraint that he had already made the keystone of his Imagism. F. S. Flint had already voiced his dissatisfaction with contemporary English poetry in the *New Age*, 'English poetry at this hour is deliquescent. There is no unity of inspiration; the words blow fitfully in all directions; and no criticism. There can be no movement, therefore . . .' Also he had made his admiration for Symbolist poetry quite plain: 'the Symbolist—and all essential poets are symbolists—takes a pure emotion and translates it by eternal images which become symbolical of man's everlasting desires and questions——' Yet Flint's early poetry, collected in a volume entitled *In the Net of the Stars* (London, 1909) is derivative, decadent and romantic. Hulme taught him to concentrate more on craftsmanship and less on inspiration. He gathered together a group of friends and although it was never formalised into a club this group met fairly regularly in the Eiffel Tower, a Soho restaurant. Hulme was the centre of these informal gatherings, the first of which is recorded as being held on 25 March, 1909. (The nucleus of this group, apart from Hulme himself and F. S. Flint, was

Francis Tancred, Edward Storer, Florence Farr and Joseph Campbell.)
He dominated the discussions and argued endlessly and dogmatically
about poetic tradition and poetic form, and tirelessly impressed upon
those present his idea of the new classicism. Poems were read and
passionately discussed, but Hulme himself dictated the terms of the
meetings and even insisted on the kind of poems written.

The image was thought of as something hard and limited evolved
from the flux of reality, the 'expression and communication of momen-
tary phases in the poet's mind'. Poetry was not a matter of self-
expression, a mode of action, but a question of a precise impression
involving a fresh sense of the relation of language and meaning. The
poem should hand over sensations 'bodily' (a response of the total
sensibility)—the images themselves embodying the substance of experi-
ence Hulme, with his eye now always on French example, saw the
beginnings of modern art in the work of Cézanne who, reacting against
the 'fluidity' of his contemporaries, achieved a sense of 'a more solid
kind of reality' by introducing a more geometric formalism into his
compositions (*Speculations*, pp. 100–7). He wanted to make of im-
pression something solid and durable. Similarly, Hulme, beginning
negatively with a feeling of dissatisfaction with existing poetry and feel-
ing the need for the expression of a new and more intense sensibility,
looked for a more formal poetic structure. Like Cézanne he felt the
need 'to make of impressionism something solid and durable like old
art' (p. 100). This accounts largely for the experimentation in older
forms, mentioned by Flint, particularly in the 'Japanese *tanka* and
haikai'. Flint's referring to *haikai* rather than to *haiku* makes it clear that
the group discovered these forms in French and in French imitations—
the *Nouvelle Revue Française*, for instance, held *haiku* competitions. The
appeal of this form is obvious for it seemed to be made to illustrate
Hulme's theories; it was concise, precise in its imagery, which was
mainly natural, and avoided didacticism. It celebrated, for the most
part, fleeting impressions by overlaying one image on another. It was
extremely impersonal in the clarity of its form and yet communicated
impressionistically the fragile nature of reality. Moreover, to Hulme
and his friends it appeared to be written in *vers libre* (in fact, it has a fixed
syllabic basis) without rhyme or regular metre. It seemed to offer dry,
hard concrete imagery and, without losing any of the essential force of
symbolist poetry, avoided direct lyricism. It was the basic unit of the
imagistic poem, juxtapositioning two images, often in contrast, and

containing them within a brief, epigrammatic form, omitting all moral and intellectual comment and allowing the images to form a 'visual chord' in the mind—a third image that unites them—so that a 'thing outward and objective transforms itself, or darts into a thing inward and subjective' (Ezra Pound). The images are not merely decorative, they are more than a part of the poem, they *are* the poem and reveal with visual clarity a moment of intense insight into reality. It is interesting to notice that for Hulme—and for Bergson—the platonic idea of two worlds, of shadows and of reality, still persists and the artist is the man who intuits the nature of reality and communicates it in 'real' language, the language of the image.

*   *   *

Ezra Pound's introduction to the Eiffel Tower group was characteristically dramatic. Dressed like the hero of Italian grand opera, with his carroty beard waving, he read aloud his poem 'Sestina' standing on a table. He gave this dramatic monologue the full and appropriate Browning Society treatment, roaring it out until the restaurant trembled and the waiters discreetly placed screens around the tables occupied by the group. Pound could hardly have known that this kind of flamboyant behaviour was unlikely to impress a group of poets dedicated to restraint and decorum. He soon learnt, however, to restrain his rhetoric and, under Hulme's influence, began to experiment with *haiku* and short lyrics and, altogether, to adopt a more modest poetic tone. He began to talk less about 'beauty' and 'ecstasy' and more about 'precision' and 'directness'. In May, 1909, he wrote to William Carlos Williams:

> If you'll read Yeats and Browning and Francis Thompson and Swinburne and Rossetti you'll learn something about the progress of English poetry in the last century. And if you'll read Margaret Sackville, Rosamund Weston, Ernest Rhys, Jim G. Fairfax, you'll learn what the people of second rank can do, and what damn good work it is. (*Letters*, pp. 91–2)

After his meeting with the Hulme group he continued to admire Browning's use of *personae* and Swinburne's metrical experiments; and he never ceased to admire Yeats, particularly after Yeats had been persuaded by Pound to benefit from the Imagists' example and harden the structure and idiom of his poetry. As late as 1910 Pound, following Pater's lead, wrote that 'Great art is made, not to please, but to call forth, or create an ecstasy' (*The Spirit of Romance*, 1910), but then we can assume this was actually written before he joined the Eiffel Tower meetings for Pound soon made himself the focus of dissatisfaction with the state of English poetry and began to echo the group's demand for 'fewer painted adjectives impeding the shock and stroke of it. At least, for myself, I want it so, austere, direct, free from emotional slither.' He joined in their demand for a new kind of poetry 'as much like granite as it can be' (*Prolegomena*).

Of course Pound was accessible during this period to influences other than those of Hulme and his friends. He had already undertaken a study of Provençal poetry and the whole field of poets represented in *The Spirit of Romance*. He himself expresses his indebtedness to a bewildering multiplicity of sources but, in particular, to Ford Madox Hueffer (Ford), and to Fenollosa whose papers on the Chinese written characters he edited. But these influences tended to reinforce and extend and, to some extent, modify the doctrine of the Image as expounded by Hulme. Indeed it is a curious fact, attributable no doubt to some incident in his personal life rather than in his poetic career, that the militancy with which he institutionalised and publicised these views is offset by his reluctance to acknowledge their source. He said that the doctrine of the image was derived direct from Aristotle: 'Aristotle will tell you that' the apt use of metaphor being as it is, the swift perception of relations, is the true hall-mark of genius: 'That abundance, that readiness of the image is indeed one of the surest proofs that the mind is upborne upon the emotional surge' (*The Serious Artist*, p. 195). This is not Aristotle but is, in its emphasis on the 'swift perception of relations', close enough to Hulme to be Hulme's. Similarly, while on the one hand he praised Hueffer as the 'critical light' of this period, on the other the objections which he forwarded to Hueffer's impressionism in poetry are purely Hulme's: 'The *conception* of poetry is a process more intense than the *reception* of an impression. And no impression, however carefully articulated, can, recorded, convey that feeling of sudden light which the works of art should and must convey' (*Poetry Review*, March, 1912, p. 134). Later, after working on Fenollosa's papers, he talked more about the 'ideogram' and less about the 'image' but in some curious way the 'ideogram' accumulated all those attributes that Hulme had associated with the 'image' except, of course, that Hulme did not derive them from the Chinese written character.

Nonetheless, there is no doubt that with the recruitment of Pound to its ranks, Imagism gained a poet of stature and a formidable impresario. The whole thing grew from a côterie interest to a vital movement of international dimensions. If there is any justice in Hulme's and Flint's suspicions that Pound had borrowed their ideas—and there does, on the face of it, seem a good deal of evidence for such a charge—then Pound could certainly reply that when he took over Imagism it was scarcely a going concern.

In the light of all this it is ironically appropriate that Pound should have launched Imagism formally in an appendix. In November, 1912, he published a volume of poems entitled *Ripostes* to which he appended five short poems under the heading 'The Complete Poetical Works of T. E. Hulme' and a prefatory note in which he introduced *Les Imagistes* as descendants of Hulme's Eiffel Tower group. Hulme is reported as being very angry with what he thought to be Pound's impertinence and even F. S. Flint thought that Pound's prefatory remarks were meant as a joke at Hulme's expense. The 'descendants of the forgotten school of 1909' who according to Pound have the future 'in their keeping', were clearly, apart from himself, poets such as Richard Aldington and Hilda Doolittle (H. D.) whom Pound was collecting together under the banner of Imagism in preparation for an assault on the establishment of English and American poetry. This assault was organised mainly through the pages of Harriet Monroe's *Poetry* where the idea of Imagism was forced on the readers' attentions—and on the editor's—by Pound. In March, 1913, there appeared in *Poetry* a short essay by F. S. Flint called 'Imagisme' and a note entitled 'A Few Don'ts by an Imagiste' in which Pound defined the image as 'that which presents an intellectual and emotional complex in an instant of time—it is the presentation of such a "complex" instantaneously which gives that sense of sudden liberation; that sense of freedom from time limits and space limits; that sense of sudden growth, which we experience in the presence of the greatest works of art'. In America, the press were very quick to seize the hint and something like an Imagist rage followed, *Poetry* being filled with an astonishing number of Imagistic poems. But, nonetheless, the centre of the movement was Pound and Pound was in London, where he recruited poets both English and American to the cause of Imagism. *The Egoist* which began publication in January, 1914, became the outlet for Pound's Imagism and poets such as F. S. Flint, H. D., Richard Aldington, J. G. Fletcher, William Carlos Williams, Amy Lowell and D. H. Lawrence, fired by an enthusiasm for the new forms and that 'sense of sudden liberation' they give, began to experiment. In the spring of 1914 Ezra Pound anthologised these Imagistic poems in *Des Imagistes* and the movement was finally formalised under Pound's direction. The market for such an anthology had been proved already by Edward Marsh's *Georgian Poetry* which had been launched in 1912 and sold some 15,000 copies. Indeed, the Georgians themselves thought that Pound's anthology had only been started because the Imagists had not been invited to contribute to their anthology (Pound alone was invited to contribute but refused). Pound drew up an Imagist Manifesto in 1913 and reprinted it in the Imagist anthologies of 1915 and 1916:

1. Direct treatment of the 'thing', whether subjective or objective.
2. To use absolutely no word that did not contribute to the presentation.
3. As regarding rhythm: to compose in sequence of the musical phrase, not in sequence of a metronome.

They held also a certain 'Doctrine of the Image', which they had not committed to writing; they said that it did not concern the public, and would provoke useless discussion.

In spite of the somewhat sinister mystery with which Pound managed to shroud the image, the lines of definition are fairly clear. The emphasis is on directness, conciseness and an avoidance of traditional forms and metres. The poem was to set up its own particular metrical patterns which would follow the meaning and not the accepted rules of prosody. Pound followed Hulme in his insistence on free verse though Pound realised that verse was never free in rhythms which are always tied to the musical structure of the poem. What they both agreed was that the rhythmic pattern of verse should be much more varied and supple than the traditional metres seemed to allow for and both agreed that rhyme was not a necessary part of that rhythmical structure.

There were eleven contributors to *Des Imagistes*, Aldington, H. D., F. S. Flint, Pound, Amy Lowell, William Carlos Williams, Skipwith Cannell, Allen Upward, John Cournos, James Joyce and Ford Madox Hueffer (Ford), and the poems were varied in form and direction and did little to harden the outlines of the manifesto. Imagism as represented here by poems had become considerably modified and bore only a passing resemblance to the austere hardness and clarity on which Hulme insisted. There were some examples of *haiku* and a good deal of free verse, but there were also prose poems and poems in strictly traditional rhymed metres. The line between Hulme's Imagism and French Symbolism were blurred by poems such as Joyce's 'I Hear an Army' and softened by Amy Lowell's Keatsian images. It seems clear that Pound had used Imagism to launch the work of those poets of whom he approved.

The last stage of Imagism was managed by the indefatigable Amy Lowell, who was too democratic to allow Imagistic precepts to stand in the way of her choice of contributors. Against Pound's expressed wishes she adopted the name Imagist for her anthologies and without a complete understanding of the term—except, perhaps, an understanding of its value as publicity—she published in 1915, 1916 and 1917 volumes entitled *Some Imagist Poets*. These volumes were published in Boston and by now the whole movement had become more important to American poetry than to English. Amy Lowell encouraged both J. G. Fletcher and D. H. Lawrence to contribute to her anthologies as well as the original members of Pound's anthology—Aldington, H. D., F. S. Flint and Amy Lowell herself, but the three anthologies represented the differing directions in which its contributors were developing rather than a coherent movement. Indeed, in the 1916 and 1917 volumes it became clear that the contributors found the tenets of Imagism too constricting and were breaking out of what had become a new and restraining formalism. Pound would have nothing to do with Amy Lowell's Imagism and had involved himself with Gaudier-Brzeska and Wyndham Lewis in the new and more dynamic Vorticism. Hulme had long ago lost interest in poetry except in so far as it could be regarded as a branch of metaphysics. The 1914–18 war which disrupted the general movement of art in Europe would have brought Imagism to an end anyway; though in America and in the hands of Amy Lowell it died more gradually and, perhaps, more naturally. Indeed only after it had died as a movement did it begin to exert its full influence, for many poets who would probably not have subscribed to the doctrine of the image now saw how they could use the fruits of this experimentation in their own work; thus Marianne Moore, E. E. Cummings, Wallace Stevens and Archibald Macleish were all indebted to the Imagists though they never involved themselves in Imagism.

Perhaps the most important single fact about Imagism is its Anglo-American character. English and American poets worked together with the feeling of a common tradition—or lack of tradition—behind them and common objectives before them, thus the two literatures were brought into an association so close that there is no feeling of national differences. Moreover, although the movement was based largely on a rejection of nineteenth-century romanticism they were different from their predecessors, to adapt T. S. Eliot's dictum, in everything but essentials. In effect they showed how the decadence of romanticism could be brought into alignment with the twentieth-century sensibility and revitalised. Their insistence on craftsmanship and the poet's skills was balanced against the nineteenth century's sense that poetry was inspired, although in fact the image was the means by which the poet 'seized' on intuition in language, a more acceptable terminology to define what their predecessors had meant by inspiration. Their insistence on clarity, economy and precision of language could well have been derived from Flaubert and offsets the Swinburnian prolixity of later romanticism. Their insistence on impersonality was only an impersonality of method and presentation, for they were still much concerned with the act of poetic creation and the poet as creator. It is clear, however, that in austerely pruning away the worst excesses of predecessors they also cleared and charted the ground on which their successors, and particularly T. S. Eliot, have built. Eliot in fact in his early poems is experimenting largely in Imagistic techniques and has constantly reiterated his debt to what he considered to be the pioneers of twentieth-century poetry. If they produced no single poem of stature or, in the end, no really coherent theory of poetry, they did produce a large number of fresh and beautifully wrought verses and threw up most of the questions with which twentieth-century poetry has been concerned. If they provided nothing else they did provide poetry with sufficient impetus to thrust it from the nineteenth into the twentieth century.

*   *   *

In its original phase, under the direction of T. E. Hulme, the poets were mainly concerned with establishing the primacy of the impersonal, hard, dry image and with ridding poetry of the distinction between form and content. They abhorred didacticism in poetry and believed that the form should be dictated solely by the demands of content and would, therefore, be different for every poem. In many ways Hulme was trying to achieve in poetry that stark directness of statement that he had seen his friend Jacob Epstein achieve in stone. He tended to think about poetry in terms drawn from the plastic arts, particularly from sculpture, and looked to Imagist poetry to provide a similarly visual impact and appropriate aesthetic self-sufficiency. The art that he admired was essentially non-naturalistic, exemplified particularly by such works as Epstein's 'Rock-drill' and Gaudier-Brzeska's 'Red Dancer', abstract carvings of dynamic internal relationships between lines and planes and far from the traditionally representational sculpture. But whereas it is possible to argue for abstract art as being impersonal and autonomous, a complete fusion of form and content, the argument cannot be trans-ferred too easily to poetry. The sculptor's medium is itself inert, his art clearly visual, whereas language is dense with history and humanity and is not, of course, primarily visual. However, in abandoning traditional poetic forms, the Imagists also abandoned an obvious source of 'shape-fulness'. that might have enabled them to achieve something of the solidity and tension that Epstein managed in his carvings.

Although Hulme saw only too clearly the limitations of nineteenth-century poetics he never really broke with it except in so far as he stressed some of its elements to the exclusion of others.[3] Thus he rejected the romantic 'I'—the identification of poet and reader—re-introduced wit and intelligence, loosened the traditional rhythmic structure and insisted on the virtues of concentration and precision, but largely main-tained a nineteenth-century diction with its exclamations, inversions and poeticisms. In fact Hulme, judged by his own standards, had a decadent predilection for romantic poetical devices. His brief but highly wrought poems are studded with lines that, at least so far as phrasing and rhythm are concerned, may well have come direct from the poetry he despised: 'Strange to me sounds the wind that blows'—'Maybe 'tis the sea whistling—feigning joy'—'Now pass I to the final river'. Even in his briefest fragments he did not escape from the poetical inversion. In his *haiku*, for example:

> Old houses were scaffolding once
> and workmen whistling.

or

> Three birds flew over the red wall into the pit
> of the setting sun.
> O daring, doomèd birds that pass from my sight.

---

[3] Cf. the discussion of anti-romanticism in Chapter VI, pp. 137-9, below.

These epigrammatic lines well exemplify the basis of the Imagistic poem. The two images are juxtapositioned in such a way as, to use Ezra Pound's definition, 'a thing outward and objective transforms itself, or darts into a thing inward and subjective'. Such poetry has the surprise and the immediacy of the metaphysical image. But the 'poetical' quality of Hulme's language is immediately obvious if set beside William Carlos Williams's *haiku*, 'The Red Wheelbarrow':

> so much depends
> upon
>
> a red wheel
> barrow
>
> glazed with rain
> water
>
> beside the white
> chickens

Indeed, in spite of his insistence on free verse as the new poetic medium —he compared its 'discovery' to the Elizabethan 'discovery' of blank verse—Hulme uses it with an eighteen-ninetyish dying fall. His verses carry a strong conviction of literary phrasing but very little sense of the human voice. The freedom of the verse is little more than a freedom from rhyme and that of taking traditional liberties with the iambic pentameter. Moreover, in typical images such as 'the wistful stars/With white faces like town children' he even achieves a characteristic note of nineteenth-century pathos. Hulme did nothing 'to purify the dialect of the tribe' and the romanticism that his poetic theory confronted is there in his poems.

The fundamental mode of Imagistic poetry is the elementary figure of personification, the humanising, anthropomorphic tendency of the human mind which Hulme found so basic and so deplorable a feature of romantic art. 'Autumn', the first and best-known Imagist poem is based solidly on the personification of the moon:

> I walked abroad,
> And saw the ruddy moon lean over a hedge
> Like a red-faced farmer.

The effect of such an image is the reverse of what Hulme's theories seem to demand, for the incomprehensible universe is made domestic and cosily accommodated to fit a nineteenth-century rural landscape. Certainly the effect is one of diminution rather than expansiveness—none of the flying off into the circumambient gas he saw to be a feature of romantic poetry—the moon is comfortably adjusted to a human landscape:

> Above the quiet dock in midnight,
> Tangled in the tall mast's corded height,
> Hangs the moon. What seemed so far away
> Is but a child's balloon, forgotten after play.
>
> ('Above the Dock')

Such an image only appears to deny the traditional symbolism of the moon on which it depends for its effect. Richard Aldington develops the idea further in the next stage of Imagism by insisting on the personification more firmly:

> The moon
> With a rag of gauze about her loins
> Poses among them, an awkward Venus—
>
> And here am I looking wantonly at her
> Over the kitchen sink.   ('Evening')

In making the implications of his image more explicit, Aldington's moon loses a good deal of its effect which, in the final stages of Imagism, Amy Lowell tries to recapture by a strained, over-reaching of the image:

> The white mares of the moon are all
>   standing on their hind legs
> Pawing at the green porcelain doors of
>   the remote Heavens.   ('Night Clouds')

D. H. Lawrence, on the other hand, shows how a poet of powerful, personal vision can give the image a distinctive and individual direction:

> Slowly the moon is rising out of the ruddy haze,
> Divesting herself of her golden shift, and so
> Emerging white and exquisite; and I in amaze
> See in the sky before me, a woman I did not know
> I loved, . . .
>
> ('Aware')

Lawrence's poem is rhymed and regular in its metre and Georgian in its diction but he lends the image a fresh distinction and immediacy in seeing the moon perhaps more traditionally, as 'a woman I did not know/I loved'. T. S. Eliot also uses a Hulme-like moon image in 'Rhapsody on a Windy Night' and in 'Conversation Galante'. In 'Rhapsody on a Windy Night' the moon is deliberately anti-romantic but just as mock-heroic is parasitic on the genuine heroic, so the anti-romantic depends for its impact on romanticism. The texture of the image is certainly denser, but basically the image works in the same way as Aldington's:

> 'Regard the moon,
> La lune ne garde aucune rancune,
> She winks a feeble eye,
> She smiles into corners.
> She smooths the hair of the grass.
> The moon has lost her memory.
> A washed-out smallpox cracks her face,
> Her hand twists a paper rose,
> That smells of dust and eau de Cologne,
> She is alone
> With all the old nocturnal smells
> That cross and cross across her brain.'

This is a long way from Ben Jonson's 'huntress, chaste and fair' though it is in opposition to such associations that Eliot's image makes its impact. The moon image brings the real and the ideal together in such a way as to suggest that the ideal is not only false but, indeed, in Aldington and in Eliot at least, more squalid generally than reality. Eliot's more characteristic method for deflating false ideals is seen in his treatment of the moon image in 'Conversation Galante' which is conversational, urbane and ironic in tone:

> I observe: 'Our sentimental friend the moon!
> Or possibly (fantastic, I confess)
> It may be Prester John's balloon
> Or an old battered lantern hung aloft
> To light poor travellers to their distress.'
> She then: 'How you digress!'

Thus the moon becomes the focus of differing attitudes and values while the detached and ironic tone of the poet as narrator is inclusive enough to suggest that all attitudes are possible but that he is committed to none of them. Thus he avoids the somewhat melodramatic strain imposed on the image in 'Rhapsody on a Windy Night' and avoids the fundamental failing of Imagistic poetry generally which is that it presents such a simplified and definite image—which is not lyrically sustained—as to constitute a severely distorted and unacceptable version of reality. In many ways Imagism represents a reaction away from a Mallarmé-type symbolism of infinite suggestibility towards something close to allegory. Later poets learnt how to use Imagist techniques while complicating the texture of their poems, thus combining hard and lucid imagery with complexities of tone and attitude.

A poet such as E. E. Cummings releases the romanticism latent in Imagism and allows it free lyrical play; the image in 'Spring omnipotent goddess' is characteristic:

> spring slattern of seasons you
> have dirty legs and a muddy
> petticoat, drowsy is your
> mouth your eyes are sticky
> with dreams and you have
> a sloppy body
> from being brought to bed of crocuses.

Cummings's idiosyncratic phrasing and typography often save his poems from the sentimentality towards which such romanticism inevitably tends. But poets such as William Carlos Williams, Wallace Stevens and Marianne Moore while incorporating Imagist techniques in their poems load their images with a far greater complexity of attitudes, and never allow the images to function mechanically. Marianne Moore's poem 'To a Steam Roller' is, fundamentally, a contrast between two attitudes of mind represented by the steamroller which crushes 'all the particles down/into close conformity', and the principle of life itself, by the butterfly. Her language, though, is hard and objective, it assimilates quotations from journals and philosophical tracts without a qualm, and seems to cut short, and certainly controls the implications of the Imagistic structure. Stevens, in his earlier phase, in poems such as 'Thirteen ways of looking at a Blackbird' or 'Domination of Black', organises a number of images around a particular theme in the attempt to achieve the single impact of the poem. Also, Stevens's images are not particularly visual and except in his sensitivity to the use of colours he tends to avoid concrete, visual images, or, at least, seems to prefer symbols of a more abstract quality. He explicitly refuses to personify the world around and outside himself, though he does so in a poem that is based on the kind of personification he is rejecting. He addresses a star:

> Lend no part to any humanity that suffuses
> You in its own light.
> Be not chimera of morning,
> Half-man, half-star.
> Be not an intelligence,
> Like a widow's bird
> Or an old horse.
>   ('Nuances of a Theme by Williams')

Stevens develops towards the confidence of direct symbolism. William Carlos Williams, however, builds his poems on a series of overlaying images, one breaking into the other, though all are controlled by a dominant Imagistic framework. In his poem 'Daisy', for example, he finds many images to expand his theme and in the first stanza introduces the image of the sun which he breaks into with the idea of love and women:

> The sun is upon a
> slender green stem
> ribbed lengthwise.
> He lies on his back—
> it is a woman also—
> he regards his former
> majesty and
> round the yellow centre,
> split and creviced and done into
> minute flowerheads, he sends out
> his twenty rays——

This is precise, accurate observation of the kind Hulme demanded from poetry. The image—not without its whimsy—leads into other images so that the poem as a whole is a nexus of images. Williams, like Stevens or Marianne Moore or any other good twentieth-century poet, has achieved his own fresh, individual voice, but we could not say with confidence that he would have done so without the impetus and example of the Imagist experiment.

The community of feeling among poets both English and American during the first forty years of the century is so strong that when

Archibald Macleish came to write his own 'Ars Poetica' he did so in Imagistic terms. Interestingly he used the original moon image as his basic figure:

> A poem should be motionless in time
> As the moon climbs
>
> Leaving, as the moon releases
> Twig by twig the night-entangled trees,
>
> Leaving, as the moon behind the winter leaves,
> Memory by memory the mind——
>
> A poem should be motionless in time
> As the moon climbs
>
> . . . . . .
>
> A poem should be equal to:
> Not true.

A poem, Macleish concludes, 'should not mean/But be', thus grasping the central principle of the primacy of the image in terms of an Imagist poem. For however much we may bridle at the assumptions of the doctrine of the image, or object that none of the original group were really capable of realising their theories poetically, it is equally clear that the theory and the practice of Imagism has been vigorously infective in modern poetry on both sides of the Atlantic—so much so that both its admirers and its detractors have to start their defence of, or attack on, modern poetry with the Imagism conceived by Hulme and his friends in the Eiffel Tower. No one now would dispute T. S. Eliot's assertion that 'The *point de repère* usually and conveniently taken as the starting-point of modern poetry, is the group denominated "Imagist" in London about 1910'. Moreover, because of this common beginning we are enabled to see modern English and American poetry as part of a common tradition whose allegiance is not based nationally but linguistically. Thus the question as to whether T. S. Eliot, for example, is writing as an American or an Englishman hardly arises, except academically, for he is writing in the Imagist tradition of the language.

Note

Biographies. William Carlos Williams (1883–1963) was born in Rutherford, New Jersey, and after training in New York and visiting Europe, has practised as a doctor in his home-town.
E. E. Cummings (1894–1964) was born in Cambridge, Massachusetts, and studied at Harvard before serving in the Ambulance Corps in the first world war, and suffering a period in a detention camp. After the war he lived in New York and Paris; he wrote a travel book, a play, a ballet scenario; and he painted.

Works. Williams's first volumes were *Poems* (1909) and *The Tempers* (1913); most of his shorter verse is in *The Collected Earlier Poems* (1951) and *The Collected Later Poems* (1950). His long poem *Paterson* was first planned in four Books, and these were all published by 1951; a further book followed in 1958, and notes and drafts for a 6th Book were published posthumously (1963). There is an admirable *Selected Poems* with an Introduction by Randall Jarrell (1949), in paperback (1963); the complete *Paterson* is also available in paperback (1963).
Williams's other publications include two novels and *The Autobiography* (1951); *In the American Grain*, essays on American culture (1925); *Many Loves and other plays* (1961); *Selected Essays* (1954); *Selected Letters* (1957).
Cummings's first book was *Tulips and Chimneys* (1923); most of his verse is available in *Poems 1923–1954* (1954), *95 Poems* (1958) and *73 Poems* (1963). The novel, *The Enormous Room* (1934), a verse play called *Him*, and *i :six nonlectures* (1953) are among his other publications.

Criticism. Two commentaries on Williams are by Vivienne Koch (1950) and J. M. Brinnin (1963); Randall Jarrell has written on the poems and *Paterson* in *Poetry and the Age* (1953). Sister M. Bernetta Quinn's *The Metamorphic Tradition in Modern Poetry* (1955) is relevant.
Among work on Cummings may be recommended: N. Friedman, *E. E. Cummings: the Art of his Poetry* (1960); C. Norman, *The Magic-Maker* (1958) and R. P. Blackmur, 'Notes on E. E. Cummings' Language', *The Double Agent* (1935).
T. S. Eliot's poetry and criticism have been amply studied; recommended studies include N. Frye, *T. S. Eliot* (1963), Helen Gardner, *The Art of T. S. Eliot* (1949), H. Kenner, *The Invisible Poet* (1959), F. O. Matthiessen, *The Achievement of T. S. Eliot* (1958), G. C. Smith, *T. S. Eliot's Poetry and Plays* (1956). There is *A Collection of Critical Essays*, ed. H. Kenner (1962).

VI

The Diction of American Poetry

DAVID FERRY

★

AMONG the aspects of American poetry that are most often noticed is the freedom with which the poets use colloquial, slangy and generally non-literary language as an ordinary part of their style. As instances of this tendency one thinks at once of William Carlos Williams, E. E. Cummings and the young T. S. Eliot. These three poets represent in various ways important things about what modern American poetry feels like; they are related in their attitudes towards what kind of diction is permissible in poetry; and they also differ significantly.

For a number of reasons, this chapter will focus primarily on Williams, and will discuss the other two poets mainly in relation to him. The reasons will make themselves plain, I hope, as the discussion moves along, but we can say at the outset that there are respects in which he is perhaps the most successful employer of a diction and an idiom that we can confidently identify as American in the twentieth century; and we can say that he is, of the most respectable figures in modern American poetry, perhaps the most thoroughly concerned with what it means to be an American poet. Obviously, when I contrast him in these respects with Eliot I am not making distinctions in terms of value. Eliot is in almost every way a more considerable poet. When I contrast him with Cummings, however, I am making distinctions in terms of value. To set the work of Cummings alongside that of Williams throws a strong light on Williams's peculiar virtues.

Before I get to the main part of my discussion, I want to discuss briefly some matters which will be perfectly well known already to the reader, but which will perhaps give us a context sufficiently large and general that anything we may say later will not be in much danger of exaggeration or distortion. For example, it is plain that the use, if not of colloquial and slangy, at least of a 'generally non-literary' language is something that happens over and over again in literary history. It is symptomatic of a continuing and probably permanent impulse in literary history: the reaction against the style of a preceding generation, the reaction against a style, whatever its particular characteristics, which is felt to have become 'literary' in the sense of 'unreal', no longer responsive to the data of experience, no longer faithful to the truth; merely conventional, merely rhetorical, style subsisting on itself, so to speak, or on the memory of what once was valid in what it had to say. Probably even those generations whose ideal has been the extremely stylised, the arcane, the remote, the conventional carried to its furthest implications, have held to their ideal in the name of some dissatisfaction with an earlier style whose realism, whose 'naturalness', has been felt to have become 'literary' in the sense that it no longer could successfully express some exciting truth. It was long before Yeats turned 'realistic' that he took to sleeping on a board to discipline his style. This is an old story which needs no elaboration. But to remind ourselves of it is useful if it keeps us from taking our present subject-matter too seriously, or seriously in the wrong way.

On the other hand, there would not be much point in saying, just another phase, just another revolution, just the old story all over again, and letting it go at that. It has been our revolution, and it has been a revolution in the language of poetry at a particularly important time. At a time when, it is commonly agreed, the language of public affairs and of private intercourse is threatened as never before, by standardisation, by sentimentalism, by vulgarisation. At such a time the services of lines like

> Let us go then, you and I,
> When the evening is spread out against the sky
> Like a patient etherized upon a table;
> (T. S. Eliot, 'The Love Song of J. Alfred Prufrock')

are incalculable, introducing as they do new ways of expressing spiritual predicaments, importing as they do new possibilities of feeling and subject-matter into poetry, and thus perhaps renewing the strength of poetry to affect the language of public affairs and of private intercourse. At such a time it is easy to see the value of and to be grateful for such a plain satire of the public language as:

> next to of course god america i
> love you land of the pilgrims' and so forth oh
> say can you see by the dawn's early my

country 'tis of centuries come and go
and are no more what of it we should worry. . . .
(E. E. Cummings, 'next to of course god america i')

One of the principal tendencies of twentieth-century poetry has been the implicit and explicit criticism of the usual language of the time. Indeed the language, language itself, has become one of the great fields for study in this century, bringing together many disciplines and engaging many different kinds of energies, gathering around itself dignities comparable to those of physics and metaphysics. By the time Eliot, late in his career, was able to put his protagonist's spiritual struggle in terms of a struggle with the language, he could be pretty sure of an audience which would not be at all surprised to hear it put in those terms and which would have its sympathies already fully trained to respond:

Trying to learn to use words, and every attempt
Is a wholly new start, and a different kind of failure
Because one has only learnt to get the better of words
For the thing one no longer has to say, or the way in which
One is no longer disposed to say it.

('East Coker')

We are by now trained to respond with sympathy to Wallace Stevens's 'The Man Whose Pharynx Was Bad', whose trouble is that he is too dumbly in his being pent, for his trouble is the trouble of his times. The problem has itself been vulgarised and sentimentalised, of course—it is a sign of the success of the revolution that it has been so—but the problem is not less real therefore. 'To purify the dialect of the tribe' remains a central concern of twentieth-century poetry; there is a heightened consciousness, almost no matter where one looks in modern literature, of the intimate relation between our fate and the forms of our expressions, and it is the greatest service of our literature that it has concentrated upon this relation.

★   ★   ★

The ways in which the purification of the dialect of the tribe has been attempted are of course too various to be numbered here. Eliot's procedures in 'The Love Song of J. Alfred Prufrock', and, say, 'Rhapsody on a Windy Night' are fair samples, however. The voice is 'colloquial' enough, if we mean by that that it is in many respects like the voice we hear in more or less realistic novels, and that its tones are contrasted, explicitly or implicitly, to those of the heroic or romantic past: ' "That is not what I meant at all;/That is not it at all" '; or, 'And would it have been worth it, after all'; or, 'Shall I say, I have gone at dusk through narrow streets/And watched the smoke that rises from the pipes/Of lonely men in shirt-sleeves, leaning out of windows?' Rather elegant voices, to be sure, but well within the conventions of 'the language of ordinary conversation', as the novel has trained us to hear that language. And all this is made 'prosier' by the avoidance of a fixed iambic pentameter and by the use of rhyme schemes so elaborate that they give the effect, at any rate, of irregularity and therefore of freedom. The voice which is dramatised here is the characteristic early Eliot voice of one who at once participates in the exhausted and ineffectual society around him and satirises it. Sometimes his effects are more elaborately subtle, as in 'Rhapsody on a Windy Night':

> The memory throws up high and dry
> A crowd of twisted things;
> A twisted branch upon the beach
> Eaten smooth, and polished
> As if the world gave up
> The secret of its skeleton,
> Stiff and white.
> A broken spring in a factory yard,
> Rust that clings to the form that the strength has left
> Hard and curled and ready to snap.

The sea as memory, 'poetic' enough: but the conversational, flat, wry 'high and dry' warns us a little about what is to come; then a piece of what sounds at first like conventional 'nature description' leading to a conventional Romantic perception—the essential meaning of the universe revealing itself in a natural scene—yet with nothing of the traditional Romantic in its phraseology. The essential structure of the universe is not a dark inscrutable workmanship that reconciles discordant elements, but a skeleton, 'Stiff and white', and the branch has been '*Eaten* smooth'. The language has the deliberate sharpness of the realistic or naturalistic; it is calculated deliberately to disappoint whatever Romantic expectations we might have. The passage concludes with a comparison of the natural thing, the branch thrown up by the sea, to an ugly human artifact, the broken spring in the factory yard. When Eliot says elsewhere in the poem, 'The moon has lost her memory', we are free to understand the line as being as plainly about the predicament, and the resources, of modern poetry as it is about any subject-matter wholly contained by the poem. It is like 'the moon and moon,/The yellow moon of words about the nightingale' that Wallace Stevens speaks of, the romantic moon of nineteenth-century poetry which has lost its memory and which needs to be spoken of now in a new vocabulary. In Stevens it is the voice of the grackle which replaces that of the nightingale, and the voice of the grackle 'grates these evasions of the nightingale'. The job of work that is being done by 'Prufrock' and 'Rhapsody' is a job of retraining the sensibilities of readers who are accustomed to the softnesses and enhancements of an exhausted roman-ticism, who are accustomed to a language which had to exclude from itself the rusty spring, the yellow soles of feet, the branch left 'high and dry', ancient women in vacant lots, and the exhausted, nervous, wry, self-mocking flat un-heroic tones of Prufrock.[1]

It is a job that was being done in many ways in many arts and in several countries, and it has by no means been an exclusively American job. It is interesting that, though most of Eliot's earliest poems have apparently to do with Boston, we are not encouraged, by and large, to think of them as poems whose principal reference is to American life. Their meaning is far more general: it is the sickness of 'our age', of 'the Western world', of 'modern man'. For a sense of what the new uses of the language might be, as they specifically apply to American experience, we must turn to Williams.

*   *   *

We can derive the fervency of some of Williams's critical writings about poetry from just this sense of the crucial importance of the language, and of what it means to be attentive to the health of the language, especially with reference to America and American history. For example, in his essay on Ezra Pound and Gertrude Stein he says:

> For everything we know and do is tied up with words, with the phrases words make, with the grammar which stultifies, the prose or poetic rhythms which bind us to our pet indolences and medievalisms. To Americans especially, those who no longer speak English, this is especially important. We need too often a burst of air in at the win-dow of our prose. It is absolutely indispensable that we get this before

---

[1] Cf. the discussion of Hulme's anti-romanticism in Chapter V, pp. 127-8, above.

we can even begin to think straight again. It's the words, the words we need to get back to, words washed clean. Until we get the power of thought back through a new minting of the words we are actually sunk. This is a moral question at base, surely, but a technical one also and first.   (*Selected Essays*, p. 163)

The sense of being at the mercy of a language with whose hampering restrictions we must strenuously contend, of feeling the necessity of a violent airing or cleansing of our powers of expression, is characteristic 'twentieth century' in its direction. But the attitude that it is especially an American problem is characteristic Williams. And it is an attempt which we are tempted at first to take much too simply, to identify with a sort of jingoism or chauvinism, or with the sentimentality that talks, for example, about things like 'the poetry of American names'. What Williams says about America ordinarily has more complex and interesting meanings, which he is willing to face. This is hinted, perhaps, in his use of the word 'technical', in the passage just quoted; it is hinted in the following passage, from his essay on Mencken's *The American Language*:

> It is bred of the bone of the country itself, nurtured from its plains and streams. It is its spittin' self and under that—the rest of it. But we're still a colony as far as our badly tutored minds are concerned. We don't quite dare, do we? to say that we have a language that is our own. Surely, we wouldn't be that vulgar. We might, we just possibly might, come to a realization of ourselves that would blast the very rules of prosody out the window.
>
> (*Selected Essays*, p. 173)

Here again, the voice sounds at first as naïve (or false-naïve) as any of the folksier American poets, in 'spittin' self' and in the heavy irony of 'Surely, we wouldn't be that vulgar.' But more is involved here than mere Yankeeism. To assert that America has its own language is not merely to make declarations about it, in his view, nor is it a simple matter of some changes in vocabulary. It is to reappraise the art itself as practised in America, and to do so in terms of a view of American history much more complex and less sentimental than these quotations might by themselves suggest. He has outlined this view of American history most clearly, perhaps, in a long and significant essay called 'The American Background', where he describes the whole of our history as a struggle, mostly so far a losing struggle, to establish an authentic and identifiable American culture, a 'related' culture capable of withstanding the pressures of a culture imposed from without, an 'unrelated' culture. Speaking of the first settlers to land in New England, he says:

> They saw birds with rusty breasts and called them robins. Thus, from the start, an America of which they could have had no inkling drove the first settlers upon their past. They retreated for warmth and reassurance to something previously familiar. But at a cost. For what they saw were not robins. They were thrushes only vaguely resembling the rosy, daintier English bird. Larger, stronger, and in the evening of a wilder, lovelier song, actually here was something the newcomers had never in their lives before encountered. Blur. Confusion. A bird that beats with his wings and slows himself with his tail in landing. (*Selected Essays*, p. 134)

He begins the essay by talking about a confusion in names, by identifying a cultural problem directly with a verbal one, and yet he is not here concerned with the more general 'twentieth-century' problems we discussed earlier. He is concerned with something much more particular and local, though through that he intends to be concerned with something much more nearly universal, for he has said that the universal grows only out of the truly local. The settlers arrived on these shores and their first task was to name a bird, and the name they chose was an error. The power of what Williams is saying resides in his tenderness towards these settlers, in his awareness of the need which forced them to rely on the terms of a culture to which they were already, by force of their circumstances, becoming alien, without having as yet anything with which to replace it: 'They retreated for warmth and reassurance to something previously familiar.' But for all his tender awareness of their need, he asserts also that the blur and confusion is already beginning, the conflict between the old English culture and the new American one. It is a vision not unlike that of Frost in 'The Gift Outright':

> The land was ours before we were the land's.
> She was our land more than a hundred years
> Before we were her people . . .
>
> . . . . . .
>
> Something we were withholding made us weak
> Until we found out that it was ourselves
> We were withholding from our land of living.

'The American Background' is an account of the difficulties that have been thrown in the way of the American effort to develop a related culture of its own, 'a relation to the immediate conditions of the matter in hand, and a determination to assert them in opposition to all intermediate authority'. The actual bird the settlers saw beating with its wings and slowing itself with its tail in landing is an emblem of those immediate conditions. To name that bird rightly, without accepting the vague equivalence of 'robin', would be an assertion of those immediate conditions in opposition to the intermediate authority of the old culture from which the settlers had fled. The heroic—and technically inventive—experience of Daniel Boone in the wilderness is one instance of naming the bird rightly; so are the many small rural communities that sprang up under difficulties in America, forced by their hard conditions to respond with arts appropriate to those conditions. Nevertheless there was still the nostalgia for the old culture, expressing itself for example in the genteel versifiers of the nineteenth century. And as that century progressed there was the growth of a new industrial civilisation, a money culture whose power over and over again was demonstrated in enticing men away from the 'culture of immediacy', away from the concrete and particular, to the city with its relatively indifferent and generalised life, in which it is all too easy to 'retreat for warmth and reassurance to something previously familiar'. The new industrial civilisation was a new version of that 'intermediate authority' against which it is necessary to strive. It is a familiar diagnosis, to be sure. Our point here is the passion that Williams invests in it and the use that he makes of it in his poetry.

Williams's response to the difficulties of American culture is strikingly positive and energetic. He does not permit himself any easy nostalgia about the old pioneers and the old folk arts. He asserts the necessity of finding, in the city if need be, the qualities of life that are there, of establishing in poetry the values of which he is an advocate. What has been lost in America time and again is that culture which is

the realization of the qualities of a place in relation to the life which occupies it; embracing everything involved, climate, geographic position, relative size, history, other cultures—as well as the character of its sands, flowers, minerals and the condition of knowledge within its borders. It is the act of lifting these things into an ordered and utilized whole which is culture. It isn't something left over afterward. That is the record only. The act is the thing. It can't be escaped or avoided if life is to go on. It is in the fullest sense that which is fit.   (*Selected Essays*, p. 157)

Williams's poems at their best are the sort of acts which he describes, and the 'realization of the qualities of a place in relation to the life which occupies it' is almost an ideal formula for these poems. The places he celebrates are by no means the 'related cultures' he would have wanted. But there is life in them, concrete and particular, and it is this which he seeks to discover and to keep alive in his poems.

Williams was stung to the quick that Eliot spoke of him as a poet 'of local interest perhaps', for it is just the word 'local' that counts, it is just that which distinguishes him from Eliot, it is just the values of the local which are so important to him. In a famous passage from the *Autobiography* he says:

> Then out of the blue *The Dial* brought out *The Waste Land* and all our hilarity ended. It wiped out our world as if an atom bomb had been dropped upon it and our brave sallies into the unknown were turned to dust.
>
> To me especially it struck like a sardonic bullet. I felt at once that it had set me back twenty years, and I'm sure it did. Critically Eliot returned us to the classroom just at the moment when I felt that we were on the point of an escape to matters much closer to the essence of a new art form itself—rooted in the locality which should give it fruit. I knew at once that in certain ways I was most defeated.
>
> If with his skill he could have been kept here to be employed by our slowly shaping drive, what strides might we not have taken! We needed him in the scheme I was half-consciously forming. I needed him: he might have been our advisor, even our hero. By his walking out on us we were stopped, for the moment, cold. It was a bad moment. Only now, as I predicted, have we begun to take hold again and restarted to make the line over. This is not to say that Eliot has not, indirectly, contributed much to the emergence of the next step in metrical construction, but if he had not turned away from the direct attack here, in the western dialect, we might have gone ahead much faster. (pp. 174-5)

It was, for one thing, the international character of *The Waste Land* that was disturbing to Williams, its abandonment of 'the locality which should give it fruit'; and related to this is the disillusionment he found in that poem, which in Williams's view would inevitably follow from its internationalism, from its indifference to locality; the third thing that disturbs him is its genius, which for Williams expresses itself most relevantly in 'the emergence of the next step in metrical construction' and all the promise of that step for a new idiom, a new voice, in poetry.

Like Williams, Eliot saw that there was no mere problem of vocabulary; there were larger problems of form, more complex problems of technique in allowing for new possibilities for the speaking voice. Eliot's awareness of this is his tantalising promise to Williams; unrelated to 'locality', his promise had to be, from Williams's point of view, unfulfilled. Williams says, in a letter to Kay Boyle in 1932:

> Poetry is creation of new form—
> A minimum of present new knowledge seems to be this: there can no longer be serious work in poetry written in 'poetic' diction. It is a contortion of speech to conform to a rigidity of line. It is in the newness of a live speech that the new line exists undiscovered. To go back is to deny the first opportunity for invention which exists. Speech is the fountain of the line into which the pollutions of a poetic manner and inverted phrasing should never again be permitted to drain.
> That T. S. Eliot knows this (mainly) is at present the sole reason for reading him. He is concerned with the line as it is modulated by a limited kind of half-alive speech. (pp. 174–5)

To say that it is 'half-alive' is not to deny that it is genuine. It only points to a wholly different spirit in Eliot's early career from that of Williams, at least as Williams sees it. For Williams's powers depend on a positive assertion of the life that is there in the situations he describes, the life that is there locally, concretely, growing out of the most simple facts; his powers depend on 'the realization of the qualities of a place in relation to the life which occupies it'. In his (over-simple) view of Eliot, Eliot is wasting his powers on the realization of that which is dead, or only half-alive, in human experience.

One thing that is implied when we say that Williams's poetry is a series of 'acts' is that many of them, taken in isolation, will be both slight and tentative, and may seem to be less dignified and interesting than they are as contributions to his continuing effort towards 'the realization of the qualities of a place in relation to the life which occupies it'. An obvious example is 'The Red Wheelbarrow', quoted on p. 128, above. Out of context this looks to be a fairly standard example of a fairly standard kind of 'imagistic' writing, and it seems the kind of writing one calls at once 'experimental'. Out of context, it might well have been written by a lady in jade earrings, and I think this is in fact one reason why it has been in so many anthologies. Nor would I argue very earnestly for its final excellence among this writer's works; its fame is

I think to some degree accidental. But in the context of Williams's writings as a whole, it can be understood as one more effort to find and celebrate the life that is there in the locality in which the life is lived. It is yet another attempt, by the isolation of accurately observed detail, to establish a relation 'to the immediate conditions of the matter in hand, and a determination to assert them in opposition to all intermediate authority'. The determination is asserted in the originality of the form and in the avoidance of suggestive 'literary' associations. It is yet another bird that beats with his wings and slows himself with his tail in landing; it is yet another attempt to withstand the temptation to call a particular kind of thrush a robin. Out of context, the line 'so much depends' is at once vague and arty; in the context of Williams's continuing effort, we know that just the sort of culture, the related culture, that he has in mind depends on responsiveness to accidental juxtapositions like this of the white chickens, the red wheelbarrow, and the rainwater. They are among 'the qualities of a place in relation to the life which occupies it'.

The trouble with most 'experimental' writing of the sort with which I am contrasting Williams—the trouble with most 'imagist' poetry, for example—the vulgarity of it is that it allows itself to feel freer to manipulate experience than it actually is. The experimentalist of this sort feels that he has more choices than he has, he feels no burden on himself of the unchosen circumstances of life, and this is a way of refusing to take life seriously. If we read Williams properly, we feel the burden on him of the unchosen circumstances of his locality, the burden on him of the unrelated culture, and a full sense of the painfulness and difficulty of creating a truly related culture; and this keeps him from the vulgarity and sentimentality of 'experimentalism'.

Williams says of other writers that he fears them 'if they write well'. It is a characteristically open and unashamed remark. But he goes on to say:

> But they have no access to my sources.
> Let them write then as they may and
> perfect it as they can they will never
> come to the secret of that form
>
> interknit with the unfathomable ground
> where we walk daily and from which
> among the rest you have sprung
> and opened flower-like to my hand.   ('The Curve')

The ground is unfathomable because the knowledge, the opportunity for poems, is endless so long as it remains local and familiar to the man who is living his life there. It must be the ground 'where we walk daily', and only from such ground, only from the concrete sense of the actuality of all things as they live in their particular places is it possible for 'you' to 'have sprung/and opened flower-like to my hand.' The life lived there will be thoroughly rich and individual and need fear no other; and its meanings will be unfathomably rich.

Williams has said that 'each speech having its own character the poetry it engenders will be peculiar to that speech also in its intrinsic form' and that 'it is in the intimate form that works of art achieve their exact meaning . . . , to give language its highest dignity, its illumination in the environment'. The highest dignity of the American language, in Williams's theory and practice, is not in the display of some special provincial vocabulary, full of words and phrases that fall oddly on English ears. Nor is it in any New World freedom about the use of the colloquial. This is not at all what he means by 'the western dialect'. It is poetry so deeply dedicated to 'its illumination in the environment' that everything about it is affected, everything the expression of its dedication. In one sense, then, it is important to say that there isn't much to tell about Williams's diction, since his diction is inseparable from everything else about his poems. It is not the words themselves, for the most part, which strike us as characteristic of Williams when we isolate them. Yet his language, as we experience it in the poems, has the effect of being strikingly original and individual.

Look at his poem 'The Young Housewife', for example:

> At ten a.m. the young housewife
> moves about in negligée behind
> the wooden walls of her husband's house.
> I pass solitary in my car.
>
> Then again she comes to the curb
> to call the ice-man, fish-man, and stands
> shy, uncorseted, tucking in
> stray ends of hair, and I compare her
> to a fallen leaf.
>
> The noiseless wheels of my car
> rush with a crackling sound over
> dried leaves as I bow and pass smiling.

Nothing could be less pretentious. The poem is perhaps a very distant cousin of all those more literary poems in which the admirer observes his lady from afar, admires her beauty, which is unattainable by him, and sees in her the first faint signs of her mortality. But the young house-wife's beauty consists in her untidiness, her shyness, her homely gestures, her homely tasks, the sense of the privateness of her life behind the 'wooden walls of her husband's house.' Her admirer is merely the local doctor, perhaps barely acquainted with her, whose passings-by on his rounds punctuate her day. There is nothing of more than 'everyday' significance here, but in that everyday significance there are tactful suggestions of something sexual in his feeling for her, ex-pressed not only by the way he imagines her without seeing her, in her negligée in the house, and by 'uncorseted' in stanza two—and in-deed by the very loving particularity of his description of her at the curb—but also perhaps by 'her husband's house', suggesting her un-attainability, and by the emphasis on 'solitary' as he describes him-self in his car. He compares her to a fallen leaf; she is, like all creatures, mortal. And she inhabits a street where there are actual fallen leaves; it is an environment of mortal things. His formal and genial bow to her as he passes is a formal and genial bow to all these qualities in her, the tactful acknowledgment of the creatureliness of a fellow-creature.

The homeliness and flatness of the language is part of the quality of beautiful restraint in the poem. There is nothing much in the diction which we would single out as 'colloquial' or even as especially 'non-literary', but the poem has the effect of being so because of the way its language is managed, by the directness and simplicity of the word order, the loose conversational grammar of 'ice-man, fish-man,' and by the avoidance, in the rhythm of the poem, of conventional rhythms with 'literary' associations. Yet though the poem cannot be regularly scanned, the dominant four-stress pattern makes itself felt. And there is a tautening formality in the discreet rhyme patterns, or patterns of off-rhyme, as in 'solitary', 'car', 'compare', 'her', 'car', 'over', for example, or 'stands' and 'ends'.

★　　★　　★

One way to describe more exactly the nature of Williams's poetic practice, the effects of his 'poetic voice', is by comparing him with Cummings, another poet who frequently uses unorthodox verse forms and a 'generally non-literary language'. Williams felt a close affinity to Cummings. In 1946, in a little magazine called *Harvard Wake*, he said:

> To me, of course, e. e. cummings means my language. It isn't, of course, mine so much as it is his, which emphasizes the point. It isn't, primarily, english. It isn't at all english. Not that superb inheritance—which we both, I am sure, stand before in amazement and wonder, knowing the dazzling achievements of which it is the living monument. We speak another language; a language of which we are so jealous that we won't even acknowledge that we hold it in common.

And again:

> I think of cummings as Robinson Crusoe at the moment when he first saw the print of a naked human foot in the sand. That, too, implied a new language—and a readjustment of conscience.

And again: 'He avoids the cliché first by avoiding the whole accepted modus of english' (*Selected Essays*, pp. 263–5).

I think all this reflects Williams's gratitude at finding a man of talents comparable to his own who seems at least as dissatisfied as himself with 'the accepted modus of english'. Cummings is also a poet who talks a good deal about America and who frequently chooses for his subject-matter scenes from everyday life. But I think Williams is quite mistaken, not perhaps about the talent, but about the degree and seriousness of Cummings's dissatisfaction with the 'accepted modus'.

Cummings is usually most successful in three kinds of poems. The first is a sweet and rather cloying, but melodious and pleasant lyricism of an obviously traditional sort—for example, 'somewhere i have never travelled, gladly beyond', or 'you shall above all things be glad and young', where the rhythms are fairly conventional and the verbal tricks, if not absent, at least at a minimum. The second is the broadly comic burlesque turn or musical comedy show-stopper, like 'Jimmie's got a goil/goil/goil', or 'may i feel said he/i'll squeal said she'. The personality expressed in this second kind is loudly clear and simple, easy to take, sometimes hilariously funny, not much more. The third kind—closely related and sometimes fused with the second—is the fairly simple satire or parody or burlesque of some stock American attitudes, especially attitudes of cliché patriotism or cliché sexual puritanism. Generally speaking, the simpler the poems are, the better, as in:

> come, gaze with me upon this dome
> of many coloured glass, and see
> his mother's pride, his father's joy,
> unto whom duty whispers low
>
> 'thou must!' and who replies 'I can!'
> —yon clean upstanding well dressed boy
> that with his peers full oft hath quaffed
> the wine of life and found it sweet—
>
> a tear within his stern blue eye,
> upon his firm white lips a smile,
> one thought alone: to do or die
> for God for country and for Yale.
>   ('come, gaze with me upon this dome')

or as in 'next to of course god america i/love you'. These are expert and charming light poems, and I suppose one can say that there is some meaningful criticism in them of 'literary' language which has gone dead.

It may indeed be said that Cummings participates honourably in the renovating function in twentieth-century poetry of introducing into poetry once again 'unpoetic' terms. But this is true of him only superficially. When we look at particular poems, their power to disturb poetic history seems to be very slight. And this is true for several reasons. First, and most obvious, when he is poetic he is very poetic indeed:

> you are like the snow only
> purer fleeter, like the rain
> only sweeter frailer you
>
> whom certain
> flowers resemble but trembling. . . .
>   ('you are like the snow only')

His willingness to be so is perhaps a sign that his dedication to the renovating function is, at least, not consistently in operation. Second, his use of slang and the colloquial frequently seems like a clown's costume he has put on, for fun or for the display of his vividly theatrical poetic personality:

> buncha hardboil guys from duh A.C. fulla
> hooch kiddin eachudder bout duh clap an
> talkin big how dey could kill
> sixereight cops. . . .
>   ('buncha hardboil guys . . .')

It is at best clownish fun, but there is frequently something unpleasantly patronising about it, what R. P. Blackmur calls his 'slumming in morals along with he-men and lady social workers' (p. 14). The poems in which the most obvious examples of slang and of the colloquial occur tend to be pastoral poems of the sort in which the pastoral figure is not really taken seriously, is diminished and simplified in a way which does not permit the reader himself to take it seriously:

> 'life?
>   Listen' the feline she with radishred
> legs said (crossing them slowly) 'I'm
> asleep. Yep. Youse is asleep kid
> and everybody is.' And i hazarded
> 'god' (blushing slightly)—'O damn
> ginks like dis Gawd' opening slowlyslowly
> them. . . .   ('Five Americans: Marj')

In this kind of poem the slang and the colloquial are not even rendered very well, the speech he pretends to be reproducing is not listened to very carefully, so that it is not interesting even as parody. And yet one is very much aware of it as a feature of the poems; one feels that one is called upon to admire the virtuoso feat involved in producing it. That is to say, the consequences of 'slangy, colloquial and generally non-literary' writing are not taken very seriously, and it is precisely in this respect that Cummings stands in contrast to Williams.

*   *   *

In point of fact, the slangy and the colloquial—at least of the most obvious kind—do not occur as frequently in Williams's poetry as we might expect. When they do occur they are almost always at the service of far more serious attitudes than we find in the comparable poems of Cummings. 'Late for Summer Weather', by Williams, is a

short poem describing a low middle-class couple taking a walk in
early autumn. The end of the poem is as follows:

> Fat Lost Ambling
> nowhere through
> the upper town they kick
>
> their way through
> heaps of
> fallen maple leaves
>
> still green—and
> crisp as dollar bills
> Nothing to do. Hot cha!

This poem is pastoral too, in the sense that we feel a difference in
sophistication between the speaker and the couple he is talking about.
The couple are seen as touching and a bit comic, he in 'grey flapping
pants', she in 'an old blue coat/that fits her tight', but not comic in
a way that diminishes them. Thus 'Hot cha!' is both a rendering of
what they might say and an expression of the speaker's own, of his
sharing of their Indian summer mood of elation, an expression on the
part of a speaker whose speech is fluid and free enough to be both
more elevated than theirs might be and to be slangy and colloquial
like theirs, but without embarrassment or condescension.

In 'A Vision of Labor: 1931' he says:

> The girl lying there
> supine in the old rowboat reading an
> adventure magazine and the two guys
> —six foot three each of them
> if they were an inch—washing their
> hip-boots off in the stream jerking
> from the pump at the finished manhole,
> washing their hands, their heads
> and faces, cupping their hands to drink
> the stuff. Geezus! What the hell
> kind of water is that to drink? But
> they probably know what they're doing
> —and looking down the bank at her
> lying flat out there in the heat with
> her five-and-ten dark glasses on
> to protect her eyes from the sun's
> glare—looking down and smiling over
> her like insane men.

The slang, the colloquial, here, is a perfectly easy element in the composition, realistically rendered, made no more of than, say, 'the stream jerking/from the pump at the finished manhole'. Such language, used in such a way, is an evidence of Williams's extraordinary freedom and seriousness. It is not an evidence of a lack of self-consciousness or a lack of art in him but of the mastery of an art which has been thoroughly considered.

Restrictions of space will not permit me to print the whole poem, but 'The Horse Show', a conversation between the poet and his old mother, is a poem in which Williams's realistic powers are displayed at their fullest. Here are two stanzas:

> They come to bother us. Why? I said. I don't
> know. Perhaps to find out what we are doing.
> Jealous, do you think? I don't know. I
> don't know why they should want to come back.
> I was reading about some men who had been
> buried under a mountain, I said to her, and
> one of them came back after two months,
>
> digging himself out. It was in Switzerland,
> you remember? Of course I remember. The
> villagers tho't it was a ghost coming down
> to complain. They were frightened. They
> do come, she said, what you call
> my 'visions.' I talk to them just as I
> am talking to you. I see them plainly.

In the respect for life which is rendered in such language, and in the power to use such language to evoke a life worthy of respect, Williams's only American peer is Robert Frost.

*   *   *

I should add a note here about a matter which has no place in my essay at large, but which is always of some interest with respect to Williams and his place in the history of American letters—his relation to Whitman. The peculiar 'American' character of the subject-matter of each is one obvious likeness, the avoidance of conventional forms is another, and Randall Jarrell has aptly characterised a third, closely related to the first two, when he says:

> One has about him [Williams] the amused, admiring, and affec-
> tionate certainty that one has about Whitman: *Why, he'd say any-*

thing!—creditable or discreditable, sayable or unsayable, so long as he
believes it.   (Intro., *Selected Poems*, p. x)

The 'Whitman tradition' with its hostility to the conventional whether
in verse or in society stays wonderfully alive in Williams's poetry, and
does so far less self-consciously than is true in the poetry of, say, Carl
Sandburg. Williams has attested, in his autobiography, to his intense
reading of Whitman in his early years, and to his early imitations of
him. But one feels primarily that the likenesses are temperamental or
environmental or, one might almost say, natural, not the direct result
of poetic influence or imitation. The society still, in the instance of
Williams, has that in it which can produce a poet who is 'naturally'
going to bear some relation to Whitman in his unconventionality as a
writer of verse and in his egalitarian manners.

But if Williams is Whitman's heir in certain important ways, he is
also, after the manner of heirs, his half-enemy as well. He says, for
example:

> Free verse—if it ever existed—is out. Whitman was a magnificent
> failure. He himself in his later stages showed all the terrifying defects
> of his own method. Whitman to me is one broom stroke and that is
> all. He could not go on . . . Whitman grew into senseless padding,
> bombast, bathos. His invention ended where it began. He is almost a
> satirist of his era, when his line itself is taken as the criterion. He
> evaporates under scrutiny—crumbling not into sand surely, but into
> a moraine, sizable and impressive because of that.

And again: 'Whitman was an open but not clear-thinking rebel. He
did not know what it was all about, that our primary conception of
the prosody was at fault.' For Williams, as he makes clear in half a
dozen places, including a full-length essay in *Leaves of Grass One
Hundred Years After* (1955), Whitman is valuable in his rebelliousness
against traditional modes, forms, rhythms and corresponding social
attitudes; but for him Whitman sees poetry as in much too simple a
relation to reality, as if it were an expression of nature, not an artificial
construct, a made thing. Williams accuses Whitman essentially of
insufficient sophistication about language, about the relation of the
forms of our speaking to our lives, and thus of an unconscious betrayal
of the revolution in which he was also a leader. Here again Williams is
a representative twentieth-century figure.

Note

Biography. *Wallace Stevens* (1879–1955) was born in Reading, Pennsylvania; he was educated at Harvard and New York Law School. He combined his work as a poet with a career as a lawyer, working from 1916 onwards for an insurance company in Hartford, Connecticut, of which he became a vice-president.

Works. Stevens's first collection, *Harmonium*, was published in 1923; his *Collected Poems* in 1955 and *Opus Posthumous*, ed. S. F. Morse, in 1957. His critical works were published as *The Necessary Angel: Essays on Reality and the Imagination* (1951).

Criticism. The best introduction is F. Kermode, *Wallace Stevens* (1960); this may be readily supplemented by *Wallace Stevens: a Collection of Critical Essays*, ed. Marie Boroff (1963).
The differing accounts of 'Bantams in Pine-Woods' referred to in this chapter are from Marius Bewley's essay in *The Complex Fate* (1952) and R. H. Pearce's *The Continuity of American Poetry* (1961) which has a long and important section on Stevens's poems and poetic ideals. Further comments on this poem are to be found in M. Bradbury and F. W. Cook, 'Whose Hoo? A Reading of Wallace Stevens's "Bantams in Pine-Woods" ', *British Association for American Studies Bulletin*, IV (New Series), pp. 36–41.

VII

An Ironic Romantic:
Three Readings in Wallace Stevens

MALCOLM BRADBURY

★

THOUGH at first slow to come to serious notice, Wallace Stevens's poetry has in recent years been given plentiful discussion and commentary. It has been a considerable influence on other poets, both in the States and in England; and it has been regarded with an increasing and ever-widening respect by critics and readers of poetry in both countries. The early criticism on Stevens, appearing when he was still writing, tended to regard him as an aesthete, a dandy, a poet of fine consciousness, yet one lacking in intensity—often, in fact, as a kind of American variant of the Sitwells. As the scope, unity and consistency of his work grew more and more apparent, particularly with the publication of *Collected Poems* in 1955, that view has changed. Today, Stevens is recognised as among the most important—some critics would say *the* most important—of modern American poets. One may now find groups of dedicated Wallace-ites, devoutly committed to the later, more difficult poems, for whom his work has the status of a systematic philosophy. A major mark of academic esteem has now been awarded with the recent publication of a *Concordance to the Poetry of Wallace Stevens*—a delightful linguistic compendium revealing the wide and systematic usage of those key Stevens words (like summer, winter, green, poet, poverty, hero, fiction) and the rarer presence of those characteristic Stevens exoticisms (rattapallax, funest, hidalgo, magnifico, ephebe, girandoles, etc.) which fascinated early critics, and seemed to them fundamental to his manner, but do not in fact recur often or systematically.

The tendency of much modern Stevens criticism is to pursue the underlying intellectual system—in fact, to see his work as unitary. A good deal of recent commentary has expounded it in this way, analysing his philosophy across the range of his poems and therefore usually elevating to the centre of his work those poems which are most distinctively speculative in character. Today as a result there is something of an under-estimation of those aesthetic, dandyish elements which once fascinated critics. And though, lately, a number of writers have stressed that Stevens is, after all, in many ways essentially a comic poet and poseur, and one deeply indebted to the verbal displays and procedures of the French symbolists, the directly euphoric character and the sheer wittiness of Stevens's literary language have not been demonstrated enough. Like Hart Crane (a poet with whom Stevens has all sorts of links), one is forced when reading Stevens to return to the mode of employment of language, to the syntactical and metaphorical procedures by which he first gains our attention. And this is important because these verbal procedures have much to do with Stevens's interpretation of experience.

In fact, much modern Stevens criticism, in stressing Stevens's greatness, has tended to draw attention to his abstractness rather than to his way of encountering particular occasions, and this can take us away from his essential point. Stevens is much concerned with particular occasions, with what they demand of the poet, with a particular response at a particular time. In some of his comments on poetry, he stresses the importance for him of the unifying elements that exist in an observed thing—the parts of a scene that he is looking at, for instance— and with the sensations that the scene produces, and with the implications of those sensations for the imagination. The particular and localised is of enormous importance for Stevens because it offers a basis for saying what the *real* is, and how it interconnected with other elements of observed reality. Objects are modified by objects as well as the mind. Imitation, the poetic art, is concerned with resemblance, and with the sensations produced in recognising connection and relevance and modification. 'The morality of the poet's radiant and productive atmosphere', Stevens comments (*The Necessary Angel*, p. 58), 'is the morality of the right sensation'—an impressionist's remark.

Stevens is, of course, a philosophical poet, but a philosopher of occasions; and that is why I think it useful to take three of his short poems and offer a close reading of them, in the hope of suggesting certain of the ways in which Stevens exploits his 'philosophical' concerns in his work. I want to go on from that to indicate some of the possibilities and difficulties associated with Stevens's poetic commitment

—which seems to me heavily romantic—in the twentieth-century situation. The poems chosen are not, with the possible exception of 'Bantams in Pine-Woods', those usually considered by critics as among his major work. They are of a sort that he wrote throughout his life, lesser commentaries on the greater themes of his work, or responses to incidental occasions. It is important to see Stevens as a philosopher of poetry; it is also important to see him as a poet responding to the possibilities of each individual poem that was proposed to him by occasions in his life or by a genial delight in language.

One needs to add, however, that the response to occasions is itself philosophically conceived. He observes in 'An Ordinary Evening in New Haven':

> The poem is the cry of its occasion,
> Part of the res itself and not about it.
> The poet speaks the poem as it is,
>
> Not as it was: part of the reverberation
> Of a windy night as it is, when the marble statues
> Are like newspapers blown by the wind. He speaks
>
> By sight and insight as they are. There is no
> Tomorrow for him. . . .

This sets a very high value on the moment of response, of organisation, of creation—on the act of imagining in close consonance with reality, that is, the res itself. But the very abstractness of the statement indicates the philosophical order of communication within which so many of Stevens's words work. He is a philosophical poet; that is to say, his poems (as well as his prose) engage us with abstract conceptions of 'reality', 'the imagination' and 'poetry' itself, and with the relation of the poet to what he perceives. His poems are commonly conducted either by means of a designed though not directly logical argument in which a degree of conviction is sought from the reader, or by presenting moments of poetic discovery or insight in which, usually, we must be attentive to the method by which such discovery has occurred. The imperative voice and the doctrinal element are explicitly there, as at the end of 'The Comedian as the Letter C':

> Score this anecdote
> Invented for its pith, not doctrinal
> In form though in design, as Crispin willed,
> Disguised pronunciamento, summary,

Autumn's compendium, strident in itself
But muted, mused, and perfectly revolved
In those portentous accents, syllables,
And sounds of music coming to accord
Upon his lap, like their inherent sphere,
Seraphic proclamations of the pure
Delivered with a deluging onwardness.

The tone of discourse is almost Wordsworthian; the image of the music, detached from a heavenly sphere and placed in the individual lap, is an image of a pure wise passiveness and openness; and disguised pronunciamento is the poetic end in view.

Many of Stevens's poems—particularly his early ones—are concerned with delineating the intellectual and emotional effect of concrete objects and scenes, and Stevens clearly shares many of the concerns and techniques of his Imagist contemporaries. But (as Frank Kermode has pointed out) he differs from them in that he defends the concrete in an abstract manner, and sees the obligation to delineate and define exactly in terms of an urgent human need, an epistemological need; his poetry is repeatedly about the relation of the material of the poem—that which is perceived—to the transforming imagination which can make it meaningful, and involves the eradication of false poetic impressions which are not acts of the genuine imagination confronting what it sees. The early poems often employ an extravagant inventiveness, a *ton pierrot*, as if the world of the imagination is conceived here as a gaudy, exotic, carnival world, simply 'celebrating the marriage/Of flesh and air.' Here the imagination is readily possessed; by a kind of hey-presto, its colourful garb is put on. But this motion into imaginative creativity is, particularly in the middle and late poems, frequently presented philosophically and with a profound sense of difficulty. By the last poems, the problems of precise imaginative contact have grown so intense that the gaudiness of the earlier poems, and their use of magnificent or clown-like *personae*, have almost disappeared, the universe has grown bare, the moment of the creative acceptance of reality has become remarkably delicate and sharp, while the primary questions have now become questions about distinguishing between philosophical statements about reality and reality itself, between any predetermined account of an occasion and 'the res itself'.

From the earliest poems, Stevens proposes an imaginative ritual in which poetry affords the meaning, shape and design in the world formerly associated with religion, save that it seeks 'Nothing beyond reality. Within it,/Everything . . .' Poetry is the supreme fiction; but the fictive element is much stressed, and it represents the subjective nature of imagination and its possible misapplications—for poetry needs the control of 'reality', a control exerted so rigorously that the occasions and possibilities of poetry are offered only a small area to play in. Poetry, offering a sole substitute for the design and spiritual concern derived from faith, is thus of the most extreme importance; as Roy Harvey Pearce says, Stevens constructs 'a major apology for poetry in our time'; as Stevens himself noted: 'After one has abandoned a belief in god, poetry is that essence which takes its place as life's reality' (*Opus Posthumous*, p. 158). Thus poetry is an epistemology committed to discovering the reality of things without any prior determinants, and is regarded by Stevens as potentially utterly truthful; its aim is

> to accept the structure of things
> As the structure of ideas

and the importance of such a procedure is also made quite explicit— 'The greatest truth we could hope to discover, in whatever field we discovered it, is that man's truth is the final revelation of everything' (*The Necessary Angel*, p. 175).

If, then, in his assumption that poetry is a mode of understanding and informing reality, Stevens is a romantic, his conception goes beyond the familiar romantic formulations. There is no other evident principle of organisation in this universe; the world is contingent and fortuitous, except in those subjective situations in which it is momently thoroughly and accurately imagined; and its design thus tends to coincide only with a recognition of design that comes as a necessary activity of language, metaphor, poetry, imagination. There is no explicit assumption of one force within us and abroad, and no direct likelihood of dejection derived from the fact that nature or the world has withdrawn *its* power from *us*; instead there is a 'poverty' that comes from denying the truth of our situation, or from being inaccurate, or from being overwhelmed into silence by reality. One faces barrenness with imagination—and imagination is the power to face barrenness. Throughout his poetry, however, Stevens insists upon the importance of a close identification with the world, and the need to recognise locality, to assimilate perception, to be an innocent perceiver without predetermined values. In some of the later poems, like 'A Primitive Like an Orb', he uses the

marriage imagery of the romantic poet to describe the effective rela-
tionship with external experience, and his figurative use of summer is
often elaborated through the assumption that summer represents
nature informed and alive. He touches on the possibility of

> an inherent order active to be
> Itself, a nature to its natives all
> Beneficence

which comes with 'the poem on the whole'. On the other hand he has
a heavy commitment to disorder, which implies scope and possibility.
There is objective power invested in nature—it is reality, the fabric of
the world in which we are visitors and with which we must come to
terms—and those forces which, so to speak, transform nature (the sun
and the seasons and also locality) are of enormous importance for
Stevens, since they work by investing the world with change, and thus
exist somewhere between reality and the imagination. In 'Looking
Across the Fields and Watching the Birds Fly', the romantic liaison
between man and a possible 'pensive nature, a mechanical/And
slightly detestable *operandum*', invested with Wordsworthian associa-
tions, is explored with characteristic tentativeness, through the *persona*
of Mr. Homburg, who is in 'Concord, at the edge of things'. In their
general development from volume to volume, the poems turn in a
cycle which moves through the seasons and leads us to the poverty
and barrenness of winter, where the pole of reality rather than that of
imagination is enforced, and where we are in a mood of dejection rather
than celebration. But in a curious way, an anti-romantic way, we are
also closer to truthfulness. Likewise, they seem to shift in geographical
location, tending to move away from the gaudy south and from
Europe, towards a North which is 'leafless and lies in a wintry slime'
('Farewell to Florida'). The recognition of the formative locality is a
recognition of the contingent forces acting upon the self, and it dis-
abuses any too readily arrived at ideas of order. There is throughout,
then, an increasing sense of difficulties, and an increasing stress upon
empiricism. Nature is formative, but it is also an independent reality,
that which is not us, the locality of individual existence. The poem as
icon can, 'The Rock' suggests, redeem or cure the barrenness of nature
and the barrenness of man, whose mind can become 'the main of
things', 'that in which space itself is contained', and so be the gateway
to the variousness of nature.

It is possible to regard Stevens, especially on the strength of the early poems, as a poet celebrating nature and vigour and life. In this sense, Stevens's modern and stylised tone and diction, as expressed in his extensive use of comedy, his extravagant phraseology, his use of fancy through linguistic associationalism, his obscurities and ambiguities, his general 'gaudiness' would be the substance of the celebration. But if we regard him rather as a poet pursuing accuracy of experience and romantic insight, then the tone of celebration must seem more akin to the mode of Coleridgean fancy, with many of the connections of the poem depending upon the ostentatious display of aesthetic powers. In fact, of course, Stevens starts as a poet from a number of symbolist premises well-rooted in American verse. As a method, symbolism characteristically heightens the poet's personal, subjective powers towards the figurative; it encourages him to effect his own 'correspondences' for truth, and draws attention to the idiosyncrasy of his imagination. It enjoins upon the poet powers of discovery that are his and his alone, stressing the subjective nature of the relationship between perceiver and what he perceives. Stevens thus typically builds up a personal iconography, a typical world of figures and landscapes, and a personal method of discourse and attack. He obeys the injunction to be modern, to purify the language of the tribe, because this is a necessity of the age (poetry 'has to be living, to learn the speech of the place', he writes in the poem 'Of Modern Poetry') and because it is herein that poetry has the means to be an effective epistemology. Yet this requires a mode of precise conduct, and Stevens treats the question of his own 'gaudiness' explicitly, particularly in the essay 'The Relations between Poetry and Painting', and in the poems 'The Man on the Dump' and 'The Man with the Blue Guitar'. It is significant that in his later work he moves towards the diminution of the 'guitar' and 'summer' elements, which are associated with the most riotous displays of the imagination. And many of his poems work by limiting the dimensions of the energetic activity of the imagination in which their original conception seems to lie, by bringing the figures and inventions into contact with reality in the interests of precision. It is precisely because he does so that he seems so important a poet; the aesthetic endeavour towards figuration, inventiveness, is put in relation to an independent and extrapolated reality, introduced into poem after poem, to the end of transforming it into an empirical way of knowing. Thus, for Stevens, poetry, which reveals, enlarges and hallows reality, does so by virtue of its willingness to face the problems of its own existence, and to be taken along by the objective data of the universe which is poetry's intrinsic material. Thus the occasions of many of Stevens's poems are fancifully conceived, and the development is handled in terms of rich imagery, gaudy phraseology, extravagant *personae*. Yet a growing rigour is exerted upon these elements through the philosophical illumination of the situation; a logical limitation of the initial situation ensues and only the most precise features of the figures are allowed to survive. In the following three poems one can see different procedures of this sort, in which the demands that Stevens is prepared to place upon the gaudy imagination are shown in action.

*   *   *

Bantams in Pine-Woods

Chieftain Iffucan of Azcan in caftan
Of tan with henna hackles, halt!

Damned universal cock, as if the sun
Was blackamoor to bear your blazing tail.

Fat! Fat! Fat! Fat! I am the personal.
Your world is you. I am my world.

You ten-foot poet among inchlings. Fat!
Begone! An inchling bristles in these pines,

Bristles, and points their Appalachian tangs,
And fears not portly Azcan nor his hoos.

This poem, in Stevens's most stylish and 'gaudy' manner, is one of the many short pieces in his first volume *Harmonium* (1923). In character it resembles an Imagist poem; it is concerned with illuminating a single occasion, a complex of feeling and thought in an instant of time; its metaphors are hard and novel and provide much of the development of the poem; and it is extremely visual, seemingly avoiding vague abstraction. The first impact is made by the diction, by the word-play, jazzy rhythms, surface delights, and it has an air of modernist whimsy, the *ton pierrot*. Its movement and its rhetoric make it a comic poem, a comedy coming particularly from the idiosyncrasy of the choice of words and the rhythmic motions they make when together. It is a poem that has had considerable interest for critics, for various reasons— it makes use of figures who resemble agents in the later poems ('the giant', 'the hero', 'the fat, the roseate characters' ('Credences of Summer', etc.); it seems to show two opposed views of the relationship of individual to world which Stevens elaborates elsewhere; and it presents interesting difficulties of reading. The heavily impacted metaphors make the meaning obscure. A number of agents are named, standing in uncertain relation to one another—Chieftain Iffucan, portly Azcan; the cock; the ten-foot poet; the inchling. It is difficult to allocate lines to their speakers, if they have a speaker other than the poet. Certain words —'caftan', 'hoos'—are not only striking but rare. The occasion represented seems itself obscure, and amid all the verbal realisation the third couplet stands out as remarkably abstract. The critic must push to bring meaning into the poem.

The occasion seems to be an encounter, in the pine-woods of the Appalachian mountains of North America, between two birds. One is a cockerel and the other regards himself as vastly smaller, 'an inchling', but it is probable that both are bantams. The two figures are humanised, and each is drawn with associations that blur their animal reference— thus the cockerel is also a Mexican chieftain and a 'ten-foot poet'. The absence of quotation-marks makes it difficult to determine the speaker or speakers. The whole poem may be addressed by the poet to the chieftain-cock-poet, whom he threatens with the inchling. Or we can say that the bantam speaks the whole poem, or we can attribute some lines to the cockerel, particularly since 'I am my world' and 'I am the personal' seem to be contrasting rather than parallel statements (though I don't think they are). Further, there are important contrasted references to size, colour, relation to locale and attitude to the world in general by which we are invited to judge these figures; but since there is no elaborated ground for judgment, no direct moral criterion, we are not much helped to award our sympathies to the one or the other. Since we seem to observe from the bantam's point of view, we may take what he says to the cockerel as our line for interpreting the poet's sympathies in the poem; or we may decide to read his opinions as ironic, on the strength of other poems by Stevens; or we may see the poem simply as an image and hold the two opinions in equipoise. It is on this last question that most of the critical disagreement has arisen.

The poem is clearly enough concerned with two basic ways of approaching the world: 'Your world is you. I am my world.' Around this, four levels of imagery are set up and run together. On one level, there is the contrast between the two birds, the brightly coloured cockerel and the bantam (this seems to be the substantive level of the poem). On another, there is the contrast between the ten-foot poet and the inchling (poet?); on another, there is the contrast between the chieftain, with his extravagant garb and loud shouts, set against the unfrightened, personal inchling. On a more abstract level, there is the contrast between the 'fat' and 'thin' views of the world. If we take it that the 'I' of the poem is not the bantam but the poet then the contrasts are divided not between two but three figures. How do these meanings relate to one another? Pound described the Imagist technique of superpositioning, in which two ideas could exist simultaneously in a single Image poem. Here there are four; in the procedure of the poem, the opening figure of the Mexican chieftain is transformed into a cockerel, and then into a ten-foot poet. None of these meanings disappears, but the cockerel offers the most reliable level of meaning, thus reducing the chieftain and the ten-foot poet to the level of comic hyperboles for the bantam bird. The human associations enlarge and make whimsical the animal context, and these are drawn with a characteristically exotic touch. The strut of the cockerel is painted with the tan and henna of Mexican art, and the names—'Iffucan of Azcan'—further associate the bird with a locale in which he does not belong, for the geographical location of the poem is clear. Iffucan's clothes and colours are from other climes, and they contrast with the pine-woods of the Appalachians, in a softer, greener, more temperate part of America than Mexico. The inchling is less humanised, and also is identified with the pine-woods about him to the extent of pointing their sharp pine-needles (tangs) at the intruding figure and so not fearing Azcan's loud shouts (his hoos). That this is the level of significant contrast is supported by the central contrast of the poem: 'Your world is you. I am my world.' The cockerel dominates his environment to the point of having turned the sun into a negro servant who carries his bright tail like a train. But he stands out against his environment; he is universal, fat and foreign. The bantam is however 'the personal', in that he is responsive to environment; he does not pretend to be bigger than he is, he remains local and is able to halt Iffucan on that score.

Why is Iffucan a 'ten-foot poet among inchlings'? The line suggests that the capacity to be universal is identified with poetry; that poetry, the power to imagine, enlarges a creature beyond his size. It is around this point that critical dissent has arisen. Thus Marius Bewley, in an ingenious interpretation, says that 'Azcan remains a good giant at heart', while in proclaiming himself 'the personal', the inchling mistakes the part for the whole; his scientific bias in his insolent cry to the imaginative life, for which Azcan stands, reveals him content with fragmentary existence and consequent moral isolation. Roy Harvey Pearce, on the other hand, sees (p. 383) Azcan's claims to gianthood as 'a mishmash of ritual', and the point of the poem is thus that the inchling 'really makes of the world what he wills', because he has a better relationship to it. If Azcan were the only poet in the poem, we would, I think, be inclined to agree with Marius Bewley; but the inchling may be a poet too, and Stevens certainly is. The small creature enlarged by his poetry, made universal, could be contrasted with the poet who accepts a more minor role in consonance with his surroundings. The aggrandised figure in his exotic garb may not be heroic but comic, then, for he would represent a failure to come to terms with reality. The inchling, the creature as small as (or smaller than) his size, could be the democratic hero, the new poet. If this is so, and it is a viable reading, then the poem conspicuously modifies its own extravagances. So it is that Crispin, in the latter part of his journey in 'The Comedian as the Letter C', serves 'Grotesque apprenticeship to the chance event', discovering, when he reaches America and leaves Europe and Mexico behind, that 'his soil is man's intelligence', and that

> The man in Georgia waking among pines
> Should be pine-spokesman.

The inchling's power over the pines, in fact, would seem to indicate that Azcan's is not the only creative imagination.

The other main way to read the poem would be to take Stevens himself as the 'ten-foot poet' bantam, Azcan. He meets a real bantam in the pine-woods and imagines that he is addressed by him. The bantam would then be the reality that the poet meets, and his function would be to modify the romantic excess of the poetic imagination (ll. 3–4) by his concrete reality. The bantam dismisses the poet's instinct towards universalisation; yet, ironically, by being the point of concentration for the scene (pointing the Appalachian tangs) he enables the portly poet to shape his poems (his 'hoos').

It is characteristic of Stevens that he does not provide that kind of guidance that would enable us to assert that one or other of these readings is evidently correct. And the point is not easily resolved by reference to other poems, for we are familiar with two different representations of this situation in Stevens. In one the identification of a person with his immediate surroundings is seen as a limitation preventing the exercise of the imaginative faculty, and the figure of the hero who transcends this situation does occur in later poems—but he is treated with great equivocation. In other poems the detachment of a person from his surroundings is seen as an escape from reality. The poem 'Theory' (*Harmonium*) says 'I am what is around me'. The poem 'Tea at the Palaz of Hoon' (also *Harmonium*) seems to suggest the opposite, though the figure who descends may (or may not) be converted and changed by his 'western' locale. In fact, most other poems on like subjects prove no less difficult than this one. But it would not be at odds with the modern critical temper to propose that the poem 'lives' in this ambiguity, in the mediation of the two situations, leading to a potential metamorphosis of each by the other. Here the mediation comes in what the reader does. In later poems, however, we frequently find the metamorphosis *in* the poem.

*   *   *

The Sense of the Sleight-of-Hand Man

One's grand flights, one's Sunday baths,
One's tootings at the weddings of the soul
Occur as they occur. So bluish clouds
Occurred above the empty house and the leaves
Of the rhododendrons rattled their gold,
As if someone lived there. Such floods of white
Came bursting from the clouds. So the wind
Threw its contorted strength around the sky.

Could you have said the bluejay suddenly
Would swoop to earth? It is a wheel, the rays

Around the sun. The wheel survives the myths.
The fire eye in the clouds survives the gods.
To think of a dove with an eye of grenadine
And pines that are cornets, so it occurs,
And a little island full of geese and stars:
It may be that the ignorant man, alone,
Has any chance to mate his life with life
That is the sensual, pearly spouse, the life
That is fluent in even the wintriest bronze.

'The Sense of the Sleight-of-Hand Man' appeared in Stevens's fourth collected volume, *Parts of a World* (1942), which has the reflective character of the later books. The poem is in his more philosophical manner, and considers and illustrates concisely an abstract issue of great importance for him—the fortuitous nature of imaginative celebration in man, the relationship it may create with the external natural world, and the powers that exist objectively in that world. The poem is not *directly* located in an occasion. The 'one' of the piece is not specifically Stevens, and the extent to which the poem intends the acts of perception throughout to be located in a perceiver within the poem is blurred. Though the theme is romantic, romantic sentience is absent, and the states of feeling with which the poem is concerned in its opening and closing lines are treated with bravura rather than precision. The natural landscape is apparently a generalised one; it is precisely drawn in some of its details, but not easily visualised, not easily located; it serves a dual purpose in the poem—it provides figures for the argument and represents too that objective reality with which man in general, and the thinking poet, must come to terms. The poem moves among grand abstractions—'soul', 'life', 'myths', 'gods'—but is touched with a note of comedy that suggests our tone is more comic, our manner more empirical, but that if we can heighten this into the romantic dimension, we will do so with our honour intact. The subject is transformation, but it is characteristic that the title should see this as 'sleight-of-hand', as a cosmic confidence trick. Yet as we move to the tentative conclusion of the poem, we have acquired the conviction that this is a matter of the greatest importance, and we have done this through the hardness, the lack of sentience, in the poem, through the bright and seemingly unyielding flow of images, which seem at once to be conceptualised stages in an argument and mysteries in the natural world.

If we try to take out that conceptual argument, we might sketch it roughly as follows: moments of insight and celebration occur by chance in man's life. This can be shown in a figure; nature may be lively about an empty house. Nature indeed is power, and seems itself to celebrate. These powers are beyond our determination, and are thus apparently fortuitous also. We no longer see the powers and independent designs in nature as the functions of the gods; but the powers remain and we can still perceive them as powers. We do this by the activity of the imagination, by personal and fortuitous whimsy. And thus it may be that man, without pantheistic theory or mythical reference, isolated in a universe without support, can at any time, through the exercise of his own ungovernable inventiveness, achieve an imaginative fusion with an order of life outside himself, in nature, a life still active even when nature seems most dead or most abstracted. The subject of the poem is then chance, and the area in which fortuity, something beyond the intended activity of the self, occurs is double—it is in nature and in the unwilled powers for celebration in the imagination itself. The theme of the poem is imaginative marriage, and the larger part of it deals with the qualities of the 'sensual pearly spouse' and with the powers that may justly be attributed to her.

But does this marriage remain the same throughout? The question of the poem is whether an opposition is being proposed between the 'one' who begins the poem and the ignorant man who ends it. The ambiguity of 'alone' (it may be that *only* the ignorant man; it may be that the ignorant man in *solitude*; grammar only slightly supports the former, and it looks like a deliberate ambiguity) sharpens the point. The opening passages can refer to the imaginative man (the sleight-of-hand man), whose moments of vision are shown to be fortuitous; and he could then be compared with the ignorant man who mates simply and directly with life, without attempting to interpret it. The sense of the sleight-of-hand man might then be that he by the whimsy of his imagination distorts as well as celebrates the world he sees, and that there is a more direct marriage with reality than his own. The whimsy of lines 13–15, with their flat and excessive metaphors, would then suggest that his emotion towards the ignorant man can only be envy, that he is conscious only of the limitations of the imagination.

The complicated and difficult thing about the poem is then that the concept of fortuity occurs within a considered and quite unfortuitous notion of the role and character of the natural world. We can see this procedurally, in the way that images taken from nature have both a subjective and objective role in the poem; they represent the functioning of the poet's imagination at a deep imaginative level (as in the conception of life 'fluent even in the wintriest bronze'), they represent whimsy and sleight-of-hand ('To think of a dove with an eye of grenadine'), and they represent objective power ('Could you have said the bluejay suddenly/Would swoop to earth?'). This creates an apparent disconnectedness in the poem, so that—to take just one example—the second grammatical sentence is proposed first as an analogy, but then seems to be not just a metaphorical statement about man, but a figure for the independent power of nature. We appear to perceive through a sentient observer and 'without' him; nature is that which the poet imagines and the objective material which awaits is available to 'the ignorant man, alone'. The poem cannot work by the fortuitous methodology it describes; it cannot await the functioning of imagination, but derives, as Stevens himself proposes in his essay 'Effects of Analogy', from the poet's sense of the world, 'as he intervenes and interposes the appearance of that sense' in the form of a figurative analogue that transcends the actual world. The poem cannot see contact with nature only as a function of occasion, association, whimsy, chance 'tootings'. It must act in a fuller mode of discourse and in utter seriousness; it must locate and limit that occasion by perceiving and providing those objective powers in nature with which it makes contact; it must extrapolate from the situation that upon which the 'grand flights' depend. The power of Stevens's figurative method here is that it serves, with effective ambiguity, that double function, so that the polar opposites of the poem are reconciled in more than one form.

*   *   *

The Poem that Took the Place of a Mountain

There it was, word for word,
The poem that took the place of a mountain.

He breathed its oxygen,
Even when the book lay turned in the dust of his table.

It reminded him how he had needed
A place to go to in his own direction,

How he had recomposed the pines,
Shifted the rocks and picked his way among clouds,

For the outlook that would be right,
Where he would be complete in an unexplained completion:

The exact rock where his inexactnesses
Would discover, at last, the view toward which they had edged,

Where he could lie and, gazing down at the sea,
Recognize his unique and solitary home.

The group of poems called *The Rock* appeared as a final section to *Collected Poems* (1954), and are among Stevens's very last work. Stevens always used his poems to support one another, and conceived a part of his task as that of converting his own sense of the world into a characteristic discourse, an inseparable style. He returned repeatedly to a number of central figures and situations, and in these last poems figures of 'rock', 'mountain' and 'sea' are recurrent, and themes of barrenness, poverty, annihilation and also visionary contentment. But the poems are independent, and it is, I think, procedurally right to stay within the single poem, though the reader should at this point be particularly recommended outside it. Yet the peculiar lucidity of this poem seems to come from a reposed and subdued way with the imagery, as if Stevens felt that its essentials were familiar enough. This perhaps is why the poem works so gently and gains such complication as it possesses from the complex grammatical and tense structure and the sorts of relationship existing between the agent and the phenomenal features which surround him, which he uses and through which he moves.

A lot of Stevens's poems provoke comparisons with the great poems of the romantics, and this one reminds us of Keats's 'On First Looking into Chapman's Homer' (one might even wonder if this is not the poem referred to in the text). Certainly a comparison of the two poems would afford an interesting exercise in practical criticism. Both deal with visionary states of being, induced by reading a poem and achieved through an appreciation of the selecting and composing power of the imagination. In both the landscape is mountainous and the novelty of the discoverer's view is established. Stevens's visionary state of 'completion' resembles the Keatsian negative capability, in which visionary precision is attained without further effort, and where a personal reconcilement with the universe, with reality, takes place. In this state the composed and purified imagination would find its precise point of eminence and survey the end of its journey, unique, solitary, and fulfilled. But just as we commonly say that Keats does not offer his full commitment to the transcendent, the visionary state, so it is apparent throughout that Stevens does not. The reservations appear largely through the grammar; the final visionary state of completeness which 'he' had needed is presented in the subjunctive, so that we cannot know whether it has been achieved. We only know of the attempt made; and what the poem he reads restores, in the present event of the poem, is a former need, not the moment of vision.

In what sense can a poem take the place of a mountain? It can attempt to describe a mountain; or the mountain can be figurative, it can represent a moment of elevated imaginative insight. Yet the mountain itself is modified—the pines are *recomposed*, the rocks are *shifted*, the modifying imagination has worked on the mountain itself in order to create the possibility of completeness. If the 'he' is himself the poet, who is reading a poem he has in the past written and is recalling its procedure and inspiration, then this would create a double figure of, so to speak, the imagination modifying the imagination. The figures of the poem exist then in a curious half-world between the figurative and the real—a half-world characteristic of Stevens's poetry (and quite unlike the tactile half-worlds of Keats). In this Stevens half-world, figures can stand both for objective reality and subjective symbols. Stevens is a symbolist poet. But if he is looking at a former poem, and finding it successful, he makes that poem, too, into a figure. The poetic endeavour and the objective thing, which is also subjectivised, are interpenetrated and interfused, creating an unusual quality of statement, and also finally limiting the ideality of the poem lying in the dust on the table.

*   *   *

Stevens is in fact an habitually ambiguous poet. In the larger number of his poems he uses *personae*, colourful characters in whose profession or physical shape is implied an attitude towards the world, or more vaguely imagined agents, like the 'he' of the last poem, involved in significant moments of perception, in mobilities of the imagination, and often seeming to stand for himself. Yet the use of 'he'—rather than 'I'— is an interesting indication of the sort of distance and therefore of ambiguity he is seeking. Further ambiguities derive from his *symboliste* use of figures for representations of states of mind and for attitudes associated with a thing, and for the thing itself. He tends to present through images, but the images, though distanced by a comic irony, require a degree of philosophical assent in the reader. The problem one here confronts is that of an imaginative process yielding up images that represent unimagined reality. Like Frost, he dispenses with the pathetic fallacy in order to suggest the distinction between brute experience and the operation of the human capacity to modify and combine; but in Frost landscape functions as actuality before it becomes symbol or metaphor, as it does in, say, 'West-Running Brook'. Whitman speaks of the poet using the 'shows and forms presented by Nature' and projecting them, 'their analogies, by curious removes, indirections . . . This is the image-making faculty, coping with material creation, and rivaling, almost triumphing, over it.' The American poet has a particular obligation towards finding novel relations, in Whitman's view: 'One main contrast of the ideas behind every page of my verses, compared with establish'd poems, is their different relative attitude towards God, towards the objective universe, and still more (by reflection, confession, assumption, &c.) the quite changed attitude of the ego, the one chanting or talking, towards himself and towards his fellow-humanity.'[1] The connections between Whitman and contemporary American poetry have been well established in recent years; and there is no doubt that Stevens, in his post-romantic curiosity about the distinctions that we can make between reality and the imagination, the 'objective universe' and the perceiver creating discourse, sees the poet as a transcendentalist, attempting to reconcile the parcelled-out parts of the world. His themes are romantic and visionary ones, but his humanism and his sense of the incompleteness of any individual vision reduce his passages of exaltation to something nearer irony, while pushing his explicitly ironic poems towards the view that irony is incomplete as a vision. The important thing is that, starting from

[1] 'A Backward Glance o'er Travel'd Roads', *November Boughs* (1888); reprinted in *Leaves of Grass and Selected Prose*, ed. S. Bradley (1949).

nothing except the fabric of the world and the creative resources of the individual, he opens out the notion of an empirical and democratic marriage in which the artistic imagination has a higher function than ever before in poetry.

Note

Criticism. A useful perspective for further reading is Roy Harvey Pearce, *The Continuity of American Poetry* (1961). Other studies of American poetry in the context of critical thought are Cleanth Brooks, *Modern Poetry and the Tradition* (1948) and Randall Jarrell, *Poetry and the Age* (1953).

For a general view and examples of criticism see Walter Sutton, *Modern American Criticism* (1963) and *Modern Criticism: Theory and Practice,* ed. W. Sutton and R. Foster (1963).

Poems quoted in the chapter are in the poet's collected works or in one of the anthologies of recent verse cited in the Preface to this volume. Cumming's comment on Rilke (pp. 175-6) is quoted from *i : six nonlectures* (1953), p. 7.

VIII

Criticism and Poetry

WALTER SUTTON

★

IN America the years since the first world war have seen an unprecedented burgeoning of criticism. In growing numbers, critics have engaged in the analysis and interpretation of literature, in speculation about its nature and function, and in the judgment implicit in both these activities. It is more than coincidence that this 'age of analysis' has also seen a phenomenal upsurge in the writing of poetry to which three successive generations of poets have contributed. Yet much less attention has been paid to the relation between these parallel growths than to the frequent complaint that the critics have crippled the poets and that criticism is hostile if not fatal to the spirit of poetic creativity.

This charge is hard to justify if we look at our literary past. A century or more ago, when direct technical analysis in the manner of the New Criticism was as yet unknown, it was still natural for the poets to respond directly to the challenge of critics concerned with speculations about the qualities of a literature appropriate to a young republic founded on democratic principles. The yearning for a distinctively American style, the desire that gave William Carlos Williams his deepest theme and that confounded the genius of Hart Crane, appears both in the literary criticism of the early nineteenth century and in the verse written under the influence of that criticism. As one response to the cultural nationalism of the period, Joel Barlow composed his would-be epic, *The Columbiad*, a remote forbear of Crane's *The Bridge*. The same wish to satisfy a critical demand for an American poem of epic scope underlay Whitman's work in the middle years of the nineteenth century.

In the face of such evidence stands the official attitude of certain poets themselves. E. E. Cummings once quoted with approval a remark by Rilke: 'Works of art are of an infinite loneliness and with nothing to be so little reached as with criticism. Only love can grasp and hold and fairly judge them.' The sentiment, which Cummings endorsed as worth 'all the soi-disant criticism of the arts which has ever existed' is a familiar one. Expressed in similar ways by many poets over the past hundred and fifty years, it represents both the early romantic's distrust of the meddling intellect (which murders to dissect) and the more recent idea of a 'dissociated' modern sensibility within which the analytical mind is at war with the creative imagination. Seen in this light, Cummings's quotation is merely one expression of a common anti-intellectual position that insists upon a dichotomy between the creative and critical processes.

But such a split is certainly false to the nature of both poetic composition and criticism, which are complementary and reciprocal. The writing of poetry calls upon the poet's reserves of analysis and judgment, just as criticism can hardly remain *un*imaginative or untouched by common feelings if it is to have enduring value. To suppose that the poet and the critic must or can do their work cut off from each other is absurd. There has been a fruitful interrelationship between the writing and judging of literature at least since the time of Aristotle, and many of the greatest critics, from Dryden to Pound and Eliot, have been poets, playwrights and novelists. In both poetry and criticism there has been a continuity of themes and ideas from the remote past into the twentieth century.

For poetry in the United States the deepest sources of intermingled critical theory and poetic practice lie in the romantic tradition. As a naturalisation and broadening of English and Continental influences, the American movement received its manifesto in Ralph Waldo Emerson's essay, *Nature*. Not until this time, sixty years after the Declaration of Independence and a generation later than *Lyrical Ballads*, did the country's intellectual leadership succeed in overcoming a nagging cultural colonialism and establishing a native literary tradition flowing from the actual language spoken by Americans.

English romanticism had contributed to this development through its individualism and its stress, in Wordsworth's prefaces, on the language of common life. The same strain sounds in Emerson's rejection, in *Nature*, of a 'rotten diction' and his assertion of the 'advantage which a country life possesses, for a powerful mind, over the artificial and curtailed life of cities'. In 'The American Scholar', a cultural declaration of independence, Emerson identifies Goethe, Wordsworth and Carlyle with the romantic revolution and notes with approval the parallels between its political and literary phases. With the social and political elevation of the common man, the artist turned increasingly to the celebration of the common life. Instead of the sublime and beautiful, the writer explored and poeticised 'the near, the low, the common', seeking the meaning of 'the meal in the firkin; the milk in the pan; the ballad in the street'. This interest had further effects: it helps to explain not only the thematic celebration of the values of common life but also the use of colloquial language and sensuous imagery in modern poetry.

But the most enduring and fruitful romantic influence upon American poetry, one that has distinguished it from the poetry of other languages, including British English, is the organic theory of form, the assumptions of which lie behind the whole modernist movement. Within this movement there have been two sharply contrasting conceptions of the nature of poetic form. Certain critics and poets (most notably the New Critics), impressed by the complexity of the internal organisation of the poem, have emphasised its self-sufficiency and inviolability as a symbolic entity; they have accordingly tended to ignore if not deny its social meanings and relevance. Others, fully as concerned with the comparison of poetic and natural processes, have stressed the openness of poetic structure and the relationship of the poem to its supporting environment. For both groups, however, the organic analogy has assumed the interrelatedness of formal elements and the essential idea that form follows function.

Originating, for all practical purposes, in eighteenth-century German thought and further developed by Coleridge in *Biographia Literaria*, the organic theory found its fullest early expression in Emerson's essay 'The Poet'. Although Emerson's transcendentalist theory now seems dated, the terms in which he epitomises his idea of poetic form have not lost freshness or force: 'For it is not metres, but a metre-making argument that makes a poem—a thought so passionate and alive that like the spirit of a plant or an animal it has an architecture of its own, and adorns nature with a new thing.'

But the formulation of the principle was not enough to liberate Emerson's own verse from the often mechanical rhythm of conventional tetrameter and pentameter lines, the monotony of which oppressed the poet himself. It apparently never occurred to Emerson that his own ideal was more fully realised in the essay, which was, after all, *his* most congenial form. In his poems, however, it is only rarely that the compelling rhythm of passionate thought breaks through, as it does in some of the gnarled verses of the 'Ode' to Channing:

> The God who made New Hampshire
> Taunted the lofty land
> With little men;
> Small bat and wren
> House in the oak:
> If earth-fire cleave
> The upheaved land, and bury the folk
> The southern crocodile would grieve . . .

Yet the *idea* of organic form is often a theme of Emerson's poems, as in 'The Snow Storm', where the north wind, the creative principle in nature, is conceived as a 'fierce artificer' careless of 'number or proportion' who shapes his fantastic forms (white bastions and projected roofs) functionally and

> Leaves, when the sun appears, astonished Art
> To mimic in slow structures, stone by stone,
> Built in an age, the mad wind's night work,
> The frolic architecture of the snow.

Although Emerson was not able to realise his own precepts, a younger poet absorbed his utterances. One of the most impressive examples of the direct effect of seminal theory upon the subsequent writing of criticism and poetry can be seen in the impact of Emerson upon Walt Whitman, who later testified, 'I was simmering, simmering, simmering; Emerson brought me to a boil.' The theory of 'The Poet' has innumerable reverberations and echoes in the 1855 preface to *Leaves of Grass*. Whitman subscribes to Emerson's idea of the transcendental function of poetry and of the poet as a divinely self-sufficient seer. He also reinforces Emerson's idea of organic form:

The rhyme and uniformity of perfect poems show the free growth of metrical laws and bud from them as unerringly and loosely as lilacs or roses on a bush, and take shapes as compact as the shapes of chestnuts and oranges and melons and pears, and shed the perfume impalpable to form.

Emerson's prophetic and nationalistic conclusion struck a responsive chord in Whitman, who infused the theme with an equalitarianism alien to Emerson. To Emerson's assertion that 'America is a poem in our eyes; its ample geography dazzles the imagination, and it will not wait long for metres', Whitman echoes, 'The United States themselves are essentially the greatest poem.'[1]

But Whitman did more than echo Emerson. He also supplied the metres that Emerson sought. As an innovator, Whitman was the first to realise, in his poetic 'ensembles', the ideal of an open organic form. More sympathetic to the values of science and democracy than Emerson or most of his contemporaries and more receptive to an unrestricted range of poetic experience, the celebrator of the days of the modern stands at the head of the modern free verse movement.

His pioneering was recognised by later poets. In 'Pact', Ezra Pound hailed Whitman as a necessary breaker of the wood and called upon his own generation to do the carving—that is, to refine the free verse techniques introduced by the earlier poet. And, with Pound's strenuous support, the free verse tradition really came of age in the twentieth century, in the wake of the international Imagist revolt against conventional Victorian and Georgian poetry. The practice of the newer poets was from the beginning guided and shaped by explicit theory,[2] and long after Imagism had vanished as a movement, its 'tenets' received support and further development in the criticism that came to stand beside the new poetry as a complementary expression of the modern spirit. Actually, Imagism must itself be recognised as a movement in criticism as well as in poetry, not only because of its printed principles but also because of T. E. Hulme's posthumous *Speculations* and Pound's influential early essays.

The career of T. S. Eliot also attests the close relationship between criticism and poetry in the first half of the century. Despite some inconsistencies, the ties between Eliot's poetic style and his critical discussions of metaphysical and symbolist poetry, between his practice as a playwright and his interest in poetic drama, are by now too well known to require much comment, except perhaps to note certain unfortunate effects of his principles.

The example of Eliot is a reminder that the modernist revolt was less sweeping than that of the nineteenth-century romantics. In reacting against a romanticism gone decadent in the verbiage and sickly rhythms of Swinburne, many of the modernists invoked the spirit of classicism.

[1] Cf. Chapter II, pp. 45-7, above.
[2] See Chapter V, pp. 115-26, above.

Unlike Emerson and Whitman, who found the burden of the past galling, Eliot and followers like Allen Tate are lovers of orthodoxy who have sought to identify themselves with sustaining 'traditions' of one sort or another.

In his early essays, Eliot assumed the role of mediator between the forces of permanence and change. 'Tradition and the Individual Talent' asserted the normative influence of an existing body of literature but at the same time gave scope to innovation by recognising that the existing order is itself changed and modified by the introduction of each new work. By its very nature, however, a 'moderate' position such as Eliot's, strategically a very strong one, tends to resist revolutionary change. Although ostensibly recognising the equal claims of tradition and innovation, Eliot's theory has on the whole proved most congenial to the forces of conservatism. Reinforced by his reactionary political views, Eliot's critical thought, including his prescriptive definitions of 'impersonal' art and the 'objective correlative', has had a limiting and deadening rather than liberating influence upon later criticism and poetry.

But there were also outright rebels among the new poets. It is possible to see two strongly contrasting strains in the modernist movement, each with its own adherents, or 'party'. In keeping with the spirit of Imagism, one group has insisted upon complete freedom of individual expression through the development of experimental free verse poems. Ezra Pound, William Carlos Williams, Marianne Moore (an experimentalist if not an entirely 'free' verse poet), and some of the early Imagists constitute what might be called the radical wing, or the party of free experimentation. The most intransigent individualists among modern poets stand here. The other, more conservative party, preferring traditional themes and measures, embraces Frost (whom Pound was unable to win over to free verse), the later Eliot and Eliot's many followers, including the Southern 'Fugitive' poets.

The difference between these two groups is significant though not absolute. Pound belongs with the intransigents despite his interest in 'making new' the literature of the past through creative translation. Despite the startling 'newness' of his early verse, Eliot belongs with the conservatives because of his orthodox social and religious views and because of his movement towards greater conventionality in verse form—a shift that can be seen when The Waste Land is placed beside the Four Quartets. What is most important is the fact that Pound and

Eliot stand at the head of differing traditions in modern poetry and that within each there has been an interaction of critical theory and poetic practice.

A few poets, like Wallace Stevens and E. E. Cummings, have combined traditional and experimental modes in their work, and some, like Cummings and Frost, have argued against the relevance of criticism to poetry. But all modern poets of any account have been deeply affected by the critical thinking of their time. This is true not only of Wallace Stevens, most of whose poems are directly concerned with problems of aesthetic perception and values, but also of Robert Frost, whose most obvious subjects seem far removed from the lamp of theory and even from the modernist movement.

Frost was somewhat older than most of the new poets, and his style was already substantially formed when Ezra Pound helped him find an English publisher and belated recognition. Conservative in his choice of metrical patterns, his only concession to innovation seems to be the introduction into his traditional forms of the counterpoint of idiomatic New England speech rhythms. For the most part, Frost has been characterised as a middle-of-the-road Yankee poet whose restrained romantic enthusiasm for nature is balanced by a humanistic concern for accepted norms of social behaviour and responsibility.

But such a view fails to recognise Frost's sophisticated awareness of the aesthetic climate of his time, and his responsiveness to it. Although Frost was not officially an Imagist, Imagism helped to prepare the climate for his acceptance, and his work has affinities with its theory. There is in his poems from the beginning a concern for the evocative image that releases 'an intellectual and emotional complex' within a concentrated span, if not an 'instant' of time. This quality, which Frost stressed in his description of himself as a 'synecdochist' who uses a part to suggest the whole, can be seen in such shorter poems as 'The Pasture Spring', 'The Runaway' and 'Spring Pools'. In these a disarming simplicity and fidelity to experience conceal from the too casual reader the extent to which the poet has charged his language with complex metaphorical implications. Also, despite his preference for conventional verse patterns, Frost is like the Imagists in the economy and precision of his language, and in his endorsement of the value of functional organic form in a poem like 'The Ax-Helve' and in the more qualified prose statement of 'The Figure a Poem Makes'.

Although the forces of conservatism were gathering strength during the wartime and post-war years, the mood of the period was revolutionary and intransigent. In Chicago, where Harriet Monroe's *Poetry*, with Ezra Pound as foreign editor, upheld the cause of Imagism in its early years, there was a wartime renaissance. Besides carrying the work of the Imagists and other American poets like Marianne Moore and Wallace Stevens, the magazine helped to introduce such newer 'Chicago' poets as Vachel Lindsay, Edgar Lee Masters and Carl Sandburg.

Although *Poetry* did not long sustain its early enthusiasm, the experimental tradition was supported by other magazines, such as *The Little Review*, *Others* and *transition*. Committed to the spirit of innovation, they provided an outlet for poets as original and various as Williams, Pound and Stevens, and for the experimental writing of Gertrude Stein. In these magazines the practice of the newer poets was supported by essays and manifestos setting forth the creeds of a whole series of post-Imagist movements including Dadaism, Surrealism and Objectivism. The period was one of intellectual ferment and of an enormously productive interaction of criticism, literary theory and creative writing. Out of it emerged a number of gifted, highly individualistic American poets.

The more conservative trend within the modernist movement is represented by *The Fugitive* (1922-25).[3] The 'Fugitives'—John Crowe Ransom, Allen Tate, Donald Davidson, Merrill Moore and R. P. Warren—shared many of the rebellious attitudes of the 'twenties towards the social and aesthetic standards of the past; they proclaimed themselves 'in tune with the times in the fact that to a large degree in their poems they are self-convicted experimentalists'. Fundamentally, however, most of the Fugitives were traditionalistic in temper and more sympathetic to the Old than to the New South, with its industrialism and bourgeois levelling. When Ransom called for a programme that would be 'in manners, aristocratic; in religion, ritualistic; in art, traditional', he was following Eliot's description of himself as 'classicist in literature, royalist in politics, and Anglo-Catholic in religion'.

More than in other little magazines of the period, the metrical patterns of the verse published in *The Fugitive* tended to follow traditional models and the experimentation of the poets to take place within conventional limits, as in Merrill Moore's ingenious sonnets and Ransom's

[3] See Chapter I, *passim*.

ironic variations upon such traditional types as the elegy and the ballad. (Both 'Bells for John Whiteside's Daughter' and 'Captain Carpenter' first appeared in the magazine.) Ransom was from the beginning a champion of conventional rhyme and metre—hence his attack on *The Waste Land* for its fragmentation and neglect of traditional ordering devices. The younger Allen Tate, who had early come under Eliot's influence and who was the one editor sympathetic to experimental form, defended the poem in the magazine, arguing that 'aberrant versification' is sometimes a necessity for the modern poet.

Although *The Fugitive* introduced and helped to establish a number of new poets, it is perhaps more important that its editors provided the nucleus of the New Criticism of the late 1930's and the 1940's. The core of this movement included Ransom (who issued a book of essays entitled *The New Criticism*), Tate, R. P. Warren and Cleanth Brooks, who had also been Ransom's student at Vanderbilt. Others who became identified with the group were R. P. Blackmur and Yvor Winters.

These men were bound by the conservatism of their social and literary ideas. Ransom and his friends supported Eliot's impersonal theory and his traditionalism. From I. A. Richards's *Principles of Literary Criticism* they adopted the idea of irony as an organising principle and complexity as a standard of poetic value. They also carried forward the revival of the metaphysical tradition to which Eliot had contributed. In 'Poetry: A Note on Ontology' Ransom distinguishes three types of poetry: physical poetry, which is concerned with things (the objective Imagist's ideal); Platonic poetry, the poetry of ideas (Pippa's song is cited as a Victorian example to be shunned); and, finest of the three, metaphysical poetry, which combines idea and image through the device of sensuous metaphor and which has the further virtues of wit and complexity.

The theory formulated by the New Critics, each in his own way, can most simply be described as a poetics of *tension*, to use the term developed by Allen Tate in his essay 'Tension in Poetry'. For Tate, tension supplies the 'meaning' of poetry through the full body of all the 'extension and intension', or denotation and connotation, that we can find in it. For Ransom, the tension arises, in large part, from the interplay of the poem's 'structure' of general meaning and its decorative 'texture'. That is to say, the imagery, metrics, sound effects and so forth, supply dramatic parallels or contrasts with the sense of the lines. Ransom speaks of them as giving us a 'curious increment of riches' that no paraphrase or rational summary can convey. Cleanth Brooks thinks of 'paradox' and 'irony' as creating the tension essential to poetry as the words of the poem are 'loaded' with meanings and values through their contextual associations.

All of these ways of describing the tensional organisation of a poem are of course in the romantic tradition of Coleridge's 'balance or recon-ciliation of opposite or discordant qualities' through which the poetic imagination achieves 'unity in multeity'. This romantic principle of organic form was confirmed and reinforced by the aesthetic theory of the late nineteenth-century symbolist poets, who also defended the self-sufficiency and inviolability of the poem as image. This aesthetic purism was especially attractive to the New Critics. Eager to justify the status of poetry in an age of science, they liked to think of the poem as a self-contained language system deriving its meaning and value from the tensional interplay of its elements, without direct reference to a larger world of common experience. Although they drew support from earlier organic theory, they deliberately ignored the poem's rela-tion to its social environment and encouraged instead the idea of a hermetic or 'closed' poetic form. In doing so they were also reacting, as extremists, against the strong sociological and political stress of the criticism of the 1930's. But to deny the social relevance of poetry is in itself a social act. It is in effect a conservative defence of the social *status quo*.

Tensional theory of this kind has deeply affected both the criticism and the poetry of the past few decades. Their interrelationship can be seen in the work of the New Critics who are also poets. In 'Narcissus as Narcissus', Allen Tate explicates his own poem, 'Ode to the Con-federate Dead' and describes its structure as the 'objective frame for the tension between the two themes, "active faith" which has decayed, and the "fragmentary chaos" which surrounds us'.

This statement of theme points to an obvious influence upon the poem, one not mentioned in the essay but unmistakable in the Eliot-like imagery and elegiac tone of the ode. The rhythms and the images of Eliot's poems of the *Waste Land* period are evoked in

> The hound bitch
> Toothless and dying, in a musty cellar
> Hears the wind only.

And in the 'Gerontion'-like lines that Tate regards as 'the gathering up of the two themes, now fused, into a final statement':

> What shall we say who have knowledge
> Carried to the heart? Shall we take the act
> To the grave? Shall we, more hopeful, set up the
> grave
> In the house? The ravenous grave?

Although in his earlier years Tate was strongly influenced by Eliot, he was close enough to him in age to share the original impetus of the modernist revolt and to engage in it as a participant. He was also old enough to escape the limitations of subject enforced by the theory to which he contributed.

The members of a slightly younger generation were less fortunate. Born, most of them, during the decade of the first world war and the revolution in the arts, they grew up in the shadow of Eliot, Pound and other leaders of the movement. They were nurtured on 'Tradition and the Individual Talent', but they tended to place more weight than their elders had on tradition and less on experimentation. Reacting against the liberty of free verse, most of them turned to conventional rhyme and metre, finding the model of Ransom more congenial than that of Pound and the early Eliot. Perhaps because of the mood of post-war disillusion in which they passed their youth, they did not attempt large social themes but limited themselves instead to the realm of personal feeling and personal experience. They were not and could not be individualists of the stamp of many of their rebellious 'fathers'.

If we look even briefly at such poets as Randall Jarrell and Robert Lowell, at Richard Wilbur or Theodore Roethke, at Delmore Schwartz or Karl Shapiro, at Hyam Plutzik or others of the 'middle generation', as George P. Elliott has called them, we shall not find them remarkable for technical innovation. Although they have written with authority within the realm of their interests, their achievements are less impressive than their elders'. They did not have to break fresh ground for their own work. Most of them accepted the traditions and the poetic theory developed by the more conservative wing of the modernist movement. Also, they are the generation of poets who followed Ransom, Brooks and Warren into the departments of English of American universities, where they have remained—a fact that may help to explain their general conservatism. Recognised academic rank

and tenure, although they do not usually provide a luxurious life, sup-
ply a measure of security incompatible with the pose of the alienated
artist favoured by an earlier and more Bohemian generation. It has
struck many observers that the writers within the university, with their
programmes, their rank, their fellowships and their prizes (all elements
of a finely graduated prestige system) constitute a well-entrenched
establishment within the Establishment.

In the manner of every younger generation, some have rebelled
against the strictures of the fathers. The critical influence of T. S. Eliot
has been resisted by Randall Jarrell and by Delmore Schwartz in an
essay entitled 'The Literary Dictatorship of T. S. Eliot'. Karl Shapiro,
who has been particularly violent in his rejection of Eliot as a 'culture
critic', has assumed a strongly opinionated anti-intellectualist position
in a collection of essays well titled *In Defense of Ignorance*. But very little
in the way of positive critical thought has been produced. For the most
part, however, the personal influence of Eliot and the impress of the
metaphysical and symbolist theories of the New Critics can be clearly
seen in the work of the middle generation poets.

A case in point is Robert Lowell.[4] Born in the year of *Prufrock and
Other Observations*, Lowell left Harvard to study under John Crowe
Ransom. In keeping with T. S. Eliot, Allen Tate and others, Lowell
became a convert to Catholicism (Roman rather than Anglican), and
his early verse reveals his inner conflicts, appropriately expressed in
metaphysical imagery reflecting, like Eliot's, an interest in mystical
experience and religious history. Lowell also shares with Eliot a sense
of the decadence of New England culture and a Puritan preoccupation
with death and the problem of personal salvation, qualities that can be
seen in poems like 'Colloquy in Black Rock' and 'The Drunken
Fisherman'. The last stanzas of these two poems are alike in their
development, within the kind of metrically regular forms favoured
by John Crowe Ransom and most of the New Critics, of imagery
suggestive of the *Waste Land* story of the Fisher King with its rebirth
theme:

> Christ walks on the black water. In Black Mud
> Darts the Kingfisher. On Corpus Christi, heart,
> Over the drum-beat of St. Stephen's choir

[4] See Chapter III, *passim*.

I hear him, *Stupor Mundi*, and the mud
Flies from his hunching wings and beak—my heart,
The blue kingfisher dives on you in fire.

and

Is there no way to cast my hook
Out of this dynamited brook?
The Fisher's sons must cast about
When shallow waters peter out.
I will catch Christ with a greased worm,
And when the Prince of Darkness stalks
My bloodstream to its Stygian term . . .
On water the Man-Fisher walks.

(It should be added that Lowell's more recent and freer verse does not show the same predominating influence.)

For this generation the one experience providing scope for the treatment of large social themes was the second world war, in which some, like Randall Jarrell and Karl Shapiro, served, and from which Lowell abstained. As Shapiro noted in his poem 'The Conscientious Objector', the abstainer is actually a hero of 'our cause' who stands for the conscience that 'we come back to in the armistice'. Questions of guilt and innocence and of individual moral responsibility for mass violence are introduced in Jarrell's poems dealing with the implicated yet detached members of bombing crews and in Shapiro's on action in the Pacific theatre. In 'Elegy for a Dead Soldier', Shapiro sees every fall as 'More than an accident and less than willed'. The problem of moral responsibility for a more humane world is posed in the imagined epitaph with which the poem ends:

Underneath this wooden cross there lies
A Christian killed in battle. You who read,
Remember that this stranger died in pain;
And passing here, if you can lift your eyes
Upon a peace kept by a human creed,
Know that one soldier has not died in vain.

The pressing questions of whether the dead can be thought of as dying for a 'cause' and whether it is conceivable that peace could be achieved through any socially based system of values are introduced without explicit comment or judgment. Although Shapiro is concerned with a crucial social problem, he does not assert an opinion of his own or suggest that the poem itself might influence public opinion. In his scrupulosity and detachment the poet is typical of his generation, whose major abstention has been from commitment.

Such social themes are less common in post-war poetry, in which the more limited concerns of the poets are focused often on personal love, personal religious experience and problems of academic and suburban life. Although the middle generation includes a number of gifted poets, the group tends to share an academic orientation, an affinity for traditional metrics and an acceptance of the metaphysical and symbolist poetics of Eliot and the New Critics.

The link with Eliot is especially strong, even when it is resisted, as in Hyam Plutzik's 'For T. S. E. Only'. Although resentful of Eliot's anti-Semitism and lack of human sympathy, Plutzik acknowledges an influence and an identification. He comments on the nature of Eliot's appeal to his generation and, in closing with the well-known lines that Eliot had earlier taken from Baudelaire, claims the older poet as a brother exile:

> You drew us first by your scorn, first by your wit;
> Later for your own eloquent suffering.
> We loved you for the wicked things you wrote
> Of those you acknowledged infinitely gentle.
> Wit is the sin that you must expiate.
> Bow down to them, and let us weep for our exile.
>
> I see your words wrung out in pain, but never
> The true compassion for creatures with you, that Dante
> Knew in his nine hells. O eagle! master!
> The eagle's ways of pride and scorn will not save
> Though the voice cries loud in humility. Thomas, Thomas,
> Come, let us pray together for our exile.
>
> You, hypocrite lecteur! mon semblable! mon frère!

In the life of art as in life at large, the continuing process of innovation and change, of actions that beget reactions, is irresistible. The poets of the middle generation, now in middle age, have been followed by a 'third generation', so called by Donald M. Allen, who has collected their work. Born in the 1920's and 1930's, its members share certain characteristics which distinguish them from their immediate elders and link them to the radical wing of the earlier modernist revolt, especially Ezra Pound and William Carlos Williams, and to Walt Whitman in the nineteenth century. Unlike the poets of the middle generation, they are united in their rejection of the 'tradition' of T. S. Eliot and all that it stands for. One of the newer poets, Robert Duncan, has said of the principal influences upon his work that 'the two *sure* things—Frost and Eliot—are not there'.

They also have a common bond in their rejection of traditional metrics. They favour an 'open form' which they have discussed most often in terms of what one of their leaders, Charles Olson, has called 'projective verse' and of what William Carlos Williams had to say, on numerous occasions, about the 'variable foot'. The younger poets have also rejected what they consider the bourgeois compromise of the middle generation. Although many are college graduates (often under the G.I. Bill) and although some have taught in colleges and universities, they have identified themselves with offbeat and nonconformist rather than conventional academic traditions. Their origins reach back through the Greenwich Village life of earlier years to the beer hall Bohemianism of Walt Whitman's Manhattan. They include the Beat poets so conspicuous a few years ago, and San Francisco is one of their centres, but they are not, for the most part, 'beat'.

Besides Allen Ginsberg and the somewhat older Charles Olson, who provided a focus for the group at Black Mountain College, the better-known members of the third generation include Denise Levertov, Robert Duncan and Robert Creeley. Most of this group of poets have concerned themselves with theories of technique. Experimental and unconventional in orientation, they have been much influenced by Whitman, Williams and Pound, rather than T. S. Eliot and his followers.

But in spite of a lively interest in theory, the work of most of the younger poets is not distinguished. Technically they have contributed little to the modification and further development of the free verse patterns already devised by the first generation of modernists. The writers of the Beat movement, which has perhaps a greater sociological than literary interest, have shown an affinity for a Whitmanesque rhapsodic (sometimes 'frantic') style, best seen in the ululating long lines of Ginsberg's 'Howl'. Most of the other poets have followed, with but slight variations, the models of Pound's and Williams's verse.[5]

[5] See Chapter X, *passim.*, for an account of recent poetry.

In conversation William Carlos Williams once remarked of Whitman, whose radical innovations had prepared the ground for the new poetry, 'He wanted to be himself, and he couldn't contain himself any longer. So he just leapt off, and he was driven to find a way for himself, like the American pioneers.'[6] Williams and the other best poets of his generation were like Whitman in that they too 'leapt off' and found their own ways. Most of their present admirers have not achieved the same freedom.

One of the best-known theoretical statements by a third generation poet, who by his age really belongs with the middle generation, is Charles Olson's essay on 'projective verse' or 'composition by field' (first published in *Poetry New York*, 1950, and reprinted in *The New American Poetry* anthology), which calls for an open poetic form determined by the dynamics of the poetic subject. The directness of the influences upon Olson is unmistakable. The opening of his essay not only cites Williams and Pound but even observes the typographical features of Pound's tract style:

PROJECTIVE   VERSE
(projectile   (percussive   (prospective

vs.

The NON-Projective

(*or what a French critic calls 'closed' verse, that verse which print bred and which is pretty much what we have had, in English & American, and have still got, despite the work of Pound & Williams:*

. . . . . .

Verse now, 1950, if it is to go ahead, if it is to be of *essential* use, must, I take it, catch up and put into itself certain laws and possibilities of the breath, of the breathing of the man who writes as well as of his listenings. (The revolution of the ear, 1910, the trochee's heave, asks it of the younger poets.)

The renewed emphasis by Olson and others on individual freedom and on innovation is a healthy one. But most of the third generation poets have not exercised such freedom in their own right. Their failure to do so is plain when their work is compared with that of such members of the vanguard of the modernist revolt as Ezra Pound, William

[6] See Walter Sutton, 'A Visit with William Carlos Williams', *Minnesota Review* (1961), 309–24.

Carlos Williams, Hilda Doolittle, Marianne Moore, E. E. Cummings
—each of whom early developed an unmistakable voice and manner
of his own.

Charles Olson's *Maximus Poems* have many points of resemblance to
the work of Pound and Williams. Olson's use of the Gloucester setting
is reminiscent of Williams's use of Paterson. Numerous passages, like
the following from 'The Kingfishers', suggest Pound's mannerisms and
learned allusions and Williams's fondness, in *Paterson*, for documentary
details:

> I thought of the E on the stone, and of what Mao said
> la lumiere'
>   but the kingfisher
> de l'aurore'
>   but the kingfisher flew west
> est devant nous!
>   he got the color of his breast
>   from the heat of the setting sun!
> The features are, the feebleness of the feet (syndactylism of
>   the 3rd & 4th digit)
> the bill, serrated, sometimes a pronounced beak, the wings
> where the color is, short and round, the tail
> inconspicuous.

A persistent and typical weakness of these lines is the lack of a
shaping force that can absorb 'influences' by subordinating and fusing
borrowed elements within the poet's own individual expression. There
is instead a comparatively relaxed poetic line with many unassimilated
details and echoes of the masters. Like many other poets of the third
generation, Olson has committed himself to a revolutionary theory of
organic form without having succeeded in carrying its principles into
practice.

Denise Levertov is outstanding among the younger poets. Born in
England of mixed Welsh and Russian Jewish stock and since 1948 a
resident of New York City, she has commented on her marriage to an
American and her coming to this country as a stimulating experience
that 'necessitated the finding of new rhythms in which to write,
in accordance with new rhythms of life and speech'. She has also
acknowledged the stylistic influence of William Carlos Williams
as indispensable to her development from 'a British romantic

with almost Victorian background to an American poet of any vitality'.[7]

Miss Levertov has a lyric élan, an economy and distinction in diction and phrasing, and the essential capacity for finding the metrical form most appropriate to her subject. Unlike most transplanted English writers, she has absorbed the rhythms of American life and speech. Although the influence of Williams can still be seen in her work, she has largely succeeded in developing a fully realised, and feminine, style of her own.

In 'Illustrious Ancestors', most recently reprinted in *The Jacob's Ladder*, she identifies herself with two of her forbears—the 'Rav of Northern White Russia', who understood the birds, and Angel Jones of Mold, the Welsh tailor and mystic—and through this association suggests her ideal of poetic form:

> Well, I would like to make,
> thinking some line still taut between me and them,
> poems direct as what the birds said,
> hard as a floor, sound as a bench,
> mysterious as the silence when the tailor
> would pause with his needle in the air.

In a more recent unpublished lecture, Miss Levertov has defined her conception of an 'organic' poetic form in which the metrical movement,

> the measure, is the direct expression of the movement of perception rather than, as in other approaches, the mold into which experience is cast.

The title of the lecture, 'Asking the Fact for the Form', is significantly a quotation from Emerson.

There are also a number of younger poets—notably James Dickey, James Wright, Adrienne Rich and Galway Kinnell—who have won recognition during the past five or ten years. Often their first books have been published by the Yale or Wesleyan university press, both pioneers in the establishment of special series devoted to contemporary poetry.

The vigorous interaction of experimental American and English poetry generated by the Imagist movement of the first world war

[7] Cf. Chapter VI, *passim.*

years declined during the second quarter of the century, even though Eliot remained a continuing influence in England and many Americans followed the work of English poets like Auden and Spender. One reason may be the alleged British distrust of radical innovation in art; another, the fact that the books of many American free verse poets were not easily available in England, where the work of William Carlos Williams, for example, has just begun to be published during the past few years. Recently, however, there has been a renewed inter-animation of English and American poetry. Gael Turnbull's Migrant Press in Ventura, California, has published in pamphlet form the experimental verse of a number of younger English poets. In London, *Agenda*, edited by William Cookson, has encouraged American contributions and extended the influence of Pound and Williams's open poetic form.

Like Denise Levertov, most of the younger American poets are committed to the romantic tradition of organic form as it has come down from Emerson and Whitman through Pound and Williams. It is a position that places upon the poet the obligation of devising metrical arrangements appropriate to his individual sensibility and particular subjects. If this theory is to continue to be justified in practice, it will be necessary for more younger poets to make their 'leaps' and find their own ways as their elders did before them.

It is of course no longer easy or perhaps even possible for a poet, or any man, to be an 'individual' in the old mould of intransigent self-sufficiency. (Witness Ezra Pound.) Intransigency is a difficult attitude to maintain in an atomic age in which writers and readers alike are painfully conscious of ever-present social pressures on a global scale.

But the ideal of individualism is essential to the creative process, and in this sense, and others, the arts provide not only the opportunity but the obligation of self-realisation, even in a mass society. Whatever the pressures of public opinion or aesthetic conventions, the poet, if he is to succeed, must always shape his work uniquely. His poem formally represents his own individual sensibility and outlook in its ordered arrangement of interrelated patterns of sound, syntax, image and meaning. In the act of composition he modifies and contributes something new to the culture out of which his work has come. The poet is not a passive creature but a creative participant in the process through which his society defines its values, aesthetic and social.

In championing an open organic form, the poets of the third genera-
tion have reacted against a strongly established trend in modern criti-
cism. Although earlier romantic theory accommodated and often
encouraged the idea of the social function of poetry (as in Words-
worth, Shelley, Whitman), the weight of the conservative theory of
the New Critics has been on the asocial nature of the poetic utterance.
Their poetics of tension, however defined, has emphasised the organic
self-sufficiency of a poetic structure unified by such devices as irony,
paradox and ambiguity. The stress on irony as a means of achieving
complexity and uniting contraries within the poem, in the manner
suggested by Coleridge, has discouraged the idea that the poet might
make important, and unequivocal, statements about his society and
his world or that, as a formulator of social values, he might be a legis-
lator, though in no absolute sense, for his world.

The hermetic organicism of the New Criticism has also been unduly
restrictive in establishing a literary 'canon' largely confined to poets
and works in the metaphysical and symbolist traditions, to the virtual
exclusion of other established modes or of the idea that there can be
a poetry of statement with direct reference to a common social world
that critics and poets have a part in building.

This limited theory has been giving way in very recent years to a
broader view of organic form. Critics and theorists, as well as poets
themselves, have been moving towards a conception of organicism
that recognises the necessary interpenetration of literary form and cul-
tural environment, and the corresponding interdependence of formalist
or aesthetic and historical criticism. It is to be hoped that this shift in
critical thinking will be supported and extended, as earlier changes
have been, by new developments in poetry itself. At this point in his-
tory we are badly in need of a poetry, of a literature, that can speak
powerfully as a champion of positive social and political ideals and as
a critic of their neglect.

It is remarkable that so many of the poets of the first generation of
the modernist revolt—Ezra Pound, T. S. Eliot, Hart Crane, William
Carlos Williams—took upon themselves, in a period of general dis-
illusionment, the role of epic spokesmen. In major poems they sought
to characterise their age, each in his own way, and to define and criti-
cise, poetically, its values. The poets of the middle generation, in-
fluenced by the conservative theory of the New Critics, were less
ambitious in their efforts. They confined themselves, for the most part,

to a more circumscribed realm of personal experience within which they often demonstrated considerable skill. It remains to be seen whether a younger generation sustained but also challenged by a more liberal theory of open organic form will reassert the social function of poetry and the socially creative role of the poet as a spokesman for the values by which he and his fellows must live if a human, and humane, world is to endure.

Note

Criticism. Two studies closely related to this chapter are W. H. Auden, *The Enchafed Flood* (1951) and Paul G. Stanwood, 'The Triumph of the Sea: Three Poems of John Peale Bishop', *Jahrbuch für Amerikastudien*, viii (1963).

The quotation from Auden used in this chapter is from a B.B.C. talk, 'Huck and Oliver', *The Listener*, L (1953), 1283. Works on Stephen Crane and Hart Crane that are referred to, are D. G. Hoffman, *The Poetry of Stephen Crane* (1957); Yvor Winters, 'The Significance of *The Bridge*, by Hart Crane', *In Defense of Reason* (Denver, 1947; London, 1960) and Allen Tate, 'Hart Crane', *The Man of Letters in the Modern World* (1936; paperback 1957).

Poems by living authors quoted in this chapter are found in the anthologies listed in the General Editors' Preface, except De Witt Bell's poem in *Atlantic* (September 1963) and Reed Whittemore's in *The Self-Made Man* (1959).

IX

The Dark Voice of the Sea
A theme in modern American poetry

DENNIS WELLAND

★

IN a recent poem De Witt Bell, invoking Euripides as one who 'made, like Melville, a pact with the sea', contrasts his own position with the Greek's:

> Alas! old master, comfort me—
> I write from the pack of other poets,
> and make no pact with the sea.

Without being necessarily more derivative than the poetry of other nations, American poetry has perhaps shown a greater awareness of 'the pack of other poets', and this not merely, or even primarily, in its allusiveness of technique. One can instance the ease with which it has been possible to group poets usefully into a Whitman tradition, a Poe tradition and a tradition of Emily Dickinson; one can point to the number of poets from Edwin Arlington Robinson to Louis Simpson (including Pound, Allen Tate and Hart Crane) who have either written poems on Whitman or discussed in their verse the nature of their debt to him; one can list the groups—Imagists, Fugitives, or more recently in Black Mountain, San Francisco, or around the late Theodore Roethke, for example—where poets have written in the closest critical collaboration with each other. The negative aspect of this reliance on others was summed up by John Peale Bishop (1892–1944): 'My imitation of other poets is in part a desire not to be myself. It is also due in part to the provincial's fear of lagging on his time.' Yet there are some problems which any poet has inevitably to work out for himself, and it is here that Bell's poem opens up an interesting line of speculation.

That Pound apparently found it easier to 'make a pact with you, Walt Whitman' than Bell does to 'make a pact with the sea' may tell us something about the relative stature of the two poets, but it may more

constructively point to the imaginative significance of the sea in
American poetry. An alternative starting point might have been this
stanza by Emily Dickinson (1830–86):

> I never saw a moor
> I never saw the sea
> Yet know I how the heather looks
> And what a billow be.

Many poets can draw, as Melville could, on first-hand experience of
the sea, but for many others, as for Emily Dickinson, an imagined sea
could be just as great a stimulus; and it is not the purpose of this chapter
to separate sea-faring from land-locked poets, any more than to postu-
late a concern with the sea as some magic index to poetic greatness.
That the sea is, however, much in the modern American poet's mind is
suggested light-heartedly by Reed Whittemore (1919–) in 'Waves in
Peoria':

> . . . that lumbering presence
> Has been in my ear so long that I have to say something
> Or other about it. In this respect
> It is like an unwritten poem pounding and pounding
> A vast cranial shore until nothing else
> Can be heard and the poet grows nervous.

Elizabeth B. Harrod (1920–), hearing the same pounding in 'Summer
Afternoon', tries to resist it:

> Alien by virtue of our breath,
> We must shut out with many tears
> The surging voices in our ears
> Or in sea-song be drowned to death.

What these two poets of our own day hear has been heard by many and
greater American poets in the past, and it is with some of these rever-
berations that this chapter is concerned. Whether the sea appears as the
destructive element or a unifying pathway, as chaotic experience or the
creative imagination, as eternity or isolated mortality, it seems one of
the strongest, most diversified motifs in American poetry.

*   *   *

When, compiling *The Oxford Book of American Verse* (1950), F. O.
Matthiessen tried to set Longfellow's achievement into perspective he

THE DARK VOICE OF THE SEA199

'salvaged many shorter pieces which display . . . a quickening imagina-
tion and a mastery of delicate versification' and commented that these
were especially associated with 'the themes of the sea and the night'.
For Longfellow (1807–82), however, there is no pact to be made with
the sea, for he is master, and the sea is less an independent force of
nature than a convenient source of imagery. In a poem like 'Seaweed'
the quickening of the imagination is manifested in the skill with which
the image is sustained rather than in any fundamental newness of
approach. Four stanzas describe a storm-wind lashing 'the desolate,
rainy seas' until they find ultimate repose 'in sheltered coves, and
reaches/Of sandy beaches'; these are counterbalanced by four stanzas
in which the image is applied:

> So when storms of wild emotion
> Strike the ocean
> Of the poet's soul, erelong
> From each cave and rocky fastness,
> In its vastness,
> Floats some fragment of a song.

The parallel between the two halves of the poem is re-emphasised by
the verbal and syntactical correspondence between the final stanza and
the fourth; this and the appropriate ebb-and-flow movement of the
versification testify to Longfellow's technical accomplishment. At the
same time we are aware of the almost mechanical way in which the sea
is being consciously used for allegory, much as Holmes, confronted by
a chambered nautilus, has to draw a moral lesson from it. This tendency
of course is characteristic of much American writing from the seven-
teenth century on, though Longfellow uses the sea less for moral didacti-
cism than as an analogy with the working of the imagination. 'The
Sound of the Sea', for instance, suggests this:

> So comes to us at times, from the unknown
> And inaccessible solitudes of being,
> The rushing of the sea-tides of the soul;
> And inspirations, that we deem our own,
> Are some divine foreshadowing and foreseeing
> Of things beyond our reason or control.

The rhetoric is less hollow than in some of his more hortatory work,
and Matthiessen's praise is justified, though this is not a poem he
includes. Certainly the swelling movement is in direct contrast to the

more strident quatrains of the 'Psalm of Life'. The tired metaphor of life as a 'solemn main' in that debilitated sermon and the injunction to us to leave our 'footprints on the sands of time' receive a welcome, if unintentional, refutation in a later poem where Longfellow has his eye more keenly on the object:

> Darkness settles on roofs and walls,
> But the sea, the sea in the darkness calls;
> The little waves, with their soft, white hands,
> Efface the footprints in the sands,
> And the tide rises, the tide falls.
>
> ('The Tide Rises and the Tide Falls')

Here there is a much more skilfully managed tension between the anthropomorphic element in the image and the awareness of the destructive hostility of the sea, but the ultimate effect has none of the dramatic impact of the single explosive line from one of Melville's 'Pebbles': 'Healed of my hurt, I laud the inhuman Sea'. That the rest of Melville's quatrain hardly sustains this stoic economy does not invalidate the immediacy of its suggestion that the poet really has come to terms with the sea as a force outside and inimical to himself as a human being: this is where the pact with the sea has to begin.

W. H. Auden once remarked in a totally different context:

> One of the great differences between Europe in general and America is the attitude towards nature. To us over here, perhaps, nature is always, in a sense, the mother or the wife: something with which you enter into a semi-personal relation. In the United States, nature is something much more savage: it is much more like—shall we say?—St. George and the dragon. Nature is the dragon, against which St. George proves his manhood.

Auden's point is substantiated by Melville's emphasis on the 'inhuman' sea and by Bell's necessity to make a pact with it. Antagonism is the only relation possible between man and the sea, even more than between man and the rest of nature, because, at the simplest level, of the actively destructive power of the sea in sinking ships, drowning swimmers and eroding the coastline. The idea of shipwreck is as recurrent in American as in English poetry. 'The Wreck of the Hesperus', for instance, is simple narrative; Emily Dickinson's 'Glee! The great storm is over!', though almost as sentimental, deepens the tone by its concern with 'the scant salvation'; H. D. (1886–1961) in 'Sea Heroes'

celebrates man's unending fight against shipwreck; and for Allen Tate
(1899–) in 'The Death of Little Boys' it is a vital, though subordinate,
image. More recently Robert Bly (1926–) in 'The Man whom the Sea
Kept Awake' exclaims—and he might be speaking for many—

> Whatever I see
> Increases the dream of the destructions of the sea.

In the poetry of Stephen Crane (1871–1900) the theme acquires an
intensity from the personal experience related in his short story 'The
Open Boat', though Daniel G. Hoffman finds a debt to Emily Dickin-
son as well in 'Crane's best poem' of which this is the beginning:

> A man adrift on a slim spar
> A horizon smaller than the rim of a bottle,
> Tented waves rearing lashy dark points
> The near whine of froth in circles.
> > God is cold.
>
> The incessant raise and swing of the sea
> And growl after growl of crest
> The sinkings, green, seething, endless
> The upheaval half-completed.
> > God is cold.

The pictorially Imagist quality of those lines may be more persuasive
than the somewhat crudely stated refrain, and the attempt to relate the
cruelty of the sea to the divine purpose is accomplished with more
subtlety in Robert Lowell's 'The Quaker Graveyard in Nantucket'.
Crane's poem does, however, establish the inhumanity of the sea as
wrecker, just as these lines by Emerson (1803–82) present its erosive
power as something in which it takes an inhuman pride:

> I make your sculptured architecture vain,
> Vain beside mine. I drive my wedges home,
> And carve the coastwise mountain into caves.
> > ('Seashore')

Here the sea's inhumanity is stressed paradoxically by the human
power of speech with which it is invested: nearer our own day Robinson
Jeffers (1887–1962) achieves a similar effect in 'The Eye' by attributing
to the sea the power of sight which it uses in a non-human way. He
characterises the Atlantic as 'a stormy moat' and the Mediterranean as

having for more than five thousand years 'drunk sacrifice/Of ships and blood', but he distinguishes them from the more mysterious Pacific to which 'Our ships, planes, wars are perfectly irrelevant':

> Here from this mountain shore, headland beyond stormy headland
>   plunging like dolphins through the blue sea-smoke
> Into pale sea—look west at the hill of water: it is half the planet:
>   this dome, this half-globe, this bulging
> Eyeball of water, arched over to Asia,
> Australia and white Antarctica: those are the eyelids that never
>   close; this is the staring, unsleeping
> Eye of the earth; and what it watches is not our wars.

Realistic description modulates into surrealistic image to express the poet's awe at the mystery of this wholly alien element. Peculiarly important in Jeffers's poetry, the sea, and especially the Pacific, is a valuable means of representing that disdain for human nature that informs so much of it. Throughout his work

>   the deep dark-shining
> Pacific leans on the land
> Feeling his cold strength
> To the outmost margins.
>
>   ('Night')

This is the background, geographical and spiritual, to his long narrative poems like 'Tamar', 'Thurso's Landing' and 'Give Your Heart to the Hawks', all of them set on what he calls, in 'Apology for Bad Dreams', 'This coast crying out for tragedy like all beautiful places'. The elemental force of the sea beating on the beauty of the coast is matched by the elemental violence of the human passions unleashed in the physical beauty of his characters, especially the women like Tamar Cauldwell or Fayne Fraser. The sea plays an important role in the actual narrative of these poems: by reviving Lee Cauldwell after the fall that might have killed him, it sets in train the whole tragic sequence of events, just as it provides the occasion for Fayne and Michael, swimming together, to inflame Lance's jealousy and provoke its terrible consequences. Helen Thurso drags Hester into the sea with her in what is as much a ritual immersion in the destructive element as is Tamar's dance on the seashore while 'the sea moved, on the obscure bed of her eternity'. Tamar's bathing with her brother, which marks the beginning of their incestuous

relationship, takes place in an inland pool, but is linked with the sea in
Jeffers's question:

> Was it the wild coast
> Of her breeding, and the reckless wind
> In the beaten trees and the gaunt booming crashes
> Of breakers under the rocks, or rather the amplitude
> And wing-subduing immense earth-ending water
> That moves all the west taught her this freedom?

Just as in *Desire under the Elms* the gaunt isolation of the barren New
England farm makes more credible the burden of in-turned lust, hate
and guilt under which its occupants labour, so in these poems a similar
intensity of passion and violence is linked directly to the wildness of the
landscape and motivated by the sea. This is what, in the title of another
poem, Jeffers calls 'Haunted Country':

> There are happy places that fate skips; here is not one of them;
> The tides of the brute womb, the excess
> And weight of life spilled out like water, the last migration .
> Gathering against this holier valley-mouth
> That knows its fate beforehand, the flow of the womb, banked back
> By the older flood of the ocean, to swallow it.

The imagery of parturition here contrasts with the destructive force of
the sea to suggest this end-of-the-world vision which haunts Jeffers's
poetry and is here reinforced by the reference to 'the last migration'
which evokes at one and the same time the American historical experi-
ence and the insecurity of human tenure on the globe. He sees man as

> Walking with numbed and cut feet
> Along the last ridge of migration
> On the last coast above the not-to-be-colonized
> Ocean.   ('The Loving Shepherdess')

Jeffers's vision of a desolate and hostile universe can become oppressive
in its ultimate inhumanity, but the extent to which it convinces us
depends very largely upon this use of the sea. Nor is he the only poet
to be affected in this way by the Pacific.

*   *   *

Robert Frost (1875–1963) sees the Pacific as a living thing that

> thought of doing something to the shore
> That water never did to land before.
>   ('Once by the Pacific')

Characteristically he derives more satisfaction than Jeffers from the thought of the land-mass behind him:

> it looked as if
> The shore was lucky in being backed by cliff,
> The cliff in being backed by continent;

but, as sometimes happens with Frost, the ominousness is dissipated into sententiousness in the closing lines:

> There would be more than ocean-water broken
> Before God's last *Put out the Light* was spoken.

Jeffers has not Frost's gnarled and gnomic wisdom nor his poetic range, but in apocalyptic mood he can avoid the triteness that Frost's otherwise-successful homeliness can betray him into at times. Except for this poem and 'Neither Out Far nor In Deep' Frost does not fit readily into this category of sea-poetry—homeliness does not belong with 'the not-to-be-colonized ocean'—but this illustrates the limitations of the category more than of the poet. Frost's answer to those who turn to the sea for mystery and awe might be found in his lines:

> I have it in me so much nearer home
> To scare myself with my own desert places.
> ('Desert Places')

Whitman (1819–92) in the same situation as Jeffers and Frost had seen a different vision, managing almost completely to overlook the sea:

> Facing west from California's shores,
> Inquiring, tireless, seeking what is yet unfound,
> I, a child, very old, over waves, towards the house of maternity,
>   the land of migrations, look afar,
> Look off the shores of my Western sea, the circle almost circled.
> ('Facing West . . .')

In Whitman's contracting universe the Pacific holds no terrors, for it is but one stage in the progress he was later to celebrate in the poem of which this is an extract:[1]

> Passage to India!
> Struggles of many a captain, tales of many a sailor dead,
> Over my mood stealing and spreading they come,
> Like clouds and cloudlets in the unreach'd sky.

[1] Cf. discussion of this poem in Chapter II, pp. 66–7, above.

Along all history, down the slopes,
As a rivulet running, sinking now, and now again to the
                                        surface rising,
A ceaseless thought, a varied train—lo, soul, to thee,
                                        thy sight, they rise,
The plans, the voyages again, the expeditions;
Again Vasco da Gama sails forth,
Again the knowledge gain'd, the mariner's compass,
Lands found and nations born, thou born America,
For purpose vast, man's long probation fill'd,
Thou rondure of the world at last accomplish'd.

Behind the confident swell of the rhetoric building up to the assurance
of the final line is the idea of the sea as a bridge between nations, an idea
paralleled in Emerson's 'Seashore' where it is juxtaposed effectively with
the sea as destroyer:

> I with my hammer pounding evermore
> The rocky coast, smite Andes into dust,
> Strewing my bed, and, in another age,
> Rebuild a continent of better men.
> Then I unbar the doors: my paths lead out
> The exodus of nations: I disperse
> Men to all shores that front the hoary main.

Again the nineteenth century is as much in evidence in style and idiom
as it is in sentiment, but it is worth recalling that Emerson's English
contemporary Matthew Arnold puts his emphasis on 'the unplumb'd,
salt, estranging sea' rather than on its unifying powers, of which these
American transcendentalists are the more aware. It is consistent with
nineteenth-century America's faith in man's increasing power over
nature that Whitman should reserve for the climax of his stanza 'the
knowledge gain'd, the mariner's compass/Lands found and nations
born', and that, in other respects so warmly human in his sympathies,
he should brush aside as 'clouds and cloudlets in the unreach'd sky' the
'Struggles of many a captain, tales of many a sailor dead' (the pro-
nounced and more regular rhythm of the line almost invites substitu-
tion of a facile emotional response for anything deeper or more dis-
turbing).

  To turn straight from this to 'The Yachts' by William Carlos
Williams[2] (1883–1963) is to see the more characteristic complexities of

[2] Cf. Chapter VI, pp. 139–47, above.

the twentieth-century poem, its greater and more far-reaching range of reference, and its greater reliance on imagery and irony as modes of communication. 'A poem that is a paradigm of all the unjust beauty, the necessary and unnecessary injustice of the world', Randall Jarrell has succinctly called it, in his introduction to Williams's *Selected Poems* (p. xix), but the paradigm is apprehended sensorily through the pictorial reality of its evocation of the sea. Where the more recent poems so far discussed have focused attention on the mysteriousness, the ferocity and the inhumanity of the sea as an illimitable and substantially empty expanse, this opens deceptively with a circumscribed sea-surface full of ships and a dominant impression of colour, grace and beauty. The first five lines admittedly introduce the idea of

> an ungoverned ocean which when it chooses
> tortures the biggest hulls, the best man knows
> to pit against its beatings, and sinks them pitilessly.

This, however, is the open sea from which the yachts are described as being shielded by the partially enclosing land while they contend in their races. The yachts themselves are presented as things of beauty and movement, operating in an atmosphere of bright, hard light, but an idea of transience is associated with them by the epithet 'mothlike' and by the deliberate ambiguity of the stanza division falling between 'minute' and 'brilliance': are they, as they seem at first sight, 'scintillant in the minute' or 'in the minute/brilliance of cloudless days'? (and, in this case, is the word 'mínute' or 'minúte'?): the ambivalences seem deliberate and constructive. The yachts are man-made and man-tended: if they are 'mothlike', their crews are 'ant like' in their industry, and the yachts are 'solicitously groomed' in 'a well-guarded arena of open water' and surrounded by other vessels in a sycophantic role. Thus protected it is not surprising that

> they appear youthful, rare

> as the light of a happy eye, live with the grace
> of all that in the mind is feckless, free and
> naturally to be desired.

The principle of youth and spontaneity which the yachts embody is immediately threatened, however, by the sea which

> is moody, lapping their glossy sides, as if feeling
> for some slightest flaw but fails completely.

The race is postponed, but when a rising wind enables it to take place the sea renews the attack, again unsuccessfully, because 'they are too/ well made'. It is at this point that the poem takes an unexpected and sinister turn as the sea becomes 'a sea of faces about them in agony' and 'the skillful yachts pass over' the struggling 'entanglement of watery bodies' with a cruelty that constitutes an implicit criticism of their grace. The poem is distinguished, in its own right, by its emotive force and its beauty of structure, but it is particularly interesting in the present context. The sea, instead of being the destroyer, becomes the defeated, and, by an unusual sort of back-formation, the familiar metaphor of 'a sea of faces' or 'a sea of humanity' is given an alarming literalness of application. The human beings are ridden down heedlessly by the very yachts over which they themselves swarmed earlier, 'ant like, solicitously grooming them', so that Williams's statement 'the horror of the race dawns staggering the mind' alludes both to the yacht-race and to the human race, doomed to be ridden down by its own creations of youthful beauty and energy. This association of beauty and horror might suggest Poe, but it is more effective than his often is because, as in Jeffers, the natural reality of the sea is evoked with such vividness as part of our normal experience that the less usual aspects of the poet's presentation gain in credibility.

In a much later poem, however, 'The Sea Farer', Williams exchanges horror for tragic exultation by identifying man with the rocks on which the sea pounds, and by proceeding directly to the assertion

> He invites the storm, he
> lives by it!

Unlike 'The Yachts', which makes its point by a sensitive and skilful manipulation of words and images, 'The Sea Farer' is more characteristic of Williams in its greater reliance on a deceptively simple statement of an observed analogy. Man is seen as deriving from his condition not fear but an excitement and stimulus:

> so that the rocks
> seem rather to leap
> at the sea than the sea
> to envelope them. They strain
> forward to grasp ships
> or even the sky itself that
> bends down to be torn

> upon them. To which he says,
> It is I! I who am the rocks!
> Without me nothing laughs.

These rocks straining at the ships can be related to the hands grasping at the yachts: both are doomed to destruction, but in the ecstatic buoyancy of these closing lines of 'The Sea Farer' Williams makes a pact with the sea which, in its ultimate ability to incorporate laughter and the comic in its scheme of things, recalls a poem of Emily Dickinson's.

This may at first sight seem a nursery rhyme of mere inconsequential whimsicality:

> I started early, took my dog,
> And visited the sea;
> The mermaids in the basement
> Came out to look at me.

The characteristic self-consciousness which leads her to feel that she is under observation disappears as she stands on the shore and lets the tide rise round her until she is almost engulfed; then, when it is almost too late, she turns back, pursued by the sea until she re-establishes contact with humanity (the town):

> And bowing with a mighty look
> At me, the sea withdrew.

Being looked at once more is the price she has to pay for her retreat, but the experience seems to have justified it. Like Williams's rocks she invites the sea (though not actually leaping at it) and like Jeffers's women she derives a stimulation from immersion in and surrender to the destructive element. Her timely withdrawal before the immersion becomes total and her recall to the world of men might justify associating this poem with 'My life closed twice before its close' and the other poems in which she tries to visualise a premature experience of death. Nevertheless the acute self-awareness coupled with the grotesquely comic elements of the dog, the mermaids and the courtesy of the sea's final bow all link it with the deliberate juxtaposition in Williams's final lines:

> It is I! I who am the rocks!
> Without me nothing laughs.

It would limit too narrowly the poem's significance to say that the sea *is* experience, or the sea *is* death, but once more the emphasis is on the potentiality of the sea for annihilation.

*   *   *

There is an anonymous primitive American painting of about 1860 called 'Meditation by the Sea' in which a diminutive but determined figure stands, with arms crossed, on a rock-strewn shore surveying the on-rush of highly stylised breakers. In its faintly sinister artificiality it has something of the quality of Emily Dickinson's poem, and the situation, though not the figure, recalls Whitman in 'Out of the Cradle Endlessly Rocking'. 'On the sands of Paumanok's shore gray and rustling' he hears the sea whispering to him 'the low and delicious word death':

> edging near as privately for me rustling at my feet,
> Creeping thence steadily up to my ears and laving me softly all over,
> Death, death, death, death, death.

Like Emily Dickinson's, the immersion is not total, and the sound of the sea merges with the song of the bird to awaken 'from that hour' the poet's own songs. 'Sea-Drift', the group of poems which 'Out of the Cradle' begins, may be said to fulfil Whitman's promise 'I am large, I contain multitudes' by the way in which it adumbrates many of the sea-themes that develop in later poetry. 'As I Ebb'd with the Ocean of Life' contrasts the tide of mortality with the immortality of the tides and declares 'You oceans both, I close with you'; the sea is associated with eternity, with mystery, and, most importantly, with the creative process. 'Tears' and 'On the Beach at Night Alone' are elegiac and bring, in Arnold's phrase, 'the eternal note of sadness in'. 'After the Sea-ship' seems in some ways to be moving towards 'The Yachts'. 'Song for All Seas, All Ships', with its insistence on heroism and on the 'sea that prickest and cullest the race in time, and unitest nations', looks forward to Allen Tate's 'The Mediterranean' where the sea becomes an eloquent symbol for the cultural heritage of the ancient world and its links with the American South. 'Patroling Barnegat' anticipates Jeffers's storm-seascapes, and in pictorial atmosphere suggests both the realism of Winslow Homer's paintings and the mystery of Albert Pinkham Ryder's. The most original in some respects is 'The World Below the Brine', for this attempts yet another and a different pact with the sea.

This title may suggest Poe's 'The City in the Sea', but there the resemblance ends. Poe romantically extends the obsession with death by water from the drowned mariner to the drowned city; his image of 'that wilderness of glass' where

> light from out the lurid sea
> Streams up the turrets silently

accentuates the impenetrability of the element that separates the watcher from death's dream kingdom. A similar idea finds more recent expression in 'The Open Sea' by William Meredith (1919–   ), though this time in a characteristically anti-romantic idiom:

> Oh, there are people, all right, settled in the sea;
> It is as populous as Maine today,
> But no one who will give you the time of day.

Poe's city is de-populated and he is thinking less literally of the drowned, but for both poets the shutting-off effect of the sea emphasises their own isolation. As Meredith puts it:

> We say the sea is lonely; better say
> Ourselves are lonesome creatures whom the sea
> Gives neither yes nor no for company.

Whitman's poem offers, instead of an uneasy pact by rejection, a more evolutionary relationship between man and the teeming world below the brine. A catalogue of dense and exotic undersea vegetation and of fish whose life, for all its remoteness, resembles ours in its violence and passion, gives rise to reflection on the superiority of our own existence and to brief speculation on 'The change onward from ours to that of beings who walk other spheres'. In his own century Whitman was not the only poet to be fascinated by thought of marine life. Melville (1819–91), for example, in 'The Maldive Shark', had painted a vivid picture of this 'Pale ravener of horrible meat' with his attendant shoals of 'sleek little pilot-fish', but Melville's epithets establish the shark as not merely sub-human but revoltingly anti-human.

The twentieth-century poet enjoys no such confidence in man's superiority over the creatures of the deep. W. S. Merwin's 'Leviathan', for example, has an obvious kinship with Moby Dick but none with 'The Maldive Shark' nor with Whitman's comforting chain of being. A massive grandeur of language and imagery is deployed to evoke memories of Genesis and a universe emerging from chaos. The whale floating like 'a lost angel/On the waste's unease, no eye of man moving'

brings to mind a disturbing vision of vastness and pre-lapsarian potenti-
ality which to the modern reader can be only tragic in its implications.
Merwin (1927–) is no more concerned than Melville in 'The Maldive
Shark' to draw moral analogies, but each poem belongs unmistakably
to its age. Merwin's closing lines, for instance, would have had a much
less ambiguous connotation for Melville's readers (though not, perhaps,
for Melville himself):

> The sea curling,
> Star-climbed, wind-combed, cumbered with itself still
> As at first it was, is the hand not yet contented
> Of the Creator. And he waits for the world to begin.

This whale is a very different one from that in 'The Quaker Graveyard
in Nantucket' (a poem which I have left out of account only because
its author forms the subject of a separate chapter in this volume),
but Lowell's poem is much closer to Christian doctrine than is Merwin's.[3]

The irony that I find inherent in 'Leviathan' emerges more clearly in
two pieces by Daniel G. Hoffman (1923–), where a more whimsical
fancy is used, as Emily Dickinson would have used it, for serious
purposes. 'The Seals in Penobscot Bay'

> hadn't heard of the atom bomb,
> so I shouted a warning to them.

The warning is unheeded and un-needed by the animals who are
obviously as much in their element as modern man is out of his. The
point is made, not didactically or moralistically, but by the vitality of
description which presents, with a witty exactness and as part of a
natural order, the physical appearance and behaviour of the seals. 'An
Armada of Thirty Whales' deploys a similar wit in a manner even more
baroque; it is a simple parable of sea-creatures who, dissatisfied with the
sea,

> nudge the beach with their noses
> eager for hedgerows and roses.

The moral is simple and foreseeable:

> But they who won't swim and can't stand
>
> lie mired in mud and in sand,
> And the sea and the wind and the worms
>
> will contest the last will of the Sperms.

[3] See above, Chapter III, pp. 78–9.

Poetry, as Robert Frost remarked, begins in delight and ends in wisdom: the delight of this poem lies in the humanising of 'these pilgrims' with 'dandiacal graces' and 'finfitted knees', but the wisdom begins at the same point in the suggestion that human beings are just as likely to be defeated by nature if they get out of their element. In this way Hoffman induces a sympathy with the whales, who are no more grotesque than we, but it is a sympathy wholly different from the attitudes in the Whitman and Melville poems which prompted this comparison.

Similarly Howard Nemerov (1920–) in 'I Only Am Escaped Alone to Tell Thee' is led from the mention of corsets to the realisation

> But all that whalebone came from whales,
> And all the whales lived in the sea,
> In calm beneath the troubled glass,
> Until the needle drew their blood.

The glass here, unlike Poe's, is troubled and, again unlike Poe's, affords to the world below it no immunity from the depredations of man. In another poem, 'The Lives of Gulls and Children', Nemerov describes children coming upon a dying gull on a deserted sea-coast:

> They would have reached out hands to him
> To comfort him in that human kind
> They just were learning—how anything alive,
> They thought, hated loneliness most.

The bird, of course, rejects them and they recognise this difference between humankind and 'the Atlantic kind he was'—a difference which does not prevent their 'Bearing the lonely pride of those who die', just as, in the other poem, Nemerov is aware of the imagined whales' 'black flukes of agony' and, in 'The Salt Garden', sees a gull as an 'image of the wild/Wave where it beats the air' bringing him a message, 'brutal, mysterious', of mortality. Whether it is the sea itself or the creatures of the sea, loneliness and mortality are the poet's inevitable associations. Richard Eberhart (1904–), in 'Seals, Terns, Time', makes the identification in his opening lines:

> The seals at play off Western Isle
> In the loose flowing of the summer tide
> And burden of our strange estate.

Their mortality is akin to ours, and if the poet seems to have become in recent years more sympathetic to what Eberhart invokes as 'blurred kind forms/That rise and peer from elemental water', it is because he has less to fear from the forces of nature and, like the sea-creatures, more to fear from human nature. When Santiago, in Hemingway's *The Old Man and the Sea*, talks to his fish on terms of equality and respect it is out of the same sense of identification as these poets feel. Elizabeth Bishop (1911–), a few years earlier, in 'The Fish', had described how she had

> caught a tremendous fish
> and held him beside the boat
> half out of water.

Studying him, she admires him as a living organism, visualising his internal as well as his external structure, and then notices 'five big hooks/grown firmly in his mouth':

> Like medals with their ribbons
> frayed and wavering
> a five-haired beard of wisdom
> trailing from his aching jaw.

The human imagery here anticipates the poet's conclusion: she describes a suffusion of victory without clarifying whether it is hers or the fish's, and then lets the fish go.

*   *   *

The poet today finds it less easy and less profitable than did his forbears to dwell on his solitary communion with nature, or to hymn the fierce beauty of the natural scene unencumbered by man. The sea may be no less inhuman than Melville found it, but the pact that the modern poet makes with it involves him in humanising its denizens. The seals in Penobscot Bay may be less aware of the atom bomb than the poet but they are hardly less vulnerable to it than he, and the bond between them is accentuated by another shared vulnerability. Santiago's great fish was eaten by sharks, and in the enduring human fear and hatred of the shark there may be an unconscious acceptance of the truth of Albany's lines in *King Lear*:

> It will come,
> Humanity must perforce prey on itself,
> Like monsters of the deep

Denise Levertov (1923–) in 'The Sharks' expressed, a few years ago, a Melvillean horror of these predators in a non-Melvillean idiom of conversational understatement:

> Well, then, the last day the sharks appeared.
> Dark fins appear, innocent
> as if in fair warning. The sea becomes
> sinister, are they everywhere?
> I tell you, they break six feet of water.
> Isn't it the same sea, and won't we
> play in it any more?

The childlike note in that final question introduces the theme of innocence, central to so much American literature but not so far impinging directly upon this study. The sharks appear just as the speaker has, for the first time, 'dared to swim out of my depth': the evil is recognised but not assimilated, and just as the setting is between sundown and moonrise, so perception is caught between innocence and experience and rendered with remarkable tact and delicacy. An awareness of the sea's beauty offsets the recognition of its treachery, but under the muted tones the sense of incipient horror is unmistakable as the poem continues. Once again the poet is making a pact with the sea in his own right and on his own terms, indifferent to the pack of other poets. One answer to her question, 'Isn't it the same sea?', would be that it certainly is the same as Melville's Maldive Sea, the same sea as all the other poets have experienced, but that it is seen this time in a way peculiar to Denise Levertov.

The point may be conveniently made by recalling the figure of the girl on the sea-shore implicit in this poem and explicit in many others. This figure may be the poet herself or by symbolic action such as dancing or singing may be capable of identification with the poet as creative artist:

> And when she sang, the sea,
> Whatever self it had, became the self
> That was her song, for she was the maker.

These lines are, of course, from Wallace Stevens's poem 'The Idea of Order in Key West', as is the title of this chapter. The poem begins as a critical essay in which Stevens (1879–1955) explores the relationship between the artist and his subject.[4] The opening stanza insists on their

---

[4] Cf. Chapter VII above, *passim*.

separateness: the sea cannot be identified with the human being. It may be conceived of as uttering a constant cry but it is a cry

> That was not ours although we understood,
> Inhuman, of the veritable ocean.

The second stanza in some respects epitomises much that this essay has tried to say:

> The sea was not a mask. No more was she.
> The song and water were not medleyed sound,
> Even if what she sang was what she heard,
> Since what she sang she uttered word by word.
> It may be that in all her phrases stirred
> The grinding water and the gasping wind;
> But it was she and not the sea we heard.

Literature, obliged by its nature to adopt a linear motion (proceeding 'word by word') cannot reproduce the simultaneity of our apprehension of and response to the sea in actuality, nor should it wish to. Its strength lies rather in its power for order, its ability, by what Coleridge called the shaping spirit of imagination, to make us understand more fully the significance that the sea has for us. The point is a familiar one, but it is made in a memorable way in this poem because of the perfect harmony between meditative toughness (as in the stanza quoted) and beauty of rhetoric as in the closing lines:

> Oh! Blessed rage for order, pale Ramon,
> The maker's rage to order words of the sea,
> Words of the fragrant portals, dimly-starred,
> And of ourselves and of our origins,
> In ghostlier demarcations, keener sounds.

When the woman's song is ended the poet and his companion turn back towards the town, for their position has been the one characteristically adopted by the American poet: looking out across the 'not-to-be-colonized ocean' but with the town in his view as soon as he turns round again. Only then do they perceive that, as Frank Kermode has said, 'its lights, human artifacts, have imposed an order on the night, "Mastered the night and portioned out the sea" '. Night and the sea, the themes which Matthiessen saw as stimulating Longfellow's best work, are brought to order by the creative imagination. In saying that

Longfellow makes no pact with the sea because he is master of it I meant that he imposes an artificial order upon it by confining its role in his poems to an analogical one. Stevens and his singer make no pact with it either, but their mastery of it lies in their imaginative apprehension of its natural order, which they then shape in their art. Stevens's epithets for the sea in this poem bear this out in the almost exemplary way in which, unobtrusively in their context, they bring together all the attributes which the other poets already discussed have associated with the sea: 'inhuman', 'the grinding water', 'ever-hooded, tragic gestured', 'the dark voice', 'the sunken coral, water-walled', 'meaningless plungings', 'bronze shadows heaped on high horizons', 'dimly-starred'. In this poem, says Kermode, 'the sea is reality'; it is also, however, the tragic beauty of reality, and this concept is embodied here with a Romantic richness that only one other American poet has achieved since Whitman, and that is Hart Crane.

*   *   *

Crane and the sea ought to be the topic of a wholly separate essay, and I shall say nothing of the unifying role of sea imagery in *The Bridge* except to remark that Crane's sea is directly linked to the seas of Melville, Whitman and Poe; the symbolic significance of Atlantis in that poem also deserves fuller examination. Ambitious and powerful as *The Bridge* is, Allen Tate is right when he sees it as 'a failure in the sense that "Hyperion" is a failure, and with comparable magnificence' (*The Man of Letters*, p. 237). He is right, too, in seeing Crane's genius as essentially lyrical and Crane's writing at its most distinguished 'when he writes from sensation'. What the sea meant to Crane is shown most clearly in the 1926 collection, *White Buildings*, in poems such as 'At Melville's Tomb' or the six magnificent lyrics of the 'Voyages' series. 'Voyages I' is the most straightforward: the sight of children playing on the beach arouses the poet's desire to warn them, rather as Hoffman wants to warn the seals. Could they hear him, the poet would tell them not to trust the

> Spry cordage of your bodies to caresses
> Too lichen-faithful from too wide a breast.
> The bottom of the sea is cruel.

In the tacit recognition of the futility of such a warning, as well as in the deliberately anti-romantic use of the word 'kids' and in the whole emotional pattern of the poem, Crane anticipates the similarly protective instinct of Holden Caulfield, in *The Catcher in the Rye*. If this is a fairly simple presentation of the sea as destructive influence, 'Voyages II' is considerably more complex. Yvor Winters finds it 'one of the most powerful and one of the most nearly perfect poems of the past two hundred years'. Certainly it is the high water mark of Crane's lyrical achievement. Almost the whole of Jeffers's 'The Eye' is epitomised in the opening reference to the sea as 'this great wink of eternity', and from this promising start Crane goes on to 'write from sensation' a poem that resists intellectual analysis but achieves a superb cumulative effect. Each of the first two stanzas comprises four lines of sea-description followed by a fifth line in which love is contrasted with it. The reliance on and evocation of sensory perception is exemplified by the opening of the second stanza:

> Take this Sea, whose diapason knells
> On scrolls of silver snowy sentences.

The sound of the sea is associated with its capacity for destruction, and with the arts of music and literature; and perhaps the conjunction of 'scrolls', 'silver' and 'snowy' may suggest the visual impression of foam-capped waves. The sea is capable of rending 'all but the pieties of lovers' hands', but the sea has been personified as a woman in such a way as to leave open the possibility that the poet's love for the sea is meant; the third and fourth stanzas sustain this impression, both by the continued personification of the sea and by the lyrical emphasis on its physical beauty. Throughout the poem the eternity of the sea is contrasted with human mortality, especially in the fourth stanza:

> Mark how her turning shoulders wind the hours,
> And hasten while her penniless rich palms
> Pass superscription of bent foam and wave,—
> Hasten, while they are true,—sleep, death, desire,
> Close round one instant in one floating flower.

The image of currency is important here: it begins in the oxymoron of 'penniless rich', is sustained in the verb 'pass', and is limited in 'superscription'. The use of this word parallels *Matthew* 22 where Christ uses the superscription on the penny as proof of the legal validity of the currency. In this stanza the sea is passing some of its riches to us, though, since its palms are penniless, this is clearly nothing of a material nature.

Nevertheless it is valid, not counterfeit, but its validity is determined by something as fleeting as the 'bent foam and wave'. It is this very transitoriness of emotion that guarantees the validity of the experience, and we are urged to accept it before it is too late. Time is marked by the turning shoulders of the sea, and only its beauty and the awe it inspires can persuade us to acceptance of our role in time and of our own mortality. The invocatory final stanza is a superb resolution of the theme; the sea has become a liberating agent and the familiar image of man as a voyager on the sea of life is invested with a new intensity and force:

> Bind us in time, O Seasons clear, and awe.
> O minstrel galleons of Carib fire,
> Bequeath us to no earthly shore until
> Is answered in the vortex of our grave
> The sea's wide spindrift gaze toward paradise.

With this sea no pact is needed, for hostility has given way to love, and though the theme is Whitmanesque in its reconciliatory universality the imaginative power of its statement links Crane also with Romanticism in its richest flowering. Through the transcendent powers of art and love, Crane manages to bring together the motifs his predecessors employed so variously; for the sea that was finally to give him his own death first endowed him with his richest imagery of eternity and human experience, of solitude and the creative imagination, of the paths that unite and destroy men.

What Stevens calls 'the maker's rage to order words of the sea' has been experienced by Romantic poets on both sides of the Atlantic, and like Stevens, though by a different process, Crane identifies the sea with the creative principle. The sixth 'Voyage' connects 'Creation's blithe and petalled word' with Venus rising from the sea, but in another early poem, 'The Bathers' (which he excluded from *White Buildings*), Crane had attached his own significance to the Venus myth:

> They say that Venus shot through foam to light,
> But they are wrong . . . Ere man was given sight
> She came in such still water, and so nursed
> In Silence, beauty blessed and beauty cursed.

Beauty, like the sea, is ambivalent, and the gift of creativity is also both a blessing and a curse, as the haunted genius of Hart Crane knew all too well. In Section I of *The Bridge* Columbus, between land and sky, exclaims:

> For here between two worlds, another, harsh,
> This third, of water, tests the word.

He might be speaking for all the American poets discussed here and for all the others unmentioned who have found in the sea the test of their creative power. In the final stanza of 'Voyages VI' Crane inherits Whitman's confidence in the victory of 'Word over all':

> The imaged Word, it is, that holds
> Hushed willows anchored in its glow.
> It is the unbetrayable reply
> Whose accent no farewell can know.

Note

Anthologies. Besides those anthologies listed in the Preface to this volume the following are useful for reading poets of today: *American Poems: a Contemporary Collection*, ed. Jascha Kessler (1964); *The Criterion Book of Modern American Verse*, ed. W. H. Auden (1956); *Forty Poems Touching on Recent American History*, ed. Robert Bly (1964); *Modern Poetry*, eds. Maynard Mack, Leonard Dean and William Frost (Second ed., 1961); *The Modern Poets: an American-British Anthology*, eds. John M. Brinnin and Bill Read (1963); *New Poems by American Poets 2*, ed. Rolfe Humphries (1958); *Poems of Doubt and Belief: an Anthology of Modern Religious Poetry*, eds. Tom F. Driver and Robert Pack (1964); *Twentieth Century American Poetry*, ed. Conrad Aiken (revised ed., 1963).

The poems quoted in the following chapter by Kenneth Koch, Leroi Jones, John Wieners, Ray Bremser and Charles Olson can all be read in *The New American Poetry 1945–1960*, ed. Donald M. Allen (1960); those by Karl Shapiro and John Berryman in *Poetry* (December, 1963); by Theodore Roethke in *The Modern Poets* (1963); by Richard Wilbur in *The New Yorker* (4 April, 1964); and by R. H. W. Dillard and Harriet Hodges in *New Writing, 1963*; William Meredith's poem is in his *The Open Sea*.

Criticism. A representative selection of critical studies would include: Glauco Cambon, *Recent American Poetry* (1962) and *The Inclusive Flame: Studies in American Poetry* (1963); Babette Deutsch, *Poetry in Our Time* (revised ed., 1963); Howard Nemerov, *Poetry & Fiction* (1963); *A Casebook on the Beat*, ed. Thomas Parkinson (1961); Harold Rosenberg, *The Tradition of the New* (1961); Macha Louis Rosenthal, *The Modern Poets* (1960).

X

Against the Grain
Poets writing today

GEORGE GARRETT

★

It isn't news to anyone that we live in a bad time. A bad world getting worse, and with typical modern pride we revel in it. Poets are no exception, and one of the worst things about the poetic scene, quite aside from the immemorial problem of writing a few lines of verse tolerably well, is that everybody knows it is a bad time. Everybody is so *aware*. Everybody *talks about* it. You can't turn around without bumping smack into a poet or critic, all dolled up in tailor-made sackcloth, lightly dusted with ashes, wringing his hands in public, and, with a voice like Jonah's when he tried the belly of the whale for size, bemoaning the present and foretelling doom to come. There is the story of the Distinguished American Poet who, shortly after his publicised conversion to Catholicism, was granted an audience with the Pope. The Poet announced: 'I should like to discuss with you the deplorable state of Catholic letters in America.' To which the Pontiff with tact and wisdom replied: 'Tell me, how many children do you have?'

Just for the record, I have three children. One of them, aged six, is an excellent poet. And for the record I ought to know better than to add my voice to the cacophony of claims and counter claims, poetic prayer wheels spinning round and louder and louder (*who gets the grease?*—), a roost of chicken-littles announcing that the sky is going to fall on American poetry. I do not happen to believe that.

Still, it is always much easier to talk about poetry than to write poems. And there are a few things that ought to be said.

I. OFFICIAL CLASS HISTORY

These days new literary generations appear, announce themselves, are evaluated, question that evaluation, then by inevitable compromise find a niche, and vanish with a frequency which would baffle even the most subtle demographer. Once upon a time wars, migrations, catastrophes and other great changes served as convenient boundary lines and watersheds. But something has happened in the last twenty years, since the second world war really, which makes possible the official coexistence of more than one generation at a time. One thinks of the so-called academics, those whom Donald Hall once named 'the silent generation', people who reached the age of consent and legal responsibility about the time of the Korean War; and one thinks also of the 'beat generation', the so-called *avant-garde* whose ranks include as many middle-aged men (the Archie Moores of poetry?) coming of age, as they do teenagers flaunting their rebellion with a first set of whiskers. Of course neither of these, nor any number of others which have erupted like skin rashes in the little magazines and literary press, is a real generation in either a literal or literary sense. In fact the whole concept of a *generation* is an arbitrary and abstract notion, pretending to be sundered from the weight and force of the weighty and omnipresent past, believing blindly that the future can be shaped. Nevertheless, let's pretend.

First, though, a brief sketch of the social context. Social history is admittedly a brutal process of over-simplification, frequently an elaboration of the obvious, and mostly a bore. Call this a final warning, a reader's point of no return.

Change is probably the only constant in human history, but after the second world war change was acute, radical and everywhere evident. When a whole society groans and changes, the poets reflect these changes and groans whether they want to or not. Among other things which happened right after the war, the universities discovered contemporary literature. Before that few of the American institutions of higher learning troubled themselves with twentieth-century literature. Quite suddenly and for many irrelevant reasons they had to. The effects are more interesting: (*a*) the creation of the academic specialist in modern writing; (*b*) the wedding of many writers, and especially the hand-to-mouth, ne'er-do-well country cousins, the poets, to the routine of the academic life, as teachers, lecturers, writers-in-residence, etc.; (c) the booming business for war babies in the publishing of anthologies, critical and even scholarly studies of recent writing; (d) not least important, the exposure of the young student to the *official* history of modern literature within the confines of a formal discipline. All this has been going on long enough to be called a habit.

The secondary effects are fairly obvious. The necessary simplification of the immediate past, sometimes close enough to be breathing down the neck of whatever the present is, has created the arbitrary division of 'the decade'. And, as might be expected, a retroactive, *ex post facto* re-classification, cheerfully imposed upon innocent and earlier decades, has tended to revise them all to fit our view of where it was all going. The living shoot dice with the bones of the dead, never dreaming somebody will roll snake eyes with their bones. And we have never really escaped the convenient delusion of the late nineteenth century, that evolution could and should be applied to everything. We may find it a little difficult, viewing the raw wounds and scars of this century, to believe that man is improving. But somehow we can never quite send to earth once and for all the foxy belief, which is always supported by the shabby evidence of technological progress, that intellectually and artistically things are moving along and forward chronologically. Thus, building on the ground and foundation of others, the practising poets are making a happy subdivision of somewhat shaky ivory towers. With all the modern conveniences, of course.

Whether he is fashionable or unfashionable, in or out of court, Eliot in his essays has been enormously influential in American poetry. Like him or not, he's there like the Blueridge Mountains of Virginia. Eliot's view of literary history is at barebones essentially progressive. In spite of the celebrated 'dissociation of sensibility' he noticed and then proceeded to correct. In spite of his veneration for the Middle Ages. He wrote so much about the weight of the past that we just naturally assumed his essays as part of our burden.

Side by side with the re-classification of the past has been the creation of a new pantheon—a kind of poetic hall of fame—wherein the busts of our century's masters could be displayed. Of course, these keep changing, but without much harm done. I remember an Arab sculptor I met in Rome whose job it was to make heroic statues of the leaders of the Middle East. 'You'll notice that they are all very much alike and that I am, shall we say, a little careless of *detail*', he said. Then he shrugged with the weight of centuries of wisdom and indifference. A magnificent Arab shrug. 'When the revolution comes, the statues always go first', he added, 'Well, it's a living.' Yes, I intend to imply that the poetic scene *is* a little like the Middle East. Americans, and especially the new 'generations' which grew up in the movies, dearly love the star system. Lacking royalty and nobility, some say, they settle for the fun of celebrity. Poetry has its Stars. Right after the war, the trinity was Eliot, Pound and Yeats. Only Pound remains safely. Elbowing their way into the inner sanctum are Frost, Williams, Stevens. Each has his cohort of cheerleaders.

One more consideration. After Eliot's essays, the most influential critical documents immediately following the war were the manifestos of the Fugitives: Ransom, Tate, and later, by lineal descent, Warren, Jarrell, and now James Dickey. Behind them, and this has never been fully understood, was a whole tradition of Southern poetics. The Southern tradition, in brief, makes a firm distinction between poetry and prose, insists that poetry should be in verse, musical, 'poetic', and in some sense 'universal'. And it is hierarchical, with poetry at the top of the literary heap. Add to this a whiff of grapeshot from the Eliot essays and some interest in irony and John Donne and you end up with something called The New Criticism.

The young poets who came back from the war, those who came back, were bonetired, shaken, glad to be alive and anxious to reclaim their lives, beginning at the beginning, with the small things, which, like a soldier's pair of dry socks or pack of cigarettes, are everything. Having endured much, they took life itself as a gift and a blessing. They didn't, at first anyway, want any more trouble. And they wanted to keep their sanity if possible; for it had been sorely tested. Generally speaking, these poets, in part reacting to the formless 'thirties, in part containing *themselves*, chose form, thus were influenced by our native formalists, the new critics, and by our great Native Formalist, Robert Frost.

To make a long story short, some among these soon became the Establishment in the small world of poetry. Since most of them were teachers, they had pupils. The pupils may be divided into good pupils and bad pupils; that is, those who followed and those who rejected.

All this adds up to a kind of sophistication, if sophistication means polish, a knowledge and awareness of the rules of the road and the game, and at least enough elementary self-transcendence for the player to see himself as player of the game. John Foster Dulles always used to call for a time of 'agonizing reappraisal' whenever, as they frequently did, events took a turn for the worse or the unexpected. The world of poets has learned to ape this attitude. Were not the comparison invidious to most of the poets, we might fairly call our most recent generation 'The Dulles Generation'.

Here, briefly, are a few other ways in which our poets reflect the current social scene. Believe it or not and like it or not.

(1) *The General Motors Aesthetic*

Persistence of the 'romantic' ideal of the poet as unacknowledged priest-prophet-legislator has put a premium on novelty, on 'originality'. Result? The poet is supposed to *show* that he is changing, growing, improving, maturing. Sometimes a genuine demonstration. More often this means merely the grafting of tailfins, chrome and new accessories on a basically unchanging model. I quote from the jacket of James Wright's *The Branch Will Not Break* (1963): ' "Whatever I write from now on will be entirely different", said James Wright after the publication of *Saint Judas*. "I don't know what it will be, but I am finished with what I was doing in that book." ' Second result? The poet as salesman, huckster. Leading to:

(2) *Madison Avenue Madness*

Some patient cynic ought to write a definitive study of the art of the bookjacket blurb in our time. Poets, *in character*, each seeing and praising himself in another's work. Here is a brief sample from the back of Stanley Kunitz's *Selected Poems 1928–1958*, which won the Pulitzer Prize for 1959:

(*a*) Wilbur writes: 'Kunitz has every technical virtue. What's more he can put his perfected and rather lapidary style at the service of the most fundamental themes and passions.'

(*b*) Lowell writes: 'I admire Mr. Kunitz's savage, symbolic drive.'

(*c*) Roethke writes: 'Mr. Stanley Kunitz has a bold dramatic imagination that can wrest meanings from bleak and difficult material, turn even the language of science to the lyrical purpose with speed and style.'

(*This way to the Egress!*)

Also to be noted. Use of reviews, critical essays and articles, etc., for self-advancement, for the consolidation of the Establishment. Compare with current methods for advertising dogfood, toothpaste, detergents. Use of press *media*. Compare with well-known practices of public relations specialists, gossip columnists, etc.

(3) *The Success Syndrome*

For example, the way in which simple acknowledgement that the poems in a particular volume have appeared previously, in one state or another, in magazines. How this can become a *selling point*. E.g. from the bookjacket of the latest volume by James Dickey, *Helmets* (1964). Very stylish, yet straight to the point: 'Of the poems brought together in this volume, the great majority have previously been printed in periodicals: *Poetry*, *Virginia Quarterly Review*, *Yale Review*, *Sewanee Review*, *Hudson Review*, *Paris Review*, and especially *The New Yorker*, in which not less than fifteen of them first appeared.'

(*A record as long as your arm!*)

Similarly fellowships and grants become the modern poet's campaign ribbons. E.g. from the jacket of *The Branch Will Not Break*: 'His numerous honors include a Fulbright fellowship, a Kenyon Review fellowship, a grant for creative work from the National Institute of Arts and Letters, and many other prizes and awards for individual poems and books.'

(Take *that*, all ye who used to proudly emblazon on your bookjackets: 'Mr. X. . . . has earned his bread as a pearl diver, a rodeo cowboy, a nuclear physicist and a professional agitator for underdog causes.')

(4) *The Status Seekers*

Another thing that has happened is that, even though the number of magazines where the poet can see his words in print has dwindled, the number of possible book publishers has increased. Chiefly responsible for this change have been the university presses. Once Yale stood alone, and that was a contest for *first* books of poems. Now other university presses are involved, including Wesleyan, Ohio State, Minnesota, Indiana, North Carolina, Cornell, Texas, Chicago, Michigan, Virginia and a good many others. According to *Esquire* (July, 1963) Wesleyan is the top prestige house among these. And evidently prestige is self-perpetuating for in 1964 three out of the four books published by

Wesleyan were repeats, new books by authors who had already appeared under that imprint. 'Such', writes Willard Lockwood, Director of the Wesleyan Press, 'is the price of success.'

It doesn't take Sherlock Holmes to deduce that the overall situation is good for established poets, poor for new ones. Mike Hammer could figure it out.

So much for theory.

II. SITZKRIEG; OR THE PHONEY WAR

Everybody even mildly interested in recent American poetry knows that there is a big war going on, a real fight between what are called 'the academics' and 'the beats'. In case we forget, the poets remind us in reviews and articles and often in verse.

Here is the conservative case stated by William Meredith in 'To a Western Bard still a Whoop and a Holler away from English Poetry':

> I read an impatient man
> Who howls against his time,
> Not angry enough to scan
> Not fond enough to rhyme,
>
> And I think of the terrible cry
> The brave priest Hopkins raised
> The night he raided the sky
> And English verse was praised.
>
> . . . . . .
>
> It is common enough to grieve
> And praise is all around;
> If any cry means to live
> It must be uncommon sound.
>
> Cupped with the hands of skill
> How loud their voices ring,
> Containing passion still,
> Who cared enough to sing.

Here is a part of the case for the opposition, emphatically stated by Kenneth Koch in his long poem 'Fresh Air':

> Where are young poets in America, they are trembling
>   in publishing houses and universities,

Above all they are trembling in universities, they
    are bathing the library steps with their spit,
They are gargling out innocuous (to whom?) poems about
    maple trees and their children,
Sometimes they brave a subject like the Villa d'Este
    or a lighthouse in Rhode Island,
Oh what worms they are! they wish to perfect their form.

It would seem, on the basis of the briefs, that the battle was one of
form in the eyes of the conservatives and one of engagement, involve-
ment in life, in the view of the radicals. However, both arguments are
at least in part specious and designed for public consumption, a little
like certain windy speeches in the Senate. The radicals have devoted
reams of paper, splashed gallons of ink in discussing form, their form
to be sure, but form nonetheless. Meanwhile the claim that the con-
servatives were too academic is vitiated by the fact that almost all of the
radicals are highly educated men. The grand pooh-bah of the lodge,
the big daddy, is Charles Olson, who attended the best private schools
and colleges, has spent most of his adult career as a scholar-professor
and as an official at various colleges; and he writes a complex, allusive,
learned poetry, replete with classical allusion and quotation.[1] They, as
much as their enemies, write poems about statues, museums, painters
and old myths. Gregory Corso, widely advertised as a sort of primitive,
a self-taught 'natural' poet (who spent some time hanging around
Harvard), refers quite matter of factly to the following in his brief
poem 'Botticelli's "Spring" ': Lorenzo, Ariosto, Michelangelo, Dante,
Leonardo, Raffaello, Aretino. He has written poems to 'Uccello', to
'D. Scarlatti'. The fifteen-line poem 'Paris' takes time to celebrate
Baudelaire, Artaud, Rimbaud, Apollinaire, Hugo and Zola.

In short, reader, the suit of academic vs. non-academic is at worst
utterly bogus, pure old P. T. Barnum phonus-balonus. At best it is a
kind of in-fighting. Dogs growling over the same bone. Brothers and
sisters arguing over a last will and testament.

Nevertheless, phoney or not, this little cold war has been going on for
quite a while and it behoves us to remove the neat bow ribbon, to cut
aside the tissue paper and find out what, if any, are the real differences
between these two groups.

The main battleground has been in the anthologies, especially those
published in paperback and designed to capture the expanding, omni-

---

[1] Cf. discussion of Olson in Chapter VIII, pp. 190-1, above.

vorous, already captive college market. One of the most important of these is *The New Poets of England and America* (1957), edited by a triumvirate from the ranks of the Establishment: Donald Hall, Robert Pack, Louis Simpson. This first *New Poets* selection was something of a *cause célèbre*. It was praised and blamed and often attacked in the periodicals. There was, indeed, a kind of uniformity about the poems in the book, though it resulted more from the editorial choices than from the poets themselves, who being mostly good poets and true, are far more various in matter and manner than they appear here.

This anthology was, in effect, answered by Donald M. Allen's *The New American Poetry 1945–1960*, a huge book (454 pp.), with large and representative selections of an entirely different set of poets, freighted with indices, biographical information, bibliographical lists and critical statements. Truly academic, Mr. Allen divided these poets of the *avant-garde* into five distinct groups: the Black Mountain group, the San Francisco Renaissance, the Beat Generation, the New York Poets and a catch all group which 'has no geographical definition' and 'includes younger poets who have been associated with and in some cases influenced by the leading writers of the preceding groups, but who have evolved their own original styles and new conceptions of poetry'.

A cursory view of the anthology gives us some clues as to what these 'original styles and new conceptions of poetry', shared by all five groups are. These poets are chiefly influenced by aspects of the poetry of Ezra Pound and William Carlos Williams. This dual influence shows itself in both matter and manner, creating a curious effect which might safely be called 'original'. Back of that, historically, they tend to celebrate Whitman, often in the long rhetorical line, more often by name. In language they rebel against the growing number of poeticisms in the language of the formalists. They have tried to include some of the vitality and rhythm of the living, spoken American language. Here, for example, is the opening of 'The Lordly and Isolate Satyrs' by *il maestro* Olson:

> The lordly and isolate Satyrs—look at them come in
> on the left side of the beach
> like a motorcycle club! And the handsomest of them,
> the one who has a woman, driving that snazzy
> convertible
>
> Wow, did you ever see even in a museum
> such a collection of boddisatvahs, the way

> they come up to their stop, each of them
> as though it was a rudder
> the way they have to sit above it
> and come to a stop on it, the monumental solidity
> of themselves, the Easter Island
> they make of the beach, the Red-headed Men

(Wow indeed! And also gee-whizz, golly and twenty-three skidoo! Professorial slang, of course, but anyway an idea.)

Along with this more inclusive language is an attempt (once more!) to shock the long-suffering, much-shocked and therefore relatively immune middle class, wherever it may be, which is certainly not reading an *avant-garde* anthology; and, as well, to tickle the under-graduate audience, for the public reading of modern poetry by the poets at colleges and Cultural Centres has rapidly become Big Business. If you want to be mildly shocked, a non-lethal jolt, flip through Alan Ginsberg's *Howl* and see what some of 'the best minds' of his generation were doing for leisure and amusement.

With the attempt to draw on the resources of the living, spoken language, came more various subject-matter to go hand in glove with the words. These poets still honouring the principle of decorum. Jazz, the comic strips, the good old days of radio, the picture show, all parts of the common, ordinary heritage of the mid-century American are frequently referred to. Here goes Leroi Jones swinging, 'In Memory of Radio':

> Who has ever stopped to think of the divinity of Lamont Cranston?
> (Only Jack Kerouac, that I know of; & me.
> The rest of you probably had on WCBS and Kate Smith,
> Or something equally unattractive.)
>   . . . . . .
> Saturday mornings we listened to *Red Lantern* & his undersea folk.
> At 11, *Let's Pretend* / & we did / & I, the poet, still do, Thank God!

The middle class was supposed to be shocked by *subject-matter* as well as by ordinary four-letter words. Their values were satirised and certain things were repeatedly celebrated which are not usually so treated:

(*a*) The frequent and explicit treatment of homosexuality as against the formalists' more usual practice of writing of the same subject as if it were a conventional heterosexual affair; the advance guard comes on

as 'rough trade' and proud of it. Here, for example, John Wieners
comes right to the point in 'A Poem For the Old Man':

> God love you
> > Dana my lover
>
> lost in the horde
> on this Friday night
> 500 men are moving up
> and down from the bath
> room to the bar.
> Remove this desire
> from the man I love.
> Who has opened
> > the savagery
>
> of the sea to me.

(b) Along with this came the cheerfully angry celebration of the
criminal, particularly the crime of violence without motive, rhyme or
reason. Here Ray Bremser calls up a new American hero to purge the
conscience of the land:

> praise to you, my country!
> praises, America!
> I would bequeath
> your whole to another blazer,
> Charlie Starkweather!
>
> > he would know how to handle the infinite
> > putrid scumbags somebody's mother manufactures—
> > he would annul your vast vagina
> > into a finer
> > > better business bureau box of the mange!

Chiefly, however, the poetry of this advance guard is conservative.
A return to the typography and punctuation of the 'thirties. With a
difference. It is neither social nor economic. The Working Man and
the Common Man hardly ever appear. They are squares. Why work
when you can live off a patron or a fellowship? Work, an enormous
part of the experience of most people, whether a labour of love or for
survival, seldom rears its ugly head in the poetry of either school.

The advance guard celebrates the artist, the self making up a poem
(*Look ma! I'm dancing!*) most of all. But since there is minimal drama
in a man alone with a piece of paper and the beating of his pulse, they
tend to celebrate themselves through the *persona* of the jazz musician

or the painter. Turning to the rest of the world they summon up violence and contempt. Reader, they preach love, but they do not wish you well. Here Charles Olson offers gratuitous advice to the Gloucester fishermen:

> o kill kill kill kill kill
> those
> who advertise you
> out

Which is a familiar modern way of disposing of those with whom we disagree. And also happens to be a perfectly standard literary allusion; cf. *King Lear*.

No, the *avant-garde* is not so wild and woolly as it proclaims with CAPITAL LETTERS and with exclamation points (!!!!!) all lined up like a rank of soldiers. Like their professed enemy—and not just the Leaders who have spent their lives in school, but also the young ones—they are all-too-well educated. Either school boys or runaways. The whole fight makes sense only within an academic context. Middle class, of course and mostly middle aged, long sheltered by leaded glass and barricades of books, they have discovered Real Life late in life. They are pseudo-primitives, often disguised within liberal protestations.

The battle has been fought in anthologies, the *Social Registers* of the *status quo*. It looked, briefly, as we moved into the 'sixties, as if it were another example of 'eyeball to eyeball confrontation'. But certain quick changes changed all that. First, we have to understand the growing importance of Whitman as an influence.[2] True enough, everybody claims him, just as all political parties claim George Washington. Yet his influence, various as it is, has come home to roost. Pound and Williams celebrated him as the pioneer and master, but so did Wallace Stevens; so did Hart Crane, and others. Karl Shapiro, landlocked far from his urban stamping grounds, in Lincoln, Nebraska, discovered him in the 'fifties, proclaimed his allegiance in *In Defense of Ignorance*, solidified his position with contributions to a scholarly study—*Start With The Sun: Studies in the Whitman Tradition*—and only recently found his position respectable enough to be well received by the National Council of Teachers of English Convention. (His speech, 'Is Poetry an American Art?', is printed in *College English*, March, 1964.)

Meanwhile there were changes in the ranks of the formalists. To

[2] Cf. Chapter II, above, *passim*.

begin with, since their chief influences were Frost (his form, apparent simplicity, his way with metaphor) and Stevens (his elegance, apparent sophistication, his verbal texture), they were ripe. The influence of Frost seems to be increasing among some of the more conservative poets. The effect of a close personal association with Robert Frost during the last years of Frost's life shows up clearly in recent poems by William Meredith. And the matter and manner of Frost is more evident than it was earlier in some of Richard Wilbur's new poems. Here, for example, the final stanza of Wilbur's 'Seed Leaves':

> This plant would like to grow
> And yet be embryo;
> Increase, and yet escape
> The doom of taking shape;
> Be vaguely vast, and climb
> To the tip end of time
> With all of space to fill
> Like boundless Yggdrasill
> That has the stars for fruit.
> But something at the root
>
> More urgent than that urge
> Bids two true leaves emerge,
> And now the plant, resigned
> To being self-defined
> Before it can commerce
> With the great universe,
> Takes aim at all the sky
> And starts to ramify.

They were also showing signs of wishing to create a more inclusive poetry, one which would include living speech, more variety of form, a more personal poetry, and at the same time trying their hands at the narrative. Case in point: Louis Simpson's *A Dream of Governors* (1959), especially the long narrative poem set in the second world war, 'The Runner'. Simpson's latest book *At the End of the Open Road*, which was awarded the Pulitzer Prize for 1963, also contains narrative experiments. Another significant case in point: Robert Bagg's series of narrative 'adventures' which appeared in *Madonna of the Cello* (1961). Robert Lowell was beginning to fiddle with freer verse forms, a more particular and personal view which soon appeared in *Life Studies* (1959). Another leader, younger but influential, W. S. Merwin followed suit with *The Drunk in the Furnace* (1960). James Merrill, almost a symbol of the flagrantly baroque, proved *he* could turn a gutsy poem with the best of them in *Water Street* (1962).

Out of the wilderness of Minnesota came Robert Bly with his magazine *The Fifties* (now *The Sixties*). With a plot to take over Poetry, an announced plot. Like the Black Muslim's announced intention to overthrow violently the American government, Bly's plot was taken lightly. After all, he had been to Harvard too. He had even studied under Richard Wilbur. He was sassy and irreverent, but then, aren't the young always so? Relax? The triumph of Bly is all too obvious in the 'new' James Wright. Wright began as a disciple of Frost, developed as one of the finest poets we have. But *The Branch Will Not Break* is quite close in style and mannerism and even subject-matter to Bly's *Silence in the Snowy Fields*; and, in fact, one of the poems is called 'Mary Bly', after Bly's daughter. 'I have been interested in the connection between poetry and simplicity', Bly wrote for the jacket of *Silence*. It is a concern and interest that relates his work and Wright's new work to that of such new forces to be reckoned with as Robert Creeley or the prolific Denise Levertov.

Up at Yale, Dudley Fitts has replaced Auden in the catbird seat as final arbiter for the Yale Series of Younger Poets, a change which immediately manifested itself in such choices as George Starbuck's *Bone Thoughts* (1960) and Alan Dugan's *Poems* (1961), for which Starbuck wrote the blurb. In both cases, free swinging, jazzy, hard-nosed verses.

What would you do if you were a bright young poet with his ear to the ground, nose to the grindstone, eye on the main chance, etc.? Why, produce a new anthology, of course! They have lately been raining down like leaves in early November. Donald Hall was involved in two. First came *New Poets of England and America: Second Selection*, this time Pack and Hall, but without Simpson. This time with the British and American poets segregated in separate sections with clear editorial responsibility for the choices. Hall picked the English, Pack the Americans. Pack introduced some new people, prizewinners who could not safely be ignored, and allowed new and old a freer, more 'representative' selection from their work. He also wrote an introduction, a last, not-too-hopeful plea for the formalists. Hall meanwhile made a somewhat different selection for his Penguin *Contemporary American Poetry*. Here a good many poets from the Donald Allen anthology appear. If you can't beat 'em, join 'em. And you can't beat 'em, they join you. John Malcolm Brinnin, an indefatigable and alert anthologiser, has risen to the occasion, producing a sumptuous anthology, *The Modern Poets: An American-British Anthology* (1963), as if to celebrate the new peace on Parnassus. It has a double standard of admission for the various poets. They are each, one and all, photographed by Rollie McKenna, who has become *the* photographer for fashionable literary people.

Quite suddenly the *sitzkrieg* is over. Peace and unity, as well as confusion prevail. To signify and symbolise this, Henry Rago, long-time editor of *Poetry* and basically a cautious one, produced a double issue of his magazine entitled 'Work in Progress'. To prove the feud is dead the reader has only to look for himself. Here is the 'new' Karl Shapiro in the opening lines of 'Basement Apartment':

Hymen's got a cold. Hymen, your nose is running.
My love, you look like Beethoven, like you were hit by a truck.

Or, regard the 'new' John Berryman, swinging into part III of 'Nine Dream Songs':

Henry Hankovitch, con guitar,
did a short Zen pray,
on his talami in a relaxed lotus
fixin his mind on nuffin, rose-blue breasts,
and gave his parnel one French kiss;
enslaving himself he withdrew from his blue

Florentine leather case an Egyptian black
and flickt a zippo.

So much for the official history. As in the case of military history, literary *communiqués* and reports do not necessarily reflect accurately what has happened. But we have to put up with them for a time (and always with an ample grain of salt) until sometime later when a patient and ruthless historian appears with no axe to grind and nothing to sell except a talent at separating the wheat from the chaff.

At the risk of the sin of repetition I would summarise as follows. We are still in the post-war period, but now a second 'generation' has arrived upon the scene. Their internecine wars brought nothing about, except, of course, sufficient ferment and excitement to alleviate some of the essential loneliness of being a poet. That precisely because of their internal squabbles they have at once increasingly isolated and become increasingly aware of the isolation of the American poet from any audience. That their thinly disguised dream is to reach an audience and say something that really matters about something real. That in order to do this they have gone back to Whitman's dream (and some few to Frost who did, after all, manage to reach a wide audience, as a public personality, if not as a poet). That they have returned to replenish themselves at the public fountains—filling their poems, as best they are able, with pure living speech, with things of this world, with common memories and fears. That there are great dangers ahead. One of these, paradoxically for those interested in *American* poetry, being that schools and groups and clubs of poets are utterly foreign to our native scene. They only occur in the textbooks which most of these poets were weaned on. And, most important, that much poetry has been written during these years, much of it good and various, almost all of it interesting. That one good sign is that these people, the very ones who made the rules and began to profit by them, have begun to question the validity of those rules and to profit enough by that questioning to continue the process. And best of all, that the future is out of their hands (and ours) anyway.

Tongues of fire, sounding brass, etc., we have a gracious plenty of. It remains to be seen if one or many of our new poets will learn enough human charity to speak to another human being and have it matter.

Of course, we all know that in spite of vast programmes, broadsides and manifestos, poets do what they can do and have to do. Our late, great poet Theodore Roethke knew it well and wrote about it so well in his *villanelle*, 'The Waking', which concludes:

> This shaking keeps me steady. I should know.
> What falls away is always. And is near.
> I wake to sleep, and take my waking slow.
> I learn by going where I have to go.

III. AGAINST THE GRAIN

It would be sheer cowardice not to take a stand, not to conclude by naming some of the younger poets who I think are good poets, working here and now and without benefit of representation in the official anthologies. There are, fortunately, many, more in fact than can be listed or mentioned in a brief essay. And, though our concern is younger poets, one should not overlook those fine poets among their elders who are still writing and creating good poems, people from the generation of elder statesmen like John Hall Wheelock and Babette Deutsch; people of the middle-aged group like Samuel French Morse, Leslie Fiedler and Elder Olson. It may be that some future reappraisal of this period will give these poets the kind of attention and appreciation they deserve.

One of the most interesting of the new poets of the 'sixties is David Slavitt whose *Suits For the Dead* appeared in Scribner's *Poets of Today, VIII* (1961). Without apparent difficulty Slavitt showed himself able to combine vernacular ease with formal grace, to write intelligently and with feeling of a wide variety of subjects while avoiding the pseudo-primitive posture or assuming any blatant *persona*. He handled narrative forms as well as lyrical. More recent poems, appearing in magazines, show a growth and maturity, deepening awareness and wit, and the courage to take risks. Everybody else has been talking about taking risks for a long time. He has simply and successfully done it. And he has begun to take risks as a reviewer and critic as well, taking the Establishment to task when it is needed and no one else has dared to. I have no doubt that during the coming years he will write important poems.

Another poet of equal promise is O. B. Hardison, Jr. His *Lyrics and Elegies* appeared in Scribner's *Poets of Today, V*. With the best command of the almost lost art of metrics, an ability perhaps superior to any living American poet, he has naturally tended towards the exploitation of the formal. Yet he has gone his own way, ignoring fashion and cliché, an example of the poet utterly unconcerned with schools and feuds. His long poem, 'Via Appia Antica', is a magnificent achievement. Subtle, understated, it is nevertheless a powerful and moving poem on Rome ancient and modern. And it contains some of the best translations of celebrated lines from the classics we have in English. Possibly because he so thoroughly integrated these fragments into the context of his work and because he did not advertise them with italics, quotation marks or even footnotes, this has gone unnoticed.

A recent and extraordinary book which has a growing underground reputation is *Notes from a bottle found on the beach at Carmel* (1963) by Evan S. Connell, Jr. *Notes* is a long (238 pp.), beautifully executed narrative poem of the size and scope of Pound's *Cantos*. It is a learned and subtle narrative poem, yet written in a style of great clarity and precision, all its virtuosity gracefully concealed. This poem could easily be the most important single poem of our period when we have enough perspective to see things clearly. That it has, so far, been ignored by most of the critics of poetry may charitably be attributed to the fact that Connell enjoys a considerable reputation as a prose writer and has published very little verse in the magazines. Meanwhile, strange as it seems, without fanfare or controversy, *Notes* has sold quite well in the bookstores.

What of the *very* new poets, those whose work has begun to appear in magazines but has not yet been collected in book form. There are, of course, many interesting new writers, and no one could honestly claim to 'keep up'. It is that interesting and promising these days. Still, as a casual reader of various literary magazines and as poetry editor of one, *The Transatlantic Review*, I keep an eye out for the young poet who seems consistently to write well and with integrity and originality.

High on my list and exemplary, I feel, of the best of the new directions is the poetry of R. H. W. Dillard. At first glance Dillard's work appears fragmentary and cryptic, but it is soon apparent that his poems are all parts of a whole, timeless in their vaguely allusive wedding of ancient and modern history, yet distinctly modern in the cinematic flow of clear and precise imagery. His work has wit and humour, the pathos of nostalgia, the power of compassion and a rare quality of childlike joy even in the treating of grim subjects. It is somewhat difficult to find a poem *by itself* which seems to demonstrate all these qualities, but 'The Signal Bells Rang Out Defeat' is at least exemplary and speaks for itself:

> The Polish sentry's gleaming heels,
> The scuff and then the sharp reports,
> The pop, pop, pop along the halls,
> The rifles of the grenadiers,
> The horsemen stretched across the hills.
>
> The ice was thick,
> The blades were dull,
> (The officer's glass was full
> As his monocle winked at the sun.)
> The blades were dull,
> The ice was thick.
>
> The masses shuffled in the square,
> A toppled statue,
> A red bandanna on the saber's tip,

The captain's single arm,
The muffled wheels,
And the dong, dong, dong of the heavy bells.

The orders were sent.
And understood.
Thunder echoed in the streets for days.

Harriet Hodges is an extremely gifted young poet. She has published very little so far, for she appears to be an extremely demanding craftsman, shaping and polishing each poem until the outward and visible signs of artifice disappear. She writes from a distinctly feminine point of view, a sensibility noteworthy for the charged power of contained, controlled and understated sensuality; an attitude at once proper and voluptuous, at once graceful and explosive; always promising. Since one should end with the thing itself, a poem, I have selected a poem of hers, 'Narcissa', as curiously relevant to the text of this essay. It is on the surface an almost flawless evocation of female narcissism, ending with a strangely satisfactory sigh of acceptance, a near turn towards pathos. Yet, and the poet knows this very well, narcissism is a larger disease and is itself a symptom of our deep ills and isolation. It can be taken quite well as illustrating rather graphically the whole ironic process of 'agonizing reappraisal' which has at once inhibited and given a subject to the poets of our time.

Narcissa

The bath steams the windows,
The outside is blotted out.
I stand at the glass on the medicine chest
My mouth a pout.
The eyes are black and heavy,
Languid, and full the lips.
Many, many mirrors have
Accomplished this.

What a rare flower
This hothouse plant I am.

Nice to have the tropics in your pocketbook.
    That handy jungle the faulted glass.
One lush breath condenses and rings you round
    with moisture.
Home at last.

Index

241

Warren, Robert Penn, 12, 13, 14, 33–42, 182–3, 185, 224
Welty, Eudora, 41
Werfel, Franz V., 82
Weston, Rosamund, 121
Wheelock, John Hall, 237
Whitman, Walter (Walt), 32, 45–67, 77, 152–3, 172, 175, 178–9, 180, 188–190, 193–4, 197, 204–5, 209–10, 212, 216, 218–19, 229, 232, 236
Whittemore, Reed, 42, 198
Wieners, John, 231
Wilbur, Richard, 42, 185, 225, 233, 234
Wilde, Richard Henry, 11

Williams, William Carlos, 70, 121, 123–4, 128, 131–4, 135, 139–48, 150–153, 175, 180, 182, 188–94, 205–9, 224, 229, 232
Winters, Yvor, 183, 217
Wolfe, Thomas, 41
Wordsworth, William, 11, 32–3, 102, 158, 160, 176, 194
Worringer, Wilhelm, 116
Wright, James, 192, 225, 234
Wyatt, Sir Thomas, 21

Yeats, W. B., 26, 39, 121, 136, 224
Young, Stark, 13